John Mercer Langston

Freedom and Citizenship

John Mercer Langston

Freedom and Citizenship

ISBN/EAN: 9783337275259

Printed in Europe, USA, Canada, Australia, Japan

Cover: Foto ©Suzi / pixelio.de

More available books at **www.hansebooks.com**

FREEDOM AND CITIZENSHIP.

SELECTED LECTURES AND ADDRESSES

OF

HON. JOHN MERCER LANGSTON, LL.D.,

U. S. MINISTER RESIDENT AT HAITI.

WITH AN INTRODUCTORY SKETCH

BY REV. J. E. RANKIN, D. D.,

OF WASHINGTON.

WASHINGTON, D. C.:
RUFUS H. DARBY, PUBLISHER.
1883.

TO THE YOUNG COLORED AMERICANS

WHO IN HOME AND SCHOOL AND COLLEGE

ARE TRYING

TO MAKE THEMSELVES WORTHY

OF

THE FREEDOM AND CITIZENSHIP

WITH WHICH

GOD AND THEIR COUNTRY

HAVE

ENDOWED THEM.

CONTENTS.

	PAGE.
DEDICATION,	5
INTRODUCTORY SKETCH,	9
THE WORLD'S ANTI-SLAVERY MOVEMENT,	41
DANIEL O'CONNELL,	69
CITIZENSHIP AND THE BALLOT,	99
BISHOP RICHARD ALLEN,	123
EQUALITY BEFORE THE LAW,	141
EULOGY ON CHARLES SUMNER,	162
OUR PATRIOT DEAD,	180
OUR POLITICAL PARTIES,	188
PACIFIC RECONSTRUCTION,	209
THE EXODUS,	232
FUTURE OF THE COLORED AMERICAN,	259

INTRODUCTORY SKETCH.

JOHN MERCER LANGSTON, one of the most remarkable colored men of his period, for he stands with the two foremost, Douglass and Bruce, was born in Louisa county, Virginia, December 14th, 1829. This date he gets from his half-sister. His father was Ralph Quarles, Esq., and his mother plain Jane Langston, of African and Indian descent, his father's favorite slave. When Mr. Quarles died he emancipated all his slaves by will, and sent them to Ohio. Of the lad Langston, who was among them, Col. William D. Gooch, a former friend of his father's, was appointed guardian by the judges of the Ross county court. By Mr. Gooch and his family he was always treated as a son. Miss Virginia Gooch, a young lady whom he distinctly remembers, taught him in the New Testament, and he never dreamed that he did not belong to them by birth.

When he was between eight and ten years of age, Colonel. Gooch took it into his head to emigrate to Missouri, a slave State. The family, with their furniture, were all packed on board a boat on the Chillicothe canal, when suddenly the sheriff, at the instance of his half-brother, William Langston, appeared with a process charging an attempt to kidnap the boy. The lad himself fearing that he was to be torn from his own family friends, clung frantically to them, and when asked by Judge Keith, before whom Colonel Gooch was taken, whether he would go with his reputed father or his half-brother, replied that he would go with Colonel

A

Gooch. Singularly enough, the lawyer who presented his half-brother's case was the now distinguished ex-Senator Thurman, who, not until within a few years, ever knew anything of the future history of the boy, when he was informed by Mr. Langston himself. The result of the business was, that Colonel Gooch continued his trip to Missouri, and the lad remained under other guardianship in Ohio. It is not to be for one moment supposed that Colonel Gooch had any dishonorable intention in the premises. But, had the boy been taken to Missouri, even if he had always remained free, his future eminence would have been impossible. In Ohio, at that time, were almost the only opportunities in the country for a young colored boy to cultivate his mind.

It is impossible to overrate the influence of Oberlin upon the welfare of Northern Ohio, and, indeed, in 1861, when came the time that tried men's souls, upon the destiny of the whole country. It was the hot-bed of the most radical sentiments in politics and religion. It was the watch-tower of freedom and righteousness. President Finney, a man who walked with God as Enoch did, though he looked upon man with rather a judicial look, was at the head of it. The pulse of his vigorous life beat in every department. To this institution young Langston was sent when he was thirteen. He went into the family, as his ward, of Prof. Geo. Whipple, afterwards for so many years the distinguished Secretary of the American Missionary Association. Professor Whipple was a fatherly and judicious counsellor and friend. After spending five years in diligent labor at his books, young Langston graduated with honor from the college in 1849. One year of law-study intervened with Judge Andrews, of Cleveland, when he returned to Oberlin and entered the theological department. From this, in due time, he graduated in 1853. How strong was his tendency to the ministry as a profession may be inferred from the theme of his commencement oration : " The Qualification of the Pulpit Orator." Of this oration, which is singularly clear and forcible, this is the last paragraph :

" Cultivated rhetoric, vigorous imagination, fine discriminating logical powers, accurate and extensive knowledge, sincere respect for his fellow-men, a soul-absorbing philanthropy, and a warm and benign earnestness; these are the qualifications of the successful pulpit orator. These were the qualities which gave such force and beauty to the discourses of Hall, such point and persuasion to the sermons of Whitefield, and such weight and fervor to the preaching of Chalmers."

If one would like some idea of what this young student meant by a soul-absorbing philanthropy, indeed, of what then passed in Oberlin for practical religion, he will find it in the following passage :

" Another qualification of the pulpit orator is a soul-absorbing philanthropy, the most glorious attribute in the character of the Pattern Minister. This was the characteristic that caused Him to feed the hungry, to clothe the naked, and to bring the riches of the gospel to the doors of the poor. Shall not the servant be as his Lord ? Indeed, the minister of the gospel, if he would be as his Teacher, if he would do his entire duty as a faithful servant, must see in every human being a brother, and adopt practically the injunction : 'Thou shalt love thy neighbor as thy self.' He must be willing to go to the dens of poverty and degradation, into the squalid hovels of the miserably poor, as well as into the spacious and elegantly furnished mansions of the rich. He must not forget them who are cast down and oppressed. He must speak in behalf of the outraged and down-trodden; in defence of the all-embracing doctrines of universal liberty. He must have the moral courage to speak against every unjust discrimination growing out of caste and accidental difference. He must stand forth in vindication of all reforms in Church and State, which are the legitimate demand of truth and love. Especially, indeed, should he speak in trumpet tones in advocacy of the rights and claims and the interests of the dumb, the disfranchised and the enslaved. In a word, being a true philanthropist, possessing a spirit akin to that of Howard and Clarkson, he should be ready to oppose every species of oppression and wrong, whether it come in the sermon of a soulless and obsequious D. D., in the speech of a heartless statesman, the enactment of a time-serving Congress, or in the huge, the colossal, the mercenary dimensions of slavery itself. The Bible, in legislating love, is the original, the God-given proclamation of independence and freedom. And he who undertakes to expound it to men ought to be thoroughly imbued with its spirit."

But, like the late President Garfield, whose thoughts were first turned to the Christian ministry, Mr. Langston was to secure his successes and rewards in another department of labor. Had he chosen the Christian ministry (as he sometimes has had lingering thoughts that perhaps he should have done) and had he been able to realize his own high ideal in it, he certainly would not have failed of similar successes and rewards. As a preacher, President Finney was in many respects Mr. Langston's model. Clear, direct, cogent, brilliant, Mr. Langston would have added that personal persuasiveness and magnetism, for which, as a lawyer he has been so distinguished, and which has made him one of the most effective of speakers upon the stump.

Having determined upon the practice of law, Mr. Langston repaired to Elyria, entered the office of Philimon Bliss, Esq., and was admitted to the bar. His first cases were in defence of the violators of the liquor license law ; for a young lawyer is compelled to take the clients who first knock at his office door. To these cases he brought such penetration and industry and persistence, that soon this first colored lawyer west of the Alleghanies had won for himself a brilliant reputation. For twelve years he remained in Ohio, adding to his resources, financial and professional, and recognized everywhere as a young man sure to rise. He was once personally insulted by a member of the bar on account of his color, to whom he administered justice with his own right hand. An effort was made by the aggrieved lawyer to have him indicted by the grand jury; but the effort failed, and Mr. Langston was privately advised, by the foreman, that if any such affront was ever put upon him again, they would indict him, unless he dealt with the offender in precisely the same manner. But he was not a professional man alone. He was all the time working for the liberation and advancement of his race. In speeches and resolutions at conventions, and on the platform he always kept his eye single to this great end. He always looked forward to that better time which he believed to be coming, as though this were his motto :

> Man's wrongs we still will right them,
>   Man's burdens help him bear,
> Man's foes, we still will fight them,
>   And make his cause our care.

Cervantes says "every man is the son of his own works." It was this constant toil and the fruit of it that prepared Mr. Langston for his part in what God was preparing for the nation. As early as 1854, in a convention to consider the wisdom of emigrating to another country, where they could be protected in their persons and rights, and have a better opportunity to rise, as they deserved, Mr. Langston .figured in what the records of the convention speak of, as " a speech replete with classic elegance." Of course he directed his eloquence against the project. And from that day to the day he left Ohio for other duties in Washington and the South, he was indefatigable in his efforts for his own people.

Among the most thrilling of the rescue cases in the country, was that of John Price, a young fugitive from slavery in Kentucky. For several years he had been living in Oberlin when one day he was observed by a Negro-catcher on the watch for some other runaway, and his supposed master was notified. The informant was promised $250 if the fugitive was returned. Getting a young man of the village to decoy the fugitive from Oberlin, a party came upon them, arrested John, and took him to a hotel in Wellington, a little town some six miles distant. Citizens from the region gathered around the hotel, asked for the warrant by which the young man was held, and, finally, without force, took him away from the United States marshal. In the company of these rescuers were some of Oberlin's best and noblest men. Immediately the whole section was on fire at the attempted outrage. This rescue has gone into history as the Oberlin-Wellington rescue, We refer to it, not merely as showing what was going on between the two sections of the country, but, also, to show what was in the blood of the Langston race. Mr. Langston's half brother, William, was the man at whose instance Colonel Gooch was arrested on the charge of kidnapping. Charles was another half-brother. That he was a man of great eloquence is evident from his

speech in the court when asked by the judge if he had anything to say why sentence should not be passed against him.
He had been convicted of complicity with others, some of
the best citizens of Oberlin, among them one who afterward
ward became Mr. Langston's brother-in-law, Hon. O. S. B.
Wall, of Washington, in this rescue. I quote from a volume which contains a full history of the affair. And I do
this not only from my own view of the fitness of the quotation, but because Mr. Langston himself, from a sense of
what he owes this half-brother and from the highest appreciation of his native gifts, has suggested it.

The scene is in Cleveland, Ohio; the date May 12, 1859,
and comment is unnecessary.

THE COURT to Mr. Charles Langston: "You have been
tried by a jury and convicted of a violation of the criminal
laws of the United States. Have you or your counsel anything to say why the sentence of the law should not be pronounced upon you?"

This was Mr. Langston's reply: "I am for the first time
in my life before a court of justice, charged with the violation of law, and am now to be sentenced. But before receiving that sentence I purpose to say one or two words in regard to the mitigation of that sentence, if it may be so construed. I cannot, and of course do not expect, that anything I shall say will in any way change your predetermined
line of action. I ask no such favor at your hands. I know
that the courts of this country, that the laws of this country,
that the governmental machinery of the country are so constituted as to oppress and outrage the colored men: men of
my complexion. I cannot, then, of course, expect, judging
from the past history of the country, any mercy from the
laws, from the Constitution, or from the courts of the
country.

"Some days prior to the 13th of September, 1858, happening to be in Oberlin on a visit, I found the country round about there and the village itself filled with alarming rumors as to the fact that slave-catchers, kidnappers, Negro-stealers, were lying hidden and skulking about, waiting some opportunity to get their bloody hands on some helpless creature, to drag him back, or to drag him for the first time, into hopeless and life-long bondage. These reports becoming current all over that neighborhood, old men and women and innocent children became exceedingly alarmed for their safety. It was not uncommon to hear mothers say that they durst not send their children to school, for fear that they would be caught up and carried off by the way. Some of these people had become free by long and patient toil at night, after working the long, long day for cruel masters, and then, at length, getting money enough to buy their liberty. Others had become free by means of the good will of their masters. And there were others, who had become free—to their everlasting honor do I say it—by the exercise of their God-given powers, by escaping from the plantation of their masters, eluding the blood-thirsty patrols and sentinels so thickly scattered all along their path, outrunning bloodhounds and horses, swimming rivers, and fording swamps, and reaching at last, through incredible difficulties, what they, in their delusion, supposed to be free soil. These three classes were in Oberlin, trembling alike for their safety, because they well knew their fate should these men-hunters get their hands on them.

"In the midst of such excitement the 13th of September was ushered in—a day ever to be remembered in the history of that place, and I am sure, no less in the history of this court—in which these men, by lying devices, decoyed into a place, where they could get their hands on him—I will not say a slave, for I do not know that; but a man, a brother, who had a right to his liberty under the law of God, under the laws of Nature, and under the Declaration of Independence.

"Many of us believed there would not be courage to make a seizure ; but in the midst of all the excitement the news came to us like a flash of lightning that an actual seizure, by means of fraudulent pretenses, had been made.

"Being identified with that man by color, by race, by manhood, by sympathies such as God has implanted in us all, I felt it my duty to go and do what I could toward liberating him. I had been taught by my Revolutionary father, and by his honored associates, that the fundamental law of this Government is, that all men have a right to life and liberty, and coming from the Old Dominion, I brought into Ohio these sentiments deeply impressed on my heart. I went to Wellington, and having learned from the men themselves by what authority they held this boy in custody, I conceived from what knowledge I had of law that they had no right to hold him. And as your honor has repeatedly laid down the law in this court, that in the State of Ohio a man is presumed to be free until he is proved to be legally restrained of his liberty, I believed that upon that principle of law those men were bound to take their prisoner before the first magistrate they found, and there establish the facts set forth in their warrant, and that until they did this, every man had a right to presume their claim was unfounded, and to institute such proceedings for the purpose of receiving such an investigation as he might find as warranted by the laws of this State. Now, sir, if that is not plain, common sense, and a correct view of the law, then I have been misled by your honor, and by the prevalent received opinion.

"It is said that they had a warrant. Why, then, should

they not establish its validity before the proper officers? And I stand here to-day, sir, to say, that, with an exception, of which I shall soon speak, to procure such a lawful investigation of the authority under which they claimed to act, was the part I took in that day's proceedings, and the only part. I supposed it to be my duty as a citizen of Ohio—excuse me for saying that, sir—as an outlaw of the United States [much sensation], to do what I could to secure at least this form of justice to my brother whose liberty was in peril. Whatever more than that has been sworn to on this trial, as an act of mine, is false, ridiculously false. When I found these men refusing to go, according to the law, as I apprehend it, and subject their claim to an official inspection, and that nothing short of a *habeas corpus* would oblige such an inspection, I was willing to go even thus far, supposing in that county a sheriff might, perhaps, be found with nerve enough to serve it. In this again I failed. Nothing then was left to me, nothing to the boy in custody, but the confirmation of my first belief that the pretended authority was worthless, and the employment of those means of liberation which belong to us all. With regard to the part I took in the forcible rescue which followed I have nothing to say, farther than I have already said. The evidence is before you. It is alleged that I said, ' we will have him any how.' This I never said. I did say to Mr. Lowe, what I honestly believed to be the truth, that the crowd was very much excited, many of them averse to longer delay and bent upon a rescue at all hazards ; and that he being an old acquaintance and friend of mine, I was anxious to extricate him from the dangerous position he occupied, and, therefore, advised that he urge Jennings to give the boy up. Further than this I did not say, either to him or to any one else.

"The law under which I am arraigned is an unjust one, one made to crush the colored man, and one that outrages every feeling of humanity, as well as every rule of right. I have nothing to do with its constitutionality; and about it I care a great deal less. I have often heard it said by learned and good men that it is unconstitutional; I remember the excitement that prevailed throughout all the free States when it was passed; and I remember how often it has been said by individuals, conventions, communities, and legislatures, that it never could be, never should be, and never was meant to be enforced. I had always believed, until the contrary appeared in the actual institution of proceedings, that the provisions of this odious statute would never be enforced within the bounds of this State.

"But I have another reason to offer why I should not be sentenced, and one that I think pertinent to the case. I have not had a trial before a jury of my peers. The common law of England—and you will excuse me for referring to that, since I am but a private citizen and not a lawyer—was that every man should be tried before a jury of men occupying the same position in the social scale with himself. That lords should be tried before a jury of lords; that peers of the realm should be tried before peers of the realm; vassals before vassals, and aliens before aliens, and they must not come from the district where the crime was committed, lest the prejudice of either personal friends or foes should affect the accused. The Constitution of the United States guarantees, not merely to its citizens, but to all persons, a trial before an impartial jury. I have had no such trial.

"The colored man is oppressed by certain universal and deeply fixed prejudices. Those jurors are well-known to have shared largely in these prejudices, and I therefore consider they were neither impartial, nor were they a jury of my peers. And the prejudices which white people have against colored men grow out of this fact : that we have, as a people, consented for two hundred years to be slaves of the whites. We have been scourged, crushed, and cruelly oppressed, and have submitted to it all tamely, meekly, peaceably ; I mean as a people, and with rare individual exceptions ; and to-day you see us thus ; meekly submitting to the penalties of an infamous law. Now the Americans have this feeling, and it is an honorable one, that they will respect those who will rebel at oppression, but despise those who tamely submit to outrage and wrong ; and while our people as a people submit, they will as a people be despised. Why, they will hardly meet on terms of equality with us in a whiskey shop, in a car, at a table, or even at the altar of God. So thorough and hearty a contempt have they for those who will meekly lie still under the heel of the oppressor. The jury came into the box with that feeling. They knew they had that feeling, the court itself has that feeling, and even the counsel who defended me have that feeling.

"I was tried by a jury who were prejudiced; before a court that was prejudiced; prosecuted by an officer who was prejudiced, and defended, though ably, by counsel that were prejudiced. And therefore it is, your honor, that I urge by all that is good and great in manhood, that I should not be subjected to the pains and penalties of this oppressive law, when I have not been tried, either by a jury of my peers, or by a jury that were impartial.

"One more word, sir, and I have done. I went to Wellington, knowing that colored men have no rights in the United States which white men are bound to respect; that the courts had so decided; that Congress had so enacted; that the people had so decreed.

" There is not a spot in this wide country, not even by the altars of God, nor in the shadow of the shafts that tell the imperishable fame and glory of the heroes of the Revolution; no, nor in the old Philadelphia hall, where any colored man may dare to ask a mercy of a white man. Let me stand in that hall, and tell a United States marshal that my father was a Revolutionary soldier; that he served under Lafayette, and fought through the whole war; and that he told me that he fought for my freedom as much as for his own; and he would sneer at me, and clutch me with his bloody fingers, and say he had a right to make me a slave ! And when I appeal to Congress, they say he has a right to make me a slave; when I appeal to the people, they say he has a right to make me a slave, and when I appeal to your honor, your honor says he has a right to make me a slave, and if any man, white or black, seeks an investigation of that claim, he makes himself amenable to the pains and penalties of the Fugitive Slave Act; for black men have no rights which white men are bound to respect. [Great applause.] I, going to Wellington with the full knowledge of all this, knew that if that man was taken to Columbus, he was hopelessly gone, no matter whether he had ever been in slavery before or not. I knew that I was in the same situation myself, and that by the decision of your honor, if any man whatever were to claim me as his slave and seize me, and my brother, being a lawyer, should seek to get out a writ of *habeas corpus* to expose the falsity of the claim, he would be thrust into prison under one provision of the Fugitive Slave Law, for interfering with the man claiming to be in pursuit of a fugitive; and I, by the perjury of a solitary wretch, would, by another of its provisions, be helplessly doomed to life-long bondage, without the possibility of escape.

"Some persons may say there is no danger of free persons being seized and carried off as slaves. No one need labor under such a delusion. Sir, four of the eight persons who were first carried back under the act of 1850 were afterwards proved to be free men. The pretended owner declared that they were not his, after his agent had 'satisfied the commissioner' that they were, by his oath. They were free persons, but wholly at the mercy of one man. And but last Sabbath afternoon a letter came to me from a gentleman in St. Louis, informing me that a young lady, who was formerly under my instruction at Columbus, a free person, is now lying in the jail at that place, claimed as the slave of some wretch who never saw her before, and waiting for testimony from relatives at Columbus to establish her freedom. I could stand here by the hour and relate such instances. In the very nature of the case they must be constantly occurring. A letter was not long since found upon the person of a counterfeiter when arrested, addressed to him by some Southern gentleman, in which the writer says:

"'Go among the niggers; find out their marks and scars; make good descriptions and send to me, and I'll find masters for them.'

"That is the way men are carried 'back' to slavery.

"But in view of all the facts I say, that if ever again a man is seized near me, and is about to be carried Southward as a slave before any legal investigation has been had, I shall hold it to be my duty, as I held it that day, to secure for him, if possible, a legal inquiry into the claim by which he is held. And I go farther; I say that if it is adjudged illegal to procure even such an investigation, then we are thrown back upon those last defences of our rights, which cannot be taken from us, and which God gave us that we need not be slaves. I ask your honor, while I say this, to place yourself in my situation, and you will say with me that if your brother, if your friend, if your wife, if your child, had been seized by men who claimed them as fugitives, and the law of the land forbade you to ask any investigation, and precluded the possibility of any legal protection or redress—then you will say with me, that you would not only demand the protection of the law, but you would call in your neighbors and your friends, and would ask them to say with you, that these your friends should not be taken into slavery.

"And now I thank you for this leniency, this indulgence, in giving a man unjustly condemned, by a tribunal before which he is declared to have no rights, the privilege of speaking in his own behalf. I know that it will do nothing toward mitigating your sentence, but it is a privilege to be allowed to speak, and I thank you for it. I shall submit to the penalty, be it what it may. But I stand up here to say, that if for doing what I did on that day at Wellington, I am to go into jail six months, and pay a fine of a thousand dollars, according to the Fugitive Slave Law, and such is the protection the laws of this country afford me, I must take upon myself the responsibility of self-protection; and when I come to be claimed by some perjured wretch as his slave, I shall never be taken into slavery. And as in that trying hour I would have others do to me, as I would call upon my friends to help me; as I would call upon you, your honor, to help me; as I would call upon you [to the district attorney] to help me; and upon you [to Judge Bliss], and upon you [to his counsel], so help me God! I stand here to say that I will do all I can, for any man thus seized and held, though the inevitable penalty of six months' imprisonment and one thousand dollars fine for each offence hangs over me! We have a common humanity. You would do so;

your manhood would require it; and no matter what the laws might be, you would honor yourself for doing it; your friends would honor you for doing it; your children to all generations would honor you for doing it; and every good and honest man would say you had done right!" [Great and prolonged applause in spite of the efforts of the court and the marshal.]

The COURT: "These manifestations cannot be allowed here. The marshal has orders to clear the room if they are repeated.

"You have done injustice to the court, Mr. Langston, in thinking that nothing you might say could effect a mitigation of your sentence. You have presented considerations to which I shall attach much weight.

"I am fully aware of the evidence that was given to the jury; of the circumstances that were related; of your action in relation to the investigation of the cause of the detention of the fugitive, and of your advice to others to pursue a legal course; and although I am not disposed to question the integrity of the jury, still I see mitigating circumstances in the transaction which should not require, in my opinion, the extreme penalty of the law. This court does not make laws; that belongs to another tribunal. We sit here under the obligations of an oath to execute them, and whether they be bad or whether they be good, it is not for us to say. We appreciate fully your condition, and while it excites the cordial sympathies of our better natures, still the law must be vindicated. On reflection, I am constrained to say that the penalty in your case should be comparatively light. It is, therefore, the sentence of the court, that you pay a fine of one hundred dollars; that you be confined in the jail at Cuyahoga county, under the direction of the marshal, for a period of twenty days from date; and that you pay the cost of this prosecution; and that in case any casualty or other occurrence should render your confinement there insecure, that the marshal see the sentence executed in any other county jail within this district."

For eleven years Mr. Langston was a member of the Board of Education at Oberlin, and when he retired from the board to answer the summons of Gen. O. O. Howard and became general inspector of education under the Bureau of Refugees, Freedmen and Abandoned Lands, they passed unanimous resolutions of confidence and regret, which only confirmed the wisdom of General Howard's selection.

For three years, from 1867, when he went to Washington, Mr. Langston served the bureau above named, visiting prominent cities in the South, and always addressing large assemblies of colored and white people wherever he went. It may well be imagined that such a representative speaker of his own race, manly, straightforward and graceful, would show the possibilities which were before them, and awaken among them great enthusiasm. This was the case. All over the South his addresses on education were warmly received and wrought wonders. Just take these selections as samples of his manner. They are extracted from an address made before the Colored Educational Convention held in Louisville, Kentucky, July 14, 1869 :

"In the spirit of liberty and charity I come to speak to you this afternoon as an earnest American citizen. Since I am earnest and you are earnest, you will not ask me to flatter you. Office I care not for; political preferment I ask not in anything, and I care not for the success of one party more than for the success of another. I simply ask that the colored American in the providence of God, coming out of slavery into the noonday of liberty, may understand what liberty is; what its responsibilities are; what duties are implied in it,

B

and meet these responsibilities and these duties with a fair
opportunity given him, to take his place, ere long, side by
side with the best men—the best men in this country or in
any other—as a man. Is achievement the measure and test
of quality ? It has been all along through the days of old
time. There has been no change made by God since our
emancipation. We are not asking to be made the social
peer of Charles Sumner, President Grant or Schuyler Colfax, or any other learned or distinguished white American
statesman. Not at all. But I am here to ask whether, with
our hair-curled and faces sooty, as they are, our condition
two hundred and forty-five years of slavery, whether we can
step out in the liberty of new life by hard work, and place
ourselves alongside with the best men of this country
and the best men of the world ? Let me illustrate. You
give a colored man that is very poor to-day exactly the
same chance you give a white man who is also very
poor. You start them in the race of life ; both go to
college together ; they leave college together, and enter
the professional school ; they enter from that into the
battle of life, both successful, and grow rapidly in the public esteem. The colored man is married the same as the
white man, and they locate in beautiful homes, with the
profits of their business. This is a law that works without
obstruction or hindrance. No man can obstruct it. One of
the finest men in this country, looking from a social standpoint, to say nothing of his moral character, nothing of his
intellectual worth, is a Negro; who, before slavery was abolished, went in the society of the best men in England and
France or in any country he visited; was the bosom-friend
of Charles Sumner and Schuyler Colfax; and when he goes
into the presence of the President of the United States, the
President, leaving his chair, advances into the middle of the

room to take the Negro by the hand. Need I call his name? What Frederick Douglass is to-day or may be to-morrow, my young friends, in the morning of life, in the midst of the new struggles and opportunities of life, may also be. Douglass did not have law and theological schools open to him. I need not exhort you to become great; you will in spite of yourselves. First, then, you must have character. Next, you must have intellectual ability. Then get money and learn how to keep it. And when you have fitted yourself for a place, when you have achieved it, society will make ready for you."

In October, 1868, the law department of Howard University was organized, and Mr. Langston was chosen dean of the department. Here he was at his best. Enthusiastically fond of the law, with a high ideal for his pupils, and with original methods of instruction, he succeeded at once in drawing some of the brightest minds of the period to himself. Indeed, for the time, this department overshadowed the other two, while the work most needed for the colored people, in the theological department, was at a disadvantage, and the work in which the university has since been so influential, namely, that of the medical department, was comparatively slight. Among Mr. Langston's methods was a lesson each Sunday morning, on the Laws of Moses—really a law lesson from the Bible. How instructive such an exercise might be made, any one familiar with the indebtedness of humanity to Hebrew legislation, as given in such a treatise as that of "Michaelis on the Laws of Moses," can readily see. It was Mr. Langston's happy faculty, too, to interest in his work such men as Senator Sumner, who once delivered an address to the graduating class, and Ralph Waldo Emerson, who once took the Sunday morning hour, and talked to the students on Reading. For a short time, also, Mr. Langston was acting-president of the university, which conferred upon him the honorary degree of LL. D.

For seven years from 1870, Mr. Langston was a member, and the law-officer of the Board of Health of the District of Columbia, and when he retired was tendered by them [an entertainment, at which they were pleased to express for him their warmest appreciation and their best wishes for his success in the new position which President Hayes had asked him to accept. That this Government should be represented abroad by some of her best colored men was the wish of both President Grant and President Hayes. For the Republic of Haiti there could be found no more suitable selection than Mr. Langston. A diplomat by very nature, of easy manner and gentlemanly address, with his ready mastery of the French, his service of more than six years has proved the wisdom of the selection. His career in Haiti opened under the most favorable auspices. Bishop Holly states that his address to the President made a profound impression on the country. The varied functions of his office, both consular and diplomatic, he has most admirably discharged. He has addressed himself to the promotion of the commercial interests of this country and to the care of distressed seamen. Through his influence American calicoes are now imported, and Haitian coffee no longer sent mainly to France and England. He has also succeeded in endearing himself to the representatives of other governments resident on the island, being their sub-dean, and sometimes acting as their presiding officer.

Though living abroad, Mr. Langston keeps up the most intimate acquaintance with the public affairs of his country, and few men, among the eminent men who have discussed such affairs, are his superiors upon the stump; and whenever he returns home for a vacation his services are always in

demand. An incident really occurring immediately after
the close of the war, and narrated in one of the local newspapers of the day, is of such thrilling interest, and is so
well told, that we transcribe it. It illustrates the extremes
of this man's life; the compensations which God has brought
in different degrees to thousands of other men. To few,
however, to such a degree as to Mr. Langston.

The Washington *Star* says :—"After the close of the War
of the Rebellion, in 1866, 1867, and 1868, when the Southern
States were temporarily under military government, I was an
army officer stationed at Gordonsville, Va., and charged with
the reconstruction affairs of Orange and Louisa counties. In
establishing schools for the newly-liberated blacks and attending to public business at the county seats, I became quite
well acquainted with the people. One of their peculiarities
was that once a month in each county on "court day" a large
part of the population assembled at the court house, some
for business, but many for a sort of holiday or social exchange,
in which the influence of intoxicating liquor was too frequently manifest. On one of these occasions it was given out that
John M. Langston, the colored orator, now United States
Minister to Haiti, would speak at Louisa court-house. The
result was an unusually large attendance of colored people,
so that the town was full. Langston was born a slave in
Louisa county, and his father, an estimable Virginia gentleman, provided in his will that he should be liberated and
educated and given a share of his estate. Although a long
while free, and honorably distinguished, there had never been
a time before when Mr. Langston could safely visit his native county. Now he was to come back a leading man of
his race, to speak in public, and to revisit the scenes and to
recall the memories of his childhood. It was therefore a
great occasion for him and for the freedmen of Louisa county.

The white people, however, took little note of it or interest in it; although I had tried among the lawyers and some of the merchants, and other principal citizens, to convey the impression that Langston was a man they should recognize and respect. I remember particularly trying to convince General Gordon, then county attorney, and an excellent man, that he might be pleased with Langston, and would be interested if he came over to hear him talk. The feeling that the Negro was in all cases necessarily inferior and totally uninteresting was, however, too strong, and the General and several others manifested impatience, if not a little indignation, at my commendatory observation about Langston. They would not have it that any 'nigger' could talk law, politics, reconstruction, or anything else with a degree of ability and intelligence to merit their attention; and they could not imagine that they themselves were soon to attest in a remarkable manner the folly of settled enmity or contempt of an entire race or class of men.

"Of course Langston would not be received at any hotel in the village, but I managed to get over that difficulty by engaging a room for myself at *The American,* inviting him into it, and quietly ordering a private luncheon for two, of the best the house afforded. With less difficulty a pleasant green, where were some shade trees and a speaker's platform, was secured for Langston's address; and after luncheon, when a crowd of colored people had assembled, I walked with him and a few white Republicans (objects of intense detestation to the mass of the people) to the platform. I noticed General Gordon and a few of the prominent citizens around the outskirts of the crowd, within hearing of the speaker, but none seemed to be really attending the meeting.

"Langston began by referring to old Virginia and Louisa county as the place of his birth, and spoke in the happiest

ı

vein and with all the elegance and oratorical art that distinguish him, of the genuine affection he felt for his native State and town, and of the pleasure it gave him to come back again to the home of his boyhood. In a few minutes he had the mastery of every one within his voice. He pictured the greatness of the State in its early days, referred to its distinguished men, and its history and national influence, spoke touchingly of its present temporary depression and distress, and most hopefully and glowingly of its future promise and possibilities as a free State. Then with admirable taste and tact he fell naturally into a discussion of the living questions of the day, avoiding all irritating points and expressions. In a little while I looked about me and saw the platform and all available space near it and around it packed with white people. The blacks, accustomed to yielding precedence, had given up all the best places and a white man was wedged into every one. More eager interest I never saw in the faces of any audience. There was General Gordon crowding near Langston with irrepressible confession of homage springing from his eyes and pouring down his cheeks, while the beautiful periods, paying honor to old Virginia, fell from the orator's lips. The address continued for two hours with unflagging interest on the part of the audience, and closed with an admirable peroration. Then followed a scene of spontaneous enthusiasm that is seldom witnessed. It was my purpose to introduce several white citizens to Langston at the close of his speech, but the excitement among them was too great. They crowded upon him, as many as could get near, and fairly overwhelmed him with the warmth and energy of their unconstrained greetings and compliments. He was borne by the pressure into the dining-room of the hotel, and a grand dinner was forthwith ordered in his honor, at which General Gordon presided, and many of the best citizens sat at the board. He was at once a guest of the town, and no attention or honor seemed too great for its good people to bestow upon him. All prejudice against color was totally extinguished. After dinner the white ladies sent a committee to wait on him, to invite him to address them at the principal church in the evening. He accepted the invitation and the auditorium was more than crowded by the people of the place. Even the windows and doorways were packed. General Gordon escorted him to the pulpit, and introduced him to the audience. The best room in the hotel was now opened to him, and the next morning carriages were provided, and in company with a numerous escort of gentlemen he was taken out to visit the homestead and tomb of his father, and he did not forget the humble grave of his darker-hued mother, who is said to have been a woman of uncommon beauty and good qualities."

Mr. Langston's political sagacity has never been at fault. He has never doubted the party of freedom. When Hon. Senator Sumner felt impelled to break with President Grant, and finally ally himself with the party which so disastrously failed under the leadership of Mr. Greeley, it was against Mr. Langston's urgent solicitation and request. Mr. Sumner hesitated and wavered. Certain influential colored men encouraged him that their people would follow. Mr. Langston was better advised. He saw in the movement only a temporary set-back to the cause of freedom, which would react upon all engaged in it. His predictions proved more than true.

The lessons, which many colored Americans should derive from Mr. Langston's career, lie upon the surface of it. He had been all his life long fitting himself for something higher and better. When in Ohio, if he had contented himself to be about an average lawyer ; if he had assumed that

his color would be an insuperable barrier to recognition and
elevation ; if he had not aimed to do his very best in every
case he had, there would have been no distinguished future
before him.   It is one of Carlyle's wise sayings, that the
history of the world is the biography of great men.   That
is, every man of eminence is bound to be in all the prominent events of his period where his name and influence may
be felt.   In his boyhood Mr. Langston remembers the time
when he did not know he had a drop of colored blood in his
veins.   Tracing his career forward through school, college,
seminary, law-office, we see how he was all the more identified with everything which concerned his own people, and
was, therefore, necessary as one of the factors which entered
into the great struggle between freedom and slavery.   As
early as 1858, as will be seen from one of the addresses in
this volume, he was discussing " The World's Anti-Slavery
Movement" as a great uplifting, under God, of the oppressed
nationalities of the world.   When the wave struck this continent he was sure to be found on the top of it.

Mr. Langston believed that the preamble of the declaration is true in this generation, as well as it was true in the
time of the Revolutionary fathers.   He believed, too, that if
God had endowed all mankind with these rights and immunities, He would not stand idly by if the oppressed made
an effort to secure what God had given and man had taken.
Indeed, Mr. Langston has never sought to rid himself of the
belief that every earnest man's life is a plan of God ; and
not a little of his courage and persistence has arisen from
this source.   This is only the Calvinism which Shakespeare
has put in this form—

> " There is a tide in the affairs of men,
>   Which, taken at the flood leads on to fortune,
>   Omitted, all the voyage of their life
>   Is bound in shallows, and in miseries.''

When the tide arose, Mr. Langston always embarked all his ventures, as though he believed that God was in it, and the result has usually shown that he was right. That the unfolding of his life has been largely the result of God's care, one can see very plainly. The manumission of his father's slaves at his death ; their going from Virginia to Ohio, where freedom was a reality, and where there was one sacred spot where a colored man could be educated ; his falling into the hands of Christian guardians, especially into the hands of so discreet and even-handed a guardian as the late Dr. George Whipple ; his training in Oberlin under such men as President Finney and Professor Morgan ; his professional life at Oberlin ; his connection with Gen. O. O. Howard, in the Bureau of the University ; his opportunities of popular address in the South ; his intimacy with executive circles in Washington, and finally, the gift to him of a position of such great dignity, and ease, and influence, as Minister Resident at Haiti : in all these events a reverent spirit may readily discern the leading of the hand of Him without whom the sparrow falleth not to the ground.

It is not claimed that Mr. Langston's character is a faultless one. It is not claimed that he has at all realized his own ideal in life. But the attention of young colored Americans is called to the fact, that beginning as he did, thirty years ago at the foot of the ladder, he has climbed so high and won such a reputation and such an influence simply, by making the best of his opportunities. In some respects, a colored man of this generation has advantages over the white man of the same character and ability. Circumstances have lifted him upon a pedestal. And if there be in him stuff to make a man of, the people will not be slow to recognize it.

When Desdemona's father was searching for Othello, Iago advised him to hide himself. His reply was:

> "Not I! I must be found.
> My parts, my title and my perfect soul
> Shall manifest me rightly."

And this certainly has been true of the colored American of our period; of the men of decided character and ability, who have found first places in the local or the general Government, that the people have not been slow to discover "the parts and title and perfect soul" of every one of them. They have had seats in both branches of the National Legis,ature; they have represented the nation abroad, and they have done it with an ability and integrity too, which is, perhaps, more remarkable, that would have brought honor to their Anglo-Saxon fellow-citizens.

Carlyle in his "Sartor-Resartus" attributes the difference between men mainly to clothes. "Consider, thou foolish Teufelsdrockh, what benefit unspeakable all ages and sexes derive from clothes. For example, when thou thyself, a watery, pulpy, slobbery freshman and new-comer in this planet, sattest mewling and puking in thy nurse's arms, sucking thy coral, and looking forth into the world in the blankest manner, what hadst thou been without thy blanket and bibs and other nameless hulls? A terror to thyself and mankind. Or, hast thou forgotten the day when thou first receivest breeches, and thy lay clothes become short? The village where thou livest was all appraised of the fact, and neighbor after neighbor kissed thy budding cheek and gave thee as handsel, silver or copper coins, on that first gala day of thy existence."

And, it is all very well for Burns to say

> "The rank is but the guinea's stamp,
> The man's the gowd for a' that."

But true as it is, the stamp is just as needful for the currency of the guinea, as the gold itself. That is the trouble with that class of men of whom the poet Gray sings:

"Far from the madding crowd's ignoble strife,
    Their sober wishes never learned to stray,
Along the cool, sequestered vale of life
    They kept the noiseless tenor of their way."

They needed the stamp to give their gold currency. There is something beside ability, which is requisite for success in life. Sometimes we call it personal magnetism; sometimes something not so flattering. Really, it is a part of what Shakespeare means when he uses the word "title" in the quotation above. Something which leads people to make way, as though in England, a nobleman were coming. Of this nameless something, which gives the world assurance of a man, Mr. Langston has his share.

It is difficult for a race to which all avenues have been open from their birth, to appreciate just what obstacles a colored man, who would rise, has had to encounter. But, perhaps, the last obstacle ever overcome is the sense that one is different from others, and the suspicion that everybody regards it a sufficient reason for keeping him back. There can be no confidence reposed in a man who is not confiding. And, if a man is all the time suspicious that people mean to affront him, he will be affronted. It is true in all social relations, that,

" Trifles light as air,
    Are to the jealous confirmations strong
    As proofs of Holy Writ."

And here is one of the great wrongs which slavery has done. It has put a mark, like the mark of Cain, upon one branch of the human family. It has made good the sentence, which was pronounced of old, upon one of the sons of Noah:

" A servant of servants shall he be unto his brethren." It has made it a presumption against any man of color, who would be anything but a field-servant, a waiter or a barber. Of course, I would not imply that any kind of work is dishonorable. But, it is a wrong, when a man who is fit for a place, or can fit himself for it, has a presumption against him because he is black. Thanks to the result of the civil war, this can never be as it has been. Mr. Langston and colored men of his period, however, had their destiny fixed before the civil war. They fought their personal battles on earlier fields. But, henceforth, it must be easier to win their early victories all over this free land.

In 1855 Mr. Langston was married to Miss C. M. Wall, of Oberlin, Ohio. The ceremony was performed by Prof. John Morgan, for whom Mr. Langston has always cherished the greatest admiration and affection. This lady, a native of North Carolina, and the daughter and slave of Col. Stephen Wall, but emancipated by him and educated among the Quakers of Harveysburgh, Ohio, and a graduate of Oberlin, has shown herself equal to the changes which have so rapidly transpired in the career of her husband, and is as much at home as the wife of Minister Resident Langston, at the Republican court of Haiti, as of lawyer Langston, of Ohio. They have had five children, four of whom are living, and all but one of whom are settled in life for themselves. Mr. Langston has always insisted that his children should have the best of society, and the best opportunities of education. Glorying in the influence of Oberlin, most of his children have been educated there. The youngest son, Frank, is in Washington learning the trade of a book-binder. Arthur, educated at Oberlin, is principal of a colored public school in St. Louis. Ralph, educated also at Oberlin, is residing at Nashville, Tennessee, where he is in the mercantile business.

and where resides his only sister, Mrs. J. C. Napier, also educated at Oberlin. Mr. Napier was one of Mr. Langston's law pupils at Howard University.

Any one acquainted with Mr. Langston will see at a glance that he represents the best type of culture among the colored people of America. Fond of books, an indefatigable student, determined to get on, ambitious for himself and for his race, with a quick and active mind, and with some of the best of America's scholars as his teachers and friends, he has enjoyed unusual advantages. But gifted as he is, his advancement has been step by step, and has been purchased by hard work. With less massive movement of mind and dignity of address than the great orator Douglass, for platform speech he is keener, and more magnetic. In person he is a little above the medium stature, slender and straight as an arrow. For suavity and grace of person he might be taken for a Frenchman. And sometimes as you look at his features you think he may be of Spanish or Italian descent. But to-day he makes his boast that he has some of the best blood of the three races, so historic in the great events of the continent: the Indian, the Negro and the Anglo-Saxon. Mr. Langston's successes have mellowed his nature and smoothed away the asperities which his early life had a tendency to provoke. His honors sit gracefully upon him, and whether at home, as an accomplished host entertaining his many friends in this District, or abroad in the service of the Government, he seems to be always a happy and contented man.

SELECTED ADDRESSES.

THE

WORLD'S ANTI-SLAVERY MOVEMENT;

ITS HEROES AND ITS TRIUMPHS.*

LADIES AND GENTLEMEN: I have selected as an appropriate theme upon which to address you on this occasion, THE WORLD'S ANTI-SLAVERY MOVEMENT; ITS HEROES AND ITS TRIUMPHS.

The anti-slavery movement, like other great movements whose aim has been the good of mankind, has not been the result of passion, has not been the invention of distempered genius. It finds its origin in the wants, the necessities of man; and its principles of love and mercy, of beneficence and good-will have their home in the bosom of God.

The paternity of the anti-slavery movement belongs to no particular individual, nation or age. Wherever oppression has exhibited its hydra-head, whether in the days of antiquity or in modern times, there the spirit that animates and energizes this grand movement, has arrayed itself in hostile and deadly conflict against it. Indeed, it has been the delight of the statesman, the philosopher, the poet, and the philanthropist of all times, to leave embalmed in his writings, as a sacred and priceless treasure to after-coming generations, the record of his deep love of freedom and his

---

* A lecture delivered at Xenia and Cleveland, Ohio, August 2d and 3d, 1858.

C

intense hatred of slavery. So we read in the writings of the great statesman of Israel words like the following: "He that stealeth a man and selleth him, or if he be found in his hand, he shall surely be put to death." And the Wise Man says: "Envy thou not the oppressor, and choose thou none of his ways." The Prophet Isaiah, too, asks with great pith and cogency: "Is not this the fast that I have chosen, to loose the bands of wickedness, to undo the heavy burdens, and to let the oppressed go free, and that ye break every yoke?" And the words of the sacred writers of a latter date are not less instinct with the same sentiment. In the New Testament the law of love is revealed in all its grandeur and beauty; for the great Nazarene Teacher declared: "Whatsoever ye would that men should do to you, do ye even so to them; for this is the law and the prophets." With great force and power, also, have the writers of Greece and Rome expressed themselves on this subject. Socrates says: "Slavery is a system of outrage and robbery." Aristotle says: "It is neither for good nor is it just, seeing all men are by nature alike and equal, that one should be lord and master over others." And Plato says: "Slavery is a system of the most complete injustice." The better judgment of Rome is expressed by her noble Cicero, in the following words: "By the grand laws of Nature all men are born free and equal, and this law is universally binding upon all men."

Nor are Germany, France, Scotland, Ireland, England, or Russia, without the distinguished honor of bearing manly testimony against oppression. Says Grotius: "Those are men stealers who abduct, keep, sell, or buy slaves or freemen. To steal a man is the highest kind of theft." And the poet Goethe says:

"Such busy multitudes I fain would see
Stand upon free soil with a people free."

A German writer of the present day uses the following truthful and glowing language : " Will you support by your vote a system that recognizes property of man in man ? A system which sanctions the sale of the child by its own father, regardless of the purpose of the buyer ? What need is there to present to you the unmitigated wrong of slavery ?" He continues : "Liberty is no exclusive property; it is the property of mankind of all ages. She is immortal; though crushed, she can never die; though banished, she will return; though fettered, she will still be free."

The Frenchman Buffon pays a deserved compliment to the colored man, and at the same time expresses commendable sympathy and tenderness of heart, when he says : "It is apparent that the unfortunate Negroes are endowed with excellent hearts, and possess the seeds of every human virtue. I cannot write their history without lamenting their miserable condition." "Humanity," he continues, "revolts at those odious oppressions that result from avarice." And Brissot says : "Slavery in all its forms, in all its degrees, is a violation of divine laws and a degradation of human nature." The brave spirit of Scotland is beautifully mirrored in the truthful words of Miller : "The human mind revolts at the serious discussion of the subject of slavery. Every individual, whatever be his country or complexion, is entitled to freedom." More than half a century ago the immortal Curran gave expression to these eloquent words : "I speak in the spirit of British law, which makes liberty commensurate with and inseparable from British soil; which proclaims even to the stranger and the sojourner, the moment he sets his foot upon British earth, that the ground on which he treads is holy, and consecrated by the genius of universal emancipation. No matter in what language his doom may have been pronounced; no matter what complexion, incompatible with freedom, an Indian or an African sun may have burnt upon him ; no matter in what disastrous battle his liberty may have been cloven down; no matter with what solemnities he may have been devoted upon the altar of slavery, the moment he touches the sacred soil of Britain the altar and the god sink together in the dust ; his soul walks abroad in her own majesty, and he stands redeemed, regenerated, and disenthralled by the irresistible genius of universal emancipation.'' Blackstone says: "If neither captivity nor contract can, by the plain law of nature and reason, reduce the parent to a state of slavery much less can they reduce the offspring." And the noble Mansfield says, in his decision in the celebrated Summerset case: "The state of slavery is of such a nature that it is incapable of being introduced on any reasons, moral or political, but only by positive law, which preserves its force long after the reasons, occasion and time itself, whence it was created, is erased from the memory. It is so odious that nothing can be sufficient to support it but positive law. Whatever inconveniences, therefore, may follow from the decision I cannot say this case is allowed or approved by the law of England, and therefore the black must be discharged."

It only remains for me to do Russia the justice to say, in this connection, that the enterprise recently inaugurated by the present Emperor for the emancipation of the serfs, gives a new lustre, a glowing halo, to her growing reputation. Nor am I unmindful of the great American declaration in favor of freedom and protestation against slavery, which is encouched in these sacred words: "We hold these truths to be self-evident : that all men are created equal, and endowed by their Creator with certain inalienable rights, among which are life, liberty, and the pursuit of happiness." Thus the great men of every nation have paid their devoirs to the Goddess of Liberty. But this love and veneration of freedom has not been confined to those who possessed mental superiority and distinguished position. The more lowly and obscure have venerated and loved that divine principle of liberty which underlies the anti-slavery movement, and whose natal day dates back to the memorable hour when God breathed into man the breath of life, and man became a living soul. And like this vital element implanted in man by Deity, and of which it is an inseparable part, liberty is itself immortal. Political assemblies can not legislate its destruction, nor can ecclesiastical decrees tarnish the glory of its existence.

The anti-slavery movement has always had its representative men ; men who have been its advocates, its champions and its heroes. Indeed, there is no department of history which the anti-slavery reformer of the present day can·read with more interest and profit than that which records the noble deeds of the brave men whose crowning honor is, that they have labored and suffered in behalf of this cause. The first representative man and hero of the anti-slavery movement of whom history makes record is the Jewish law-giver, who was appointed to appear before Pharaoh, and to demand the release of the children of Israel, and to lead them out of the land of bondage into the land of freedom. And now as we behold him " upon the misty mountain-top of antiquity " we can but admire and applaud his grand achievements. His God-appointed mission, his heroic devotion and indefatigable zeal, his untiring energy and his glorious success, render it altogether fit and proper that he should stand first among the representatives of the anti-slavery movement who conducted to triumph that movement, whose record is at once God's solemn protest against oppression and His ineffaceable and eternal proclamation in favor of the largest, the fullest freedom.

Slavery existed in Greece from her earliest history. It existed in all her various States, under different codes of laws, with more or less severity and rigor. In Chios the yoke was found too galling to be borne, and multitudes, betaking themselves to flight, found secure and permanent retreats in the mountain fastnesses of the interior of the island; and from these mountain retreats such fugitive slaves, headed by the noble Drimacos, met the expeditions of the Chians and vanquished them with great slaughter. The Chians, baffled and defeated, were glad to accept the terms, humiliating and mortifying though they were, proposed by the commander of the insurgents, and thus secure a truce. But the ardor and enthusiasm, the resolution and courage of the insurgents were inspired in a goodly degree by the valor and conduct of their brave and daring leader. Drimacos is, indeed, worthy of the highest eulogium. His moderation and wisdom, his generosity and magnanimity, his undying love of liberty and just appreciation of human rights illustrate and distinguish his character.. The very last act of his life attests the true nobility of his soul. The Chians feared his power and influence even in his old age; and, prompted by the mean spirit of oppression, they offered a great reward to any one who would capture him or bring his head. The old hero, fearing the base work of treachery, determined to make his death, as he had already made his life, a holy sacrifice to liberty. And he did. Calling to him a young man whom he greatly loved he said to him: "I have ever regarded you with a stronger affection than any other man, and to me you have been a brother. But now the days of my life are at an end, nor would I prolong them. With you, however, it is not so; youth and the bloom of youth are yours. What then is to be done? You must prove yourself to possess valor and greatness of soul; and since the State offers riches and freedom to whomsoever shall slay me and bear them my head, let the reward be yours; strike it off, and be happy." His heart-touching appeals overcame the young man; and the death of the immortal Drimacos became the price of his freedom. It is this fugitive slave, the "propitious hero," as the Chians afterwards denominated him, that I would name as another representative character and hero of the anti-slavery movement.

Roman history, also, records the life and character and conduct of a fugitive slave, who, with propriety, may be named as another hero of the anti-slavery movement. I refer to Eunus, the gallant leader of the Sicilian slaves who were twice driven to rebellion by the severity, the cruelty of their oppressors. But the noblest, the most magnificent anti-slavery struggle recorded in Roman history is that of the Gladiators, who rose in rebellion against their oppressors under the leadership of Spartacus. It is true that their plot was discovered; but a small body broke out, which was greatly increased by the rapid accession of vast numbers of other slaves, when under the courageous and skillful generalship of Spartacus, they subdued a Roman consular army, and were not themselves subdued till after a struggle of two years, and until sixty thousand of them had fallen in battle, and Spartacus himself fell fighting upon his knees upon a heap of his enemies. Possessing the strength, the size and the physical endurance that fitted him to play the part of a gladiator, he possessed, also, the courage, the skill, the energy, the resolution and the sagacity, which rendered him a brave and formidable leader. But these were not the only qualities which adorned and embellished his character. He possessed a heart full of humanity, instinct with the love of. liberty. It was this sentiment of freedom that fired and nerved his soul, that prompted every act and governed his whole life. The language of the play, then, is but the natural, the inevitable outburst of his manly spirit. In addressing his fellow gladiators he is made to say: "If ye are beasts, then stand here like fat oxen waiting for the butcher's knife. If you are men, follow me. Strike down your guard, gain the mountain passes, and then do bloody work, as did your sires at old Thermopylæ! Is Sparta dead? Is the old Grecian spirit frozen in your veins that you do crouch and cower like a belabored hound beneath his master's lash? O, comrades! Warriors! Thracians! If we must fight, let us fight for ourselves! If we must slaughter, let us slaughter our oppressors! If we must die, let it be under the clear sky, by the bright waters, in noble, honorable battle!" Among the heroes of the anti-slavery movement, whose lives and characters are portrayed in the historical annals of antiquity, a prominent and conspicuous place belongs to this fugitive gladiator.

But lest I weary your patience in dwelling too long upon the anti-slavery struggles of distant antiquity, and upon the character and lives, the daring and achievements of their master spirits, I will come at once to the history of certain anti-slavery struggles of a more recent date, whose consideration is equally fraught with interest and profit. This brings us to the fifteenth century, the last half of which is certainly distinguished for three things; first, the introduction of the African slave trade, by Antonio Gonzales, a Portuguese sea-captain; secondly, the discovery of America in 1492; and thirdly, the appropriation of the then discovered West India Islands by the Spaniards, with the reduction of the natives to slavery. These natives are said to have been a listless, improvident people, of small endurance, and ill suited to the hard labor and cruel usage of slaves. Their sad and lamentable condition aroused the sympathy of the

Dominican priest, Las Casas. Through the energetic and persevering endeavors of this advocate of the Indians, a favorable impression was made in their behalf. But "the relaxation" in favor of the Indian slave was only secured at the expense of the African. As early as 1503 a few African slaves had been brought across the Atlantic. Indeed, according to Bancroft, there were such numbers of Africans in Hispaniola at this time that Ovando, the governor of the island, entreated that the importation might nò longer be permitted. The first anti-slavery movement upon this continent, however, in favor of the African slave was an insurrection in New Segovia. Two hundred and fifty of the slaves, who belonged in the governments of Venezuela and Santa Marta, prompted not by their natural fierceness and arrogance, as the Spanish historian would have us believe, but by their love of liberty and their determination to be free, gathered themselves together and made a desperate struggle for their freedom. It is true that they were over-powered and put to the sword. But their attempt, their manly struggle, though they were defeated, challenges our admiration.

The first importation of slaves from Africa by the English was made during the reign of Queen Elizabeth in 1562. The noble Queen herself is said to have doubted the propriety and lawfulness of the procedure. Indeed, she seems to have entertained religious scruples concerning it, and to have revolted at its very thought. She imposed upon Captain Hawks, the first Englishman who transported African slaves to America, the most rigid injunctions. Fearing that the Africans would be carried away from their native land without their consent, she declared to him that "It would be detestable, and call down the very curse of Heaven upon the undertakers." Though thus early introduced there was

no well-organized or well-adjusted effort made for its overthrow till 1787.   This movement, however, had its fearless
harbingers, prominent among whom were Morgan Godwin,
Richard Baxter, Edmund Burke, and the pure-minded and
indomitable Granville Sharp, whose peculiar mission it was
to establish the principle that, according to English law, as
soon as a slave sets his foot on English territory his shackles
fall and he becomes free; thus giving a complete refutation
to the opinion of York and Talbot, that a slave by coming
from the West Indies into Great Britain or Ireland, either
with or without his master, does not become free, and that
the master may legally compel him to return to his plantation.

John Wesley, the founder of Methodism, and George Fox,
the founder of the society of Quakers, deserve special mention in this connection.   The names of others press upon
me, but I must not tarry to mention them.   In 1785 the immortal Thomas Clarkson made his appearance, and took his
position as the advocate of the outraged slaves; as the
leader of the movement in favor of the abolition of the slave
trade.   His labors were many and arduous.   But with a
zeal and devotion worthy of the noble cause which he had
espoused, he was ready to make any sacrifice and meet the
heaviest task.   The movement, however, needed a representative and hero in Parliament.   This want was supplied in
the mild and amiable, the firm and courageous, the able and
laborious Wilberforce.   It was at this time in the history of
the cause that its friends and advocates formed themselves
into an association.   Through the instrumentality of Clarkson and the members of this association outside of Parliament, and Wilberforce, Pitt, Fox and Burke, with others, in
Parliament, after a twenty-years struggle, in 1807, the slave
trade was abolished.   But the anti-slavery spirit of England

did not become extinct with the abolition of the slave trade. Its triumph there only nerved it for the work of abolishing slavery itself, which reached its consummation in the emancipation of 800,000 West India bondmen. It is the glorious triumph of this movement that we have met to-day to commemorate. And it is altogether fit and proper that we should thus commemorate it ; for it is one of the grandest achievements of the world's anti-slavery movement. It was not the result of a bloody and cruel war. Its honor and glory belong not to the prowess, the cunning and the skill of some military chieftain, It was a great moral triumph, whose power and glory belong to those "mild arms of truth and love made mighty through the living God."

Upon the consequences of this movement many interesting and important things might be said did time permit. I will only say, however, that emancipation in the West Indies has brought to the inhabitants the most beneficial results. To this assertion all persons well acquainted with the condition of the planters and laboring classes of the islands will bear the most satisfactory testimony. The emancipated classes are now enjoying the advantages of freedom; are devoting themselves to honest and profitable industry, and to the cultivation of morality and religion. Now they enjoy the elective franchise and are eligible to exalted positions of honor and trust in the State. They are not only eligible to such high offices, but many of their number are to-day filling them with great credit to themselves and honor and profit to the State. In both Houses of the Legislature of Jamaica, and in the Privy Council of the Governor, are colored men who are distinguished for their probity, sagacity, and wisdom. Indeed, the most eminent politician of Jamaica, Hon. Edward Jordon, is a colored man, and is said to be the principal member of

Governor Darling's Cabinet. He is also Mayor of Kingston. But he is not the only colored man of the island whose position entitles him to special mention in this connection. The position and services of Vickars, Price, and Walters, not to mention others, render them conspicuous and noteworthy.

But upon this subject, fruitful of thought and advantageous reflection, I cannot dwell. In leaving it I would refer the incredulous and uninformed to the able letter of S. B. Slack, of Jamaica, upon the actual results of emancipation in that island, recently published in the New York *Tribune*.

Passing over other struggles and triumphs of the anti-slavery movement, their heroes and representative men, I come at once to the bloody contest of Haiti. Unlike the peaceful triumph of the emancipation of the British West Indies, the struggle of Haiti was full of blood, carnage, and death. Unlike the emancipation movement of the West Indies, also, this movement was inaugurated and carried to triumph by colored men themselves. They caught the spirit of the French Revolution, and vowed eternal hostility to slavery. Their souls were aroused by the announcement in the celebrated Declaration of Rights, "that all men are free and equal." It was the struggle of a people who, driven to desperation by inhuman and intolerable oppression, made one last, mighty effort to throw off their yoke and gain their manhood, and assert and maintain their rights. Fired with this sentiment, they made that resolution which always brings a glad and glorious success to a people armed in a just and holy cause. The moving spirit of the first insurrection was James Oge. While residing in Paris he made the acquaintance and enjoyed the familiar friendship of Brissot, Robespierre, Lafayette, and other revolutionists connected with the society *Amis des Noirs*. From these men he learned his lessons of freedom. Resolving to become the deliverer of his race he returned to his native land on the 12th day of October, 1790, and announced himself, in the language of the historian, as the redresser of his people's wrongs. He commenced his work with a force two hundred strong. But circumstances were not yet ripe for the undertaking. Oge was defeated and compelled, with several of his companions, to take refuge in the Spanish portion of the island. He was demanded, however, from the Spaniards, and in March, 1791, was broken alive upon the wheel. A sad fate, indeed, for a man of such generous impulses and noble purpose, a hero of such self-sacrifice and benevolent enterprise, a patriot so deeply devoted to his country and the welfare of the people.

A similar though more barbarous fate was the portion of his associates, Vincent Oge and Jean Baptiste Chevanne. History nowhere records anything more cruel and inhuman than the condemnation passed by the court upon these men. The stoutest, the hardest heart must shudder at its words. They were to be conducted, according to Lacroix, "by the public executioner to the church of Cape François, and there bareheaded, *en chemise*, with a rope about their necks, upon their knees, and holding in their hands a wax candle of two pounds weight, to declare they had wickedly, rashly, and by evil instigation, committed the crimes of which they had been accused and convicted, and there and then that they repent of them, and ask the forgiveness of God, of the king, and the violated justice of the realm; that they should then be conducted to *La Place d' Armes* of the said town, and in the place opposite to that appropriated to the execution of *white men*, to have their arms, legs, hips, and thighs broken alive; that they should be placed upon a wheel with their faces toward heaven, and there remain so long as God should preserve their lives. After their death their heads were to be severed from their bodies and placed upon poles; that of Oge on the road to Dondon, that of Chevanne on the road to Grande Riviere, and the property of both was to be confiscated to the king."

It is said that Oge lost his firmness in this terrible moment, but that Chevanne died, as he had lived, the same stern, unyielding foe of his oppressors, But the martyrdom of these heroes of the first insurrection did not quench the growing determination of the people to be free. Indeed, it was the rallying-cry of the after-struggle. At this time all things in France and in the island conspired to hasten the insurrection which had been espoused by Vincent Oge before his execution. The story of the barbarous death of Oge created in France a terrible storm of popular indignation against the planters. The feeling now in favor of the colored people became intense and vehement. And the National Assembly, borne along upon the tide of popular enthusiasm, passed a decree giving citizenship to all colored persons in the colonies born of free parents, and, also, making them eligible to seats in the colonial judicatures. But when the news of the passage of this decree reached the island it filled the planters with ungovernable anger. All were for throwing off allegiance to the mother country and hoisting the English flag. Their fierce anger was at length allayed. It was not long, however, before the cry, "The blacks have risen!" sent a thrill to the hearts of the planters more terrible than the awful tread of an earthquake.

It was on the night of the twenty-second day of August, 1791, that the second Haitian insurrection broke forth. Its beginnings were of comparatively small account, but its progress was rapid and wide-spread, so that in a short time it reached "from the sea to the mountains." Destruction and devastation marked its course. Neither life nor property was spared; both were destroyed. The insurgents were determined not only to destroy their masters, but everything which reminded them of their former servile condition. They offered all things as a bloody and burning sacrifice to freedom. They made the flames that wrapt the vast fields of cane in their fiery arms, that devoured the dwellings and mills of flourishing plantations and the lowly cabins, once their own homes, to illuminate the path-way of liberty in its glorious coming to the bondmen of Haiti. To Buckman, Jean François, Jeannot and Biassou belongs the honor of conducting this movement through its first stages. They led their forces against vindictive and cruel foes; foes that would not only subjugate, but enslave them; under whom they had already felt the sharp sting of the lash, and suffered the untold agonies of slavery. It is not strange, then, that in this contest cruelty met cruelty, barbarity barbarity, and many things were done which all are forced to lament and deplore.

In the mean time many white colonists, despairing of peace and prosperity, had left the island; some coming to the United States, and others going to Great Britain and to the neighboring Island of Jamaica. Through the influence of the royalist who had gone from France to Great Britain and the colonists who had gone from Haiti, proposals were made to the British government to take possession of the island and make it a British colony. These proposals were favorably received, and accordingly a British force appeared in the island on the 20th of September, 1793. Then it was that there was to be seen upon the field of conflict four belligerent parties, the English, the French, the Spanish, and the blacks. At this time, too, great confusion and disorganization prevailed.

Then it was that the master spirit of the Haitian Revolution, Toussaint l'Ouverture, made his appearance. And his coming was like the radiance of morning, all bright and beautiful. The eyes of the whole world were upon him. God had brought him forth, "with Atlantean shoulders," strong and powerful, to bear the responsibilities of a momentous emergency. This great man, than whom a greater never lived, was born in 1743, on Count de Noes plantation, a short distance from Cape François. The son of parents purely African, he was, nevertheless, even in his boyhood, distinguished for his gentleness and stability of temper, his deep reflection, and his love and veneration for religion. These peculiarities marked his entire life. Indeed, it was these qualities of character, connected with his great genius, his remarkable patience, Christian moderation and robust constitution, that gave him such power of endurance, which made him the man for the hour; which placed him at the head of the forces fighting for freedom.

In every relation of life this man was a model man. As husband and father, he was altogether without fault, always exhibiting towards his wife the tenderest love, and towards his children the most affectionate and fatherly solicitude; while as a friend his conduct was distinguished by the most unwonted generosity and magnanimity. This is beautifully and touchingly illustrated in his behavior towards his master and family when danger threatened them, and he imperilled his own life to secure their succor. As lieutenant-governor his rigid though just discipline, his well-adjusted and judicious plans, his magical influence and power over the people, soon brought to the island peace and prosperity. But the character of this extraordinary man shines most brilliantly and beautifully in his conduct as a great military leader and hero. It was in this capacity that his wonderful originality and independence, his ingenuity and skill, his genius and power found ample scope for their display. Toussaint l'Ouverture was the most extraordinary man of his age, though he lived in an age remarkable for its extraordinary men. A slave for nearly fifty years, he stepped from slavery into freedom, and at once showed himself an intellectual and moral prodigy. Superior to Napoleon and Washington as a great military leader, he was, like Washington, inclined to the arts of peace. It is not strange that Napoleon, while he studied Toussaint as his model and patron, feared him as a rival, and did not hesitate to make use of the basest treachery to secure his overthrow and destruction. He knew full well his just title to the appellation "The Opener," and read in his great native ability and attainments the brilliant career that awaited him.

The words of Toussaint after his overthrow were full of inspiration and truth : "In overthrowing me you have overthrown only the trunk of the tree of Negro liberty in Santo Domingo. It will arise again from the roots, because they are many, and have struck deep." Indeed, slavery was never re-established in that island. Christophe, Dessalines and Clerveaux rose in arms and forty thousand Frenchmen were made an atoning sacrifice for the temerity of Bonaparte.

I will not harrow up your feelings by dwelling upon the sad fate of the great Haitian hero, upon his cruel separation from his family, nor his death in a "cold, damp and gloomy dungeon," in the castle of Joux, among the Jura mountains. Nor will I, I need not, dwell upon the success and the happy consequence of the Haitian revolution. To all people struggling for freedom, it is a glorious bow of promise, spanning the moral heavens.

Thus, whenever, wherever liberty has made a stand against oppression, whether with the arms of "truth and love," or with the sword and bayonet, she has always won the most

D

brilliant, splendid triumphs.   And in these triumphs of the
past we read the sure prophecy of " the good time coming "
to the American anti-slavery movement.

This movement also had its forerunners.   Upon their history and doings I will not tarry to say a single word.   When
the time came, however, for the movement to make a new development, to take on another type, to make a higher aim, to
assume a definite and positive character, and to receive a new
impulse, God, as in time past, raised up a man who has
shown himself equal to the arduous undertaking.   That
man was the immortal William Lloyd Garrison.   A man of
obscure parentage, without the prestige of a great name or
the magical influence of wealth, but possessing great moral
courage, stability of character, and Christian fortitude, he
came forth as the advocate of liberty, declaring : " I am in
earnest; I will not equivocate; I will not excuse; I will not
retreat a single inch; and I will be heard !"   He and his associates announced in substance, in their celebrated anti-slavery
declaration of 1833, that all men are created free and equal;
that slavery is a stupendous wrong; that it is an outrage
upon humanity and a sin against God; that no man can by
right gain property in the body and soul of his fellow, and
that slavery ought to be immediately and unconditionally
abolished.

The achievements of the American anti-slavery movement
since that time have been such as to impart hope and
courage to every heart.   Of course, I do not refer to the
achievements of any separate and distinct organization.   I
refer to the achievements of that complicated and stupendous organization composed of persons from all parts of this
country, whose aim is the abolition of slavery and the
enfranchisement of the colored American.   What, then, are
some of its accomplishments ?

In the first place, it has brought the subject of slavery itself distinctly and prominently before the public mind. Indeed, in every nook and corner of American society this matter now presents itself, demanding, and in many instances receiving, respectful consideration. There is no gathering of the people, whether political or religious, which is not now forced to give a place in its deliberations to this subject. Like the air we breathe, it is all-pervasive. Through this wide-spread consideration the effects of slavery upon the slave, the slaveholder, and society generally, have been very thoroughly demonstrated ; and as the people have understood these effects they have loathed and hated their foul cause. Thus the public conscience has been aroused, and a broad and deep and growing interest has been created in behalf of the slave.

In the next place, it has vindicated, beyond decent cavil even, the claim of the slave to manhood and its dignities. No one of sense and decency now thinks that the African slave of this country is not a man. No sensible slaveholder now dares to deny his humanity. Instead of this, the leading slaveholders now claim that *all* laboring classes, whether white or black, ought to be slaves, no longer predicating their claim to the Negro slave on the ground that he is wanting in humanity. Possessing intellect, sensibility and will, judgment, understanding and imagination, sense, consciousness and fancy, reason and conscience, the American bondman is a man capable of the most refined culture and the noblest endeavor. And the anti-slavery movement has fully attested the truthfulness of this declaration.

The anti-slavery movement has also shown the real condition of the poor non-slaveholding whites of the South ; that they have no rights which are to be respected and cared for when the interests of slavery are to be looked after ; that their right to think freely and to give free utterance to their opinions is altogether denied them ; that they have no free voice, no untrammelled utterance, in political or religious matters ; but their opinions are manufactured for them, and they must receive them at the hands of their self-styled superiors ; that they are denied all educational advantages, and their children are left to grow up in ignorance, and spend their lives in indolence and dissipation. Nor have they the means, the opportunity, of acquiring wealth. They cannot with facility gain a moderate competency. Looked at from any standpoint, their condition is truly an unfortunate one. In it we see the blighting effects of slavery upon free labor. Indeed, free labor and slavery cannot live together. This must be so ; for let the masses be educated, let them enjoy freedom of thought and freedom of speech, and slavery could not stand. This huge image of error and wrong would soon soon tremble and fall to the ground. May God hasten the day when light shall burst upon the minds of these poor whites who now sit in the shadow of death, and they, knowing their rights, shall assert and maintain them like men ; and through their enfranchisement light and liberty may come to the poor bondman ! Indeed, the poor white man of the South and the slave ought to be linked in friendship stronger than iron chains ; for a common enemy preys upon their freedom.

In like manner the anti-slavery movement has fastened the attention of the world upon the impudent and daring encroachments of slavery upon the rights and liberties of the people of the North. In doing this the deep baseness of the Florida war, the annexation of Texas, the enactment of the Fugitive Slave Law, the repeal of the Missouri Compromise, the attempt to force slavery upon the people of Kansas, and the Dred-Scott decision, have been most fully and

completely developed, while the nefarious outrage perpetrated in the practical abrogation of that clause of the Constitution which guarantees to the citizens of each State all
the rights and immunities of the citizens of the several
States, as well as the outrage perpetrated by the greedy
assumption of well-nigh all the patronage of the National
Government, has been thoroughly exposed. This has led
the people of the North to array themselves against this
common pest of the country. And now we have a North as
well as a South.

The anti-slavery movement has also offered a most triumphant vindication of the anti-slavery character of the Declaration of Independence, whose broad and comprehensive
definition of freedom includes every human being, whether
white or black, whether born in heathen lands or in the
midst of civilization and Christianity. Indeed, the Declaration is no glittering generality, no beautiful abstraction.
Its doctrines of freedom are solemn verities. It has also
vindicated, by an argument incapable of refutation, the anti-
slavery character of the Constitution of the United States,
and has met and refuted the foul aspersion of the Bible,
that it sanctions and sanctifies slavery. And now, in the
name of the Bible, the Constitution, and the Declaration,
we demand the immediate and unconditional abolition of
slavery.

Another important and splendid achievement of this movement is the establishment of its own literature—a literature
peculiar and distinct, and yet distinguished for its excellences and beauties. This could not be otherwise, for many
of the most eminent scholars, poets and philosophers of the
country are its contributors. Our anti-slavery books, full
of valuable and interesting thoughts, rendered acceptable by
an appropriate and graceful style, are not only read by all

classes, in every section of this country, but are read and admired by the common people, and the critics of other lands. These books are our constant companions. In society and solitude, the living thoughts they contain burn and glow in our hearts. The influence of our anti-slavery literature is silent, yet potential, well-nigh omnipotent. It is true that one good book is more powerful than a thousand soldiers clad in arms. The attack of an army is for the most part sudden; it may be desperate, but the influence of a book is deep, wide-spread and permanent. It is imperishable and ever active. What a wonderful, matchless influence, then, our anti-slavery publications are exerting upon the public mind ; through their stubborn facts, convincing the judgment, and through their earnest and pathetic appeals in behalf of freedom, charming and captivating the heart.

This movement also has its living orators. These orators possess the noblest of all themes—a theme whose simple announcement touches the human heart, and wakes a response deep and lasting. It is a theme, too, which affords the most ample field for the display of the stoutest faculties of thought and reason, of imagination and fancy. Upon the "resistless eloquence wielded" by these orators, their incomparable rhetoric, and its admirable effect, I need not pronounce a panegyric. The beauty and power of their productions must be admitted by all. Indeed, to them more than any other class—to Phillips and Sumner, to Parker and Beecher, to Smith and Cheever, to Douglas and Seward, to Remond and Burleigh—belong the honor of building up an aristocracy of American eloquence, whose authority and sway are extensive and influential. In its authors and orators, this movement has made one of its most imposing achievements.

More than this, the anti-slavery movement has brought to the colored people of the North the opportunities of developing themselves intellectually and morally. It has unbarred and thrown open to them the doors of colleges, academies, law schools, theological seminaries and commercial institutions, to say nothing of the incomparable district school. Of these opportunities they have very generally availed themselves; and now, wherever you go, whether to the East or the West, you will find the colored people comparatively intelligent, industrious, energetic and thrifty, as well as earnest and determined in their opposition to slavery. Indeed, they have already been able to furnish a large number of earnest, laborious and efficient workers to this cause; workers of whose endeavors and success we need not be ashamed. With the opportunities offered for their intellectual and moral development they have also had the means of acquiring wealth, which they have not failed to improve. And now their pecuniary ability is not of insignificant account. In the State of Ohio alone thirty thousand colored persons are the owners of six millions of dollars' worth of property, every cent of which stands pledged to the support of the cause of the slave. Animated by the same spirit of liberty that nerved their fathers, who fought in the Revolutionary war and war of 1812, to free this land from British tyranny, they are the inveterate and uncompromising enemies of oppression, and are willing to sacrifice all that they have, both life and property, to secure its overthrow. But they have more than moral and pecuniary strength. In some of the States of this Union all of their colored inhabitants, and in others a very large class of them, enjoy the privileges and benefits of citizens. This is a source of very great power. For next to the magical dollar, the vote is that instrumentality by which the soul of an American is led captive at one's will. This influence, too, is consecrated and pledged to the slave.   No Democratic politician; no hollow-hearted politician of any party whatever; no man who is not a devoted, laborious, anti-slavery man can ever secure our vote.   Money cannot buy it.   Flattering promises of self-aggrandizement cannot induce its desecration; for it is a sacred thing, and shall be used as Ithuriel's spear, to stab the demon of slavery. To have brought the means of education and development to such a people, a people possessing such a spirit, is certainly one of the most desirable and valuable achievements of the American anti-slavery movement.

Another achievement of the American anti-slavery movement is the emancipation of forty or fifty thousand fugitive slaves, who stand to-day as so many living, glowing refutations of the brainless charge that nothing has, as yet, been accomplished   Indeed, this movement exhibits great moral muscle and strength, shows itself a moral giant, when despite the Fugitive Slave Law and the vigilant patrol of the South, it sends its powerful and magical influences to the everglades of Florida, the cane-fields of Louisiana, and the rice swamps of South Carolina, and leads out thence the peeled and broken slave.   Nor does this movement leave the fleeing bondman without protection and care in his new home in the North.   Wherever he goes, now, whether in our large cities or into our rural districts, he finds friends either to welcome or give him help for his further journey to the freer land of Queen Victoria.

But the crowning achievement of the anti-slavery movement of this country is the establishment, full and complete, of the fact that its great aim and mission is not merely the liberation of four millions of American slaves, and the enfranchisement of six hundred thousand half freemen, but the preservation of the American Government, the preservation of American liberty itself. It has been discovered, at last, that slavery is no respecter of persons, that in its far-reaching and broad sweep it strikes down alike the freedom of the black man and the freedom of the white one. This movement can no longer be regarded as a sectional one. It is a great national one. It is not confined in its benevolent, its charitable offices, to any particular class; its broad philanthropy knows no complexional bounds. It cares for the freedom, the rights of us all. Some may call this representation a fancy sketch; rhetorical gammon. But it must be evident to every one conversant with American affairs that we are now realizing in our national experience the important and solemn truth of history, that the enslavement and degradation of one portion of the population fastens galling, festering chains upon the limbs of the other. For a time these chains may be invisible; yet they are iron-linked and strong; and the slave power, becoming strong-handed and defiant, will make them felt. This identification of the interests of the white and colored people of the country, this peculiarly national feature of the anti-slavery movement is one of its most cheering, hope-inspiring and hope-supporting characteristics. This fact is encouraging because the white Americans cannot stand as idle spectators to the struggle, but must unite with us in battling against this fell enemy if they themselves would save their own freedom. Indeed, the unchivalrous though natural behavior of the slave oligarchy has already aroused the people of the North to a consciousness of this burning truth. And the deep, solemn voice of the people as it comes thundering up from the hills of New England and from the prairies of the West is pronouncing their heroic determination to meet and overthrow this power. Their cry is: "The slave oligarchy must die; the slave oligarchy shall die!"

These are some of the achievements of the anti-slavery movements of our own country. From its very beginning it has gone steadily on in its career of triumph. No power has been able to withstand it. In its irresistible march it has split to pieces all the great ecclesiastical and political organizations of the country. It has overthrown, utterly overthrown, the old Whig party, and written across the Democratic party, the other stronger ally of slavery, in burning characters: "Thy days are numbered." It has changed the National Congress and the State legislatures into anti-slavery conventions, and has shipwrecked the fortunes of many distinguished men, who had fastened their political destinies to a blind though ardent defence of slavery. These achievements of our American movement augur and insure its ultimate success, and the triumphs of the world's great anti-slavery movement, to which allusion has been made, predict the sure coming of the millennium of liberty.

Let us, then, disfranchised Americans, take new courage; for our cause and the cause of the slave shall triumph gloriously. With hearts full of hope, and a determination to battle for the right against the wrong, let us adopt the beautiful sentiment of the poet :

> "God speed the year of Jubilee,
>   The wide world o'er !
> When, from their galling chains set free,
> The oppressed shall vilely bend the knee
> And wear the yoke of tyranny,
>   Like brutes, no more.
> That year will come, and freedom's reign
> To man his plundered rights again
>   Restore.
>
> God speed the day when human blood
>   Shall cease to flow !
> In every clime be understood
> The claims of human brotherhood,

And each return for evil, good—
    Not blow for blow.
THAT DAY WILL COME, all feuds to end,
And change into a faithful friend
    Each foe.

God speed the hour, the glorious hour,
    When none on earth
Shall exercise a lordly power,
Nor in a tyrant's presence cower,
But all to manhood's stature tower,
    By equal birth!
That hour will come, to each, to all,
And from his prison-house the thrall
    Go forth.

Until that year, day, hour arrive,
With head and heart and hand I'll strive
To break the rod and rend the gyve—
The spoiler of his prey deprive;
    So witness, Heaven!
And never from my chosen post,
Whate'er the peril or the cost,
    Be driven."

DANIEL O'CONNELL.

THE GREAT AGITATOR'S YOUNG LIFE—HIS POWER AS A STATESMAN—HIS EFFORTS AS AN ABOLITIONIST—THE EFFECT OF HIS LIFE ON THE TIMES IN WHICH HE LIVED.*

I should not describe to you my feelings if I did not at once say that I feel specially honored by the invitation which brings me before you on this occasion, and as I enter upon the duty which the acceptance of this invitation imposes, I realize most keenly my inability to meet your expectation by treating with fullness of learning and power the subject upon which I am to speak.

Masters of the pen, orators, indeed, of this and other countries have made Daniel O'Connell, his peculiarities, his virtues, his achievements, the subject of their discourse and their address. From this very platform America's most elegant, captivating and eloquent orator has dwelt with his own peculiar power, in his most happy mood, upon this theme.

Why now should I, after so much has been written, so much said, so beautifully and so eloquently, with so much truth and power, be asked to offer a humble word in eulogy

---

* A lecture delivered in Lincoln Hall, Washington, D. C., December 28, 1874.

and commendation of Ireland's greatest son? Is it because he did peculiar work in behalf of the class, citizens of our own country, with whom I am peculiarly identified ? Was he an abolitionist, demanding at Dublin and at London, among the Irish and the English, sending his voice, like that of the storm, till mankind heard it, that slavery, the chattelizing of the American Negro, be unconditionally and immediately abolished ? Was he a reformer of such large comprehension, humanity, sense of justice and right, wisdom and sagacity, that he limited in his conceptions human freedom and legal rights by no boundaries of color, nationality or caste? Or has our country reached that hour when the name of this great and good man, statesman and patriot, should be pronounced and dwelt upon to inspirit, animate and support those newly emancipated, admitted and welcomed to the body-politic with the ballot in their hands, as well as those native and naturalized, once citizens of Erin, now citizens and voters of our country, who are resolved to make this country, in its law, its religion, and its politics, pure, exalted, enduring ?

As to these questions the sequel will make my answer. Although this answer is anticipated, if not wholly, partly by your knowledge of the past history and utterances of the great agitator.

Born in 1775, Daniel O'Connell breathed from his birth an atmosphere of revolution. Change, readjustment, progress, even through blood, was seen and felt in every direction, in the midst of the leading nations of the earth. Before he had completed the first year of his age America made her memorable Declaration of Independence, and thus a nation so far discovering vigor, purpose, energy, enterprise, devotion and valor, has gone forward, advancing in years and distinguishing itself in military, commercial, scientific, literary, political and moral achievements. It is not in the power of man to estimate the influence of our own Declaration and our struggle for independence upon the youthful O'Connell. This we know, that such a declaration was never made by a nation of any lineage or tongue prior to the Fourth of July, 1776, and the world has produced no single individual who has discovered a larger and more practical knowledge of that declaration than this great man. Nor is it possible for us to estimate the influence of other reform movements among other nations preceding and reaching to and beyond the period of his birth and youth. Born at this particular juncture in the affairs of the world, with influences of the character indicated brought to bear upon him from near and far, with native endowments peculiar to the genuine Irishman : warmth of soul, vigor of intellect, ardor and susceptibility of temperament, sternness and persistency of impulse, carrying for the time being the mind and will; with affections tender, sympathy quick and abundant, it was natural—indeed it would have been contrary to all mental law had it been otherwise—that O'Connell should be in his manhood the brave, persistent leader of his race.

But in this connection we are not to forget that he sprang from a people who have given the world more great men in proportion to their numbers than any nation on the face of the earth. And many of these eminent men are peculiarly distinguished for the possession and display of those qualities of character which make the greatest men of the world. Edmund Burke, the statesman of Beaconsfield, "whose last thoughts, last wishes, like his first, were with his native land," stands as author, orator and statesman, as original thinker in the world's estimation, pre-eminent among the great men of his day. Richard Brinsley Sheridan, in delivery and effectiveness of address, in his day second to no

man in the British Parliament; Henry Grattan, the brightest
ornament of the Home Parliament, who was present when
the constitutional charter of 1782 restored Ireland to the
rank and dignity of a free nation; who was also present
when the Legislative Union was formed destroying her independence; Plunkett, Grattan's associate and friend in the
Irish and Imperial Parliaments—with Grattan in 1782, with
him in 1800, were in their endowments, achievements, their
entire life, the mirror of those elements of character which
mark real greatness.

It will be recollected that it was Plunkett who, in 1782,
pleading for the life and independence of Ireland and her
Parliament, in addressing his associates used the memorable
words: "Yourselves you may extinguish, but Parliament
you cannot extinguish. It is enthroned in the hearts of the
people; it is enshrined in the sanctuary of the constitution;
it is as immortal as the island that protects it. As well
might the frantic suicide imagine that the act which destroys
his miserable body should also extinguish his eternal soul.
Again, therefore, I warn you. Do not lay your hands on
the constitution; it is above your powers!"

Here other names which illustrate and adorn Irish history
crowd upon my memory: Curran, Shiel, Phillips, Emmet,
Moore, Doyle, McHale and others of like character and
influence. But upon these I may not dwell. The struggles
through which the Irish people have been led to pass, as well
as the peculiar elements of their national life, have tended
to produce in abundance, and with marked traits of character, leading and eminent men. National, like individual
struggles, if not indispensable to, tend to the production of
power and greatness in man and nations.

I neither sympathize with those who take simply the poetic
view of Ireland, representing her as a "mountain nymph,

with flowing garments, wavy ringlets, glowing countenance, enrapt eye and Venus-like fingers, trilling the strings of a harp," nor with those who, taking the prosaic view simply, liken her to a " mother seated on the mud floor of a log cabin, clad in rags, with disheveled hair, pinched features, eyes too hot and dry for tears, and skinny fingers, dividing a rotten potato among a brood of famishing children." Both views are too extreme. To me neither seems truthful. The first, certainly, seems unlike humanity. The latter represents a condition of want and degradation which not even the oppressed and outraged children of Ireland, as a nation, have reached. I prefer to regard Ireland as a nation of valiant sons and daughters, struggling with the hard things of life, to be sure; deserving, as they are entitled to, better things by far, but made of such excellent material, and possessed and influenced by such sterling purpose as that they produce in the throes of struggle, not a few, but a multitude of great and influential men. Such nation has given the world the immortal O'Connell.

Educated, as to academical study, at Saint Omers, in France; as to his profession, the law, in England, at London, and in the Middle Temple; seeing the men and feeling the influence of other lands than his own ; led as he was, to cultivate thought, sobriety and purpose of life, he learned neither to despise nor forget, though oppressed and lowly, the land and people of his birth and with whom he was identified in blood, achievement and destiny.

His first tutor was an Irish priest, from whom he learned early lessons, quickening to conscience, arousing patriotic devotion, and fixing the ardor, the purpose, the impulses even of his soul on the side of personal purity, fidelity and duty.

It is reported of this tutor that he was "a Christian in the

truly evangelical meaning of the word, since his faith in Christ
Jesus brought him but sneers and persecution; a scholar,
whose views were all impregnated with the salt of sound theology and whose manner of instruction was often tinctured
with the solemn gloom of the cloister. Such was the first
priest with whom the future Emancipator became acquainted,
and it would be idle to deny that this good man's character
had deeply impressed him with that high admiration, amount-
ing almost to reverence, ever manifested towards the clergy,
and that lively sense of the necessity of a Christian life, the
practice of which is one of the most glorious traits in his
character."

At Saint Omers two classes of students were educated:
the sons of Irish emigrants, long resident of France, and the
sons of Irish parents, still residents of their native land, driven
thence by the penal code to seek abroad learning, knowledge,
mental discipline, indispensable to high moral endeavor and
triumph.

Speaking of the students of Saint Omers, the author of
"O'Connell and His Friends" uses these beautiful words:
"It must have been a glorious sight to behold the amity
which subsisted between these two branches of the old Mile-
sian stock—the one flourishing in a free, foreign soil, the other
preferring to stand on Irish ground in defiance of every
storm, still aspiring under the multitude of its chains."

To the latter class, as we know full well, O'Connell belonged;
and aspiring, though under chains, he gave evidence of the
possession of that faith in himself and in the Irish people
which made him in after years their liberator, and them his
willing, confiding, ardent and admiring constituency. Returning from England, O'Connell was admitted to the Irish
bar, at Dublin, in 1798.

"The Irish bar," says McGee, "was still in the glory of its

E

independence; there was buoyancy in the national heart, and a generous emulation ran through the Senate, the bar and the press. The voice of Curran was heard in the Four Courts, drying the tears his pathos had caused. * * * The silver tones and gorgeous figures of Bushe were there in meridian brilliancy, 'charming a verdict by the silent witchery of his manner.' The morose yet unfathomable mind of Saurin, rich alike in logic and learning, made another giant figure in that group of colossal jurists; while pressing hard after them in the career of fame, came a younger and scarcely less noble race: Holmes, Thomas Addis Emmet and Louis Perrin. Such was the school to which the pupil of Saint Omers came, already rich in learning, skilled in elocution and subtle in debate. Here his first Irish lessons were received, and assuredly he has done no discredit to his instructors."

Early in his professional life, before he gained solid footing, while yet in his twenty-third year, he witnessed the defeat of the projected revolution of the "United Irishmen." Here he was taught, as some one has said, "another painful lesson in the science of reform." Quickly thereafter he witnessed with sorrowing heart what shall prove, it is to be hoped, but the seeming death and funeral of Irish independence. The actors, the scenes, the horrors of 1798 and 1800 made such an impression upon his tender but vigorous and manly soul, that he "vowed before God to devote his energies to his country and its altars, and to live but for the emancipation of both." As I dwell upon this consecration of O'Connell to the freedom of his country and countrymen, I call to mind but a single individual consecration of grander character, more excellent and beautiful. I refer to the consecration of the noble, self-sacrificing and heroic American who, forgetting the odds against him, the contempt, the ridicule, the social ostracism, the baptism of pain and suffering which awaited and which would pour like a flood upon him, became the champion of the Negro's emancipation and enfranchisement, declaring: "I am in earnest; I will not equivocate; I will not excuse; I will not retreat a single inch, and I will be heard!"

William Lloyd Garrison still lives. He rejoices in the triumph of that cause to which he dedicated the strength of his manhood and the wisdom of his age. It would have been well, as it seems to me, could Daniel O'Connell have witnessed the restoration of Irish independence, the re-establishment of her Home Parliament, as well as Catholic emancipation—the freedom of the national conscience. But hail to these sons of truth and freedom, whose bloodless weapons, wielded by strong hands, sustained by stout hearts, made powerful, omnipotent through God and the right, brought liberty and happiness to millions, sorely, bitterly oppressed.

A wise and just analysis will discover in the character of O'Connell those qualities which shine in leadership; which make greatness possible. The first of these is essential and positive individuality. Every truly great man who becomes and does that which perpetuates his name as the friend of the people, the conservator of virtue and the general good, is himself. I speak not of the first class of great men; not of those who build up the foundations of others; whose advocacy of principles or measures is by authority; but of those who remove rubbish, lay solid and enduring foundations, and rear thereupon superstructures of utility, grace, beauty and grandeur; who themselves create precedents and perpetuate their authority. Such individuality, such essence of selfhood, O'Connell possessed; and the characteristics of his nationality no more distinguished him than his individualism. He was an Irishman, but he was more; he was Daniel O'Connell. He did not fail to assert, to render positive the personality of which I speak, as his efforts in the forum, on the hustings, and in Parliament, abundantly attest. Conviction, something other and more than the intellectual recognition, acceptance even, of truth and obligation, the sense of sincerity, honesty, faith and duty burning in his soul, firing his imagination, impelling and controlling his will, is an element entering largely into that rare combination of qualities composing the very being and distinguishing the life and conduct of this great man.

Addressing his constituents at Ennis, refusing to take the oath of supremacy at the bar of the House of Commons, advancing popular reform by tongue, pen, public and private influence, he impressed and moved every one—the people, law-givers, officials, the king even—by the manifestation of the intensity, the ardor, the enthusiasm of his conviction. A learned doctor of theology once said: "My bones are on fire of the gospel; and if I preach not, I shall die." This language described the feeling, the mental condition, which I find in the moral attitude of O'Connell.

If I name courage, moral and physical, as another of the constituent elements of O'Connell's character, I refer to that quality which, to my mind, is the most brilliant and beautiful, and the one of which his life is the most fully and radiantly instinct. He possessed the highest type of moral courage, the purpose and power to do that which seemed in him, in spite of the prepossession and customs of society, right and proper. Living at a time when, and among a people by whom matters of honor were settled by duel; when he who did not accept this mode of adjusting personal difficulties was adjudged a coward, though physically brave, as demonstrated in his youth and subsequently in his mature life, after he had fought one duel successfully, he gave to his countrymen and mankind a new and better lesson on this subject. He taught his brave and fiery nation, acquainted with war and familiar with bloodshed, that "no political change is worth the shedding of one drop of human blood;" that "he who commits a crime gives strength to the enemy; that nothing can be politically right which is morally wrong." These aphorisms of his moral code, their utterance and vindication, not only demonstrate the adoption and cultivation of a wise pacific policy as to individuals and nations, but the possession of a moral courage, Christian heroism, of surpassing beauty.

The personal courage of O'Connell, not less than his love of peace, is fully and satisfactorily sustained by the facts of his history. His vow, however, against duelling, made "in a state of society and in scenes of such danger" as surrounded the English and Irish politicians of his time, required the moral courage indicated, as well as that decision and energy which are its natural and inevitable fruit.

His determination and rigor of character, prompt and ready apprehension of duty, individual and national, are worthy of special comment. His own duty made clear, either by reflection or intuition, was pursued and performed with a will and power as irresistible as the truth.

These qualities, not less than his general strength and power of character, were especially marked in great emergencies. Then he was borne, but beautifully sustained even above his usual power, great as this always was, when he made display of genius and vigor of mind, splendid and powerful in the highest sense. The first political speech of O'Connell is said to have been made against the legislative union of Great Britain and Ireland. On this occasion his whole soul was moved, and his power of argument, declamation and invective were stirred indeed. He portrayed this final degradation of Ireland by England with a master's power, and it is perhaps true that no speech of his in after years surpassed the one delivered then before the congregated thousands of Dublin. At this time, and in this effort, he gave his countrymen proof of the power of the youthful advocate and defender of Irish nationality; the world, proof of what he was capable when aroused and tested.

Another trait of character peculiarly distinguishing O'Connell, is the breadth of his humanity. He was a patriot; he loved deeply his country and his race. But his patriotism had no streak of selfishness in it. Its soul seemed that of benevolence; comprehending every child of Ireland. It did not forget nor neglect any son of mankind—enslaved or oppressed, on island or continent, whether of European, Asiatic or African extraction.

Truthfully and well has it been said: "Were those who have been benefited by his labors to assemble in congress, at the call of gratitude, an assembly would be formed without a parallel in all past history. The Asiatic of the Indian peninsula would leave his rice crops by the sacred Ganges; Africa would send forth her dusky deputies; the West Indies their emancipated dark men; Canada her grateful reformers, and Europe the noblest of her free and of her fallen races." And I may add to this list of grateful and worthy representatives assembling in the grandest international gathering the world ever saw, to honor this benefactor of so many and diversified peoples and classes, deputies of the dark-hued sons of America, whose "immediate and unconditional freedom" he demanded in fit and powerful words. His broad humanity, his far-reaching and comprehensive benevolence, his wise and deep sense of duty to the race, make us all his debtors. His individuality, conviction, moral courage, decision of character and comprehensive humanity constitute the bottom elements of O'Connell's moral nature. Such qualities were essential to his moral constitution, course of life and success.

Were I to dwell upon the intellectual qualities, the powers and peculiarities of O'Connell, I should speak of his reason, massive but acute, active and reliable, affirming moral truth in the words of wisdom itself, with the authority of inspiration; his conscience, quick and responsive, accepting and enforcing the affirmations of the reason with resistless power; his understanding, capable of the largest endeavor, the most unflagging and persistent effort, as well as the broadest, the most varied and exalted achievement; his logical acumen, as sharp and vigorous in the search for knowledge and truth as stern and positive in indicating and sustaining them; his invective, as keen as a blade; his sarcasm, scorching and burning as a fire; his imagination, as lively and radiant as the light; his sensibility, as tender as the heart of the Singer of Israel. With such powers of intellect, an industry that knew no weariness, and a physical endurance as lasting as his mental activity, O'Connell gained the largest and most varied learning, as he wielded the most telling and lasting influence. An American, having seen and heard him on more than one occasion, bears this testimony with regard to him:

"He possessed a mind of uncommon native vigor, trained by a complete education, and enlarged with a knowledge of men and things varied and ample. The versatility of his genius, his extensive information, and his capacity to adapt himself to the matter under discussion, or the audience before him, were surprising. I have heard him exhaust topics that required for their elucidation an intimate acquaintance with the Constitution of the United States, with the condition of the barbarous tribes in the interior of Africa, with the wrongs inflicted by the East India Company upon the dwellers in Hindostan, with the commercial tariffs of European nations, with the persecution of the Jews in Asia, with the causes of the opium war in China, with the relative rights of planters and laborers in the Western Archipelago, and he was at home in each. I have seen him hold the House of Commons spell-bound, call shouts from the *elite* of British intelligence and philanthropy in Exeter hall, lash into fury or hush into repose acres of wild peasantry gathered on the moors of Ireland, and he was at home with each."

The opinion is unanimous of friends and foes alike that O'Connell was a master spirit. Historically considered as Catholic, statesman, abolitionist and orator, he occupies none other than the most conspicuous place.

Perhaps there is no short-coming we are so ready to forgive and overlook in our eminent men as neglect of religious duty and culture. And it is, perhaps, equally true we are more tardy in our recognition and appreciation of exalted Christian character in such persons than any other marked peculiarity. No one, however, can fittingly and truthfully describe, portray the character of O'Connell who does not dwell with special emphasis upon his Catholic Christian devotion and consistency. In his religion, a Roman Catholic, he was not less true to his church than his country. As zealous as Paul on his way to or returning from Damascus, he was as conscientious and consistent. He was loyal to his own convictions, earnest, vigorous and faithful in his profession, and his life, like his death, reveals and illustrates the beauty and loveliness of his active religious devotion and consistency.

Indeed the church and Catholicity are largely and specially indebted to this marked and model representative for the exalted standard which he lifted up and sustained by his conversation and life, the influence he exerted and impressed in his remarkable and interesting death. With his powers of mind still strong, his faith steady and aglow, in his seventy-second year, after forty-nine years of professional and public service, he died bearing an eloquent and affecting testimony of his devotion and faithfulness to the church no less than to his country.

Both he seems to have regarded with an affection vigorous and deep, for in his last strange dispositions he remembered each in making the bequest: " My body to Ireland, my heart to Rome, my soul to Heaven."

Father Ventura, in the concluding passage of his elaborate and masterly funeral discourse upon the dead Christian hero, explains the words by saying :

" He loves his country, and therefore he leaves to it his body ; he loves still more the church, and hence he bequeathes to it his heart ; and still more than the church he loves God, and therefore confides to Him his soul."

As to whether he loved the church more than Ireland, more than independence of judgment and freedom of conscience for all, O'Connell leaves us in doubt; for he says in a speech delivered at a meeting of the Catholic board, December 24, 1813 :

" No man is ever converted from his opinions by persecution or abuse. Let all those subjects be forever banished from among us, and let us set the glorious example of preaching and practicing the doctrines of that Christianity which is founded in fraternal affection and best evidenced by fraternal charity.

" For my own part I have devoted much of my time to the Catholic cause; a time of little value, alas to my country, but of great value to myself; but I would not give up one hour of that time, or a single exertion of my mind to procure the mere victory of any one sect or persuasion over the others. No, my object is of a loftier and different nature. *I am an agitator with ulterior views.* I wish for liberty ; real liberty.

" But there can be no freedom anywhere without perfect liberty of conscience. That is of the essence of freedom in every place. In Ireland, it is eminently, almost exclusively, the hope of liberty.

" The emancipation I look for is one which would establish the rights of conscience upon a general principle to which every class of Christians could equally resort, a principle which would serve and liberate the Catholics in Ireland, but would be equally useful to the Protestant in Spain : a principle, in short, that would destroy the Inquisition and the Orange lodges together, and have no sacrilegious intruder between man and his Creator! I esteem the Roman Catholic religion as the most eligible. All I require is that the Protestant, the Presbyterian, the Dissenter, the Methodist, should pay the same compliment to his own persuasion, and leave its success to its own persuasive powers without calling in the profane assistance of temporal terrors, or the corrupt influence of temporal rewards."

Hereafter we shall more fully perceive how deeply he loved his country. Though not a Catholic, one can but admire and applaud the consistency, zeal and devotion—if not wise, earnest and genuine—of this valiant son of the church. Let every one be true to his own soul ; let him stand or fall on its judgment alone. For one true to himself cannot, will not, be false either to God or humanity. So it was with this distinguished Irish Catholic layman.

In this connection, and on this occasion, I may neither make assertion nor enter upon any discussion as to whether O'Connell might not have shown greater wisdom, have more largely secured the good of his country by accepting Protestantism and union and co-operation with its friends. I only maintain, and no man can reasonably deny, that he was faithful and loyal to the religion of his choice. Nor does it come within the line of my duty to discuss the question as to whether if the Orangemen had been given complete and undisputed control of Ireland—Catholicity being held entirely subordinate to Protestantism—the independence of the country might not have been maintained, or, if lost for a time, more speedly re-established, and the happiness of the people more securely sustained and prolonged.

Ireland has been, is to-day unfortunate. Her divisions have been sore and fruitful of great evil. But political, no less than religious differences, breed divisions which work frequently to the woe of the people. These differences among all nations, however thoughtful, enterprising and progressive, will, in the very nature of things must, exist. While .the human mind retains its present constitution, the human soul its fidelity to its own affirmations with regard to duty, there can be no absolute religious union, no subordination of all individuals of a single nation, or all nations, to the same religious belief. O'Connell favored that union, that conciliation and cordiality between Catholics and Protestants consistent with this independence of judgment, this natural difference of religious conviction. In his speech on the "French Party" he says:

"Our first desire, and the motives which govern us, are to take away from France even the hope of success by removing those excuses of distrust and dissension and weakness in this country, which at present are really so many temptations to the enemy to invade us. We would fain excite a national and Irish party, capable of annihilating any foreign oppressor whatever, and devoted to the amelioration of this our native land. This is, indeed, a French party that does exist in Ireland; a party most useful to the views and designs of France. It is the party of the present ministry; that party which exerts its vicious energies to divide, distract and oppress the realm; that loads the nation with the weight of ill-judged taxation, and employs the money wrung from poverty and distress in fomenting internal dissensions; in calumniating the Irish people to each other; accusing the Catholics of disloyalty, because they seek the rights of the constitution, charging the Protestants with bigotry, and yet encouraging them to become intolerant. It is, in fine, this party which desolates this country, and then talks to us of our growing prosperity."

George Canning, one of the first orators of Great Britain, and who frequently took part in the debates on the Catholic question, "with signal superiority of eloquence, and liberality of sentiment," makes on one occasion, when dwelling on this subject, this statement:

"The great body of Irish Catholics are, it is said, in the hands of agitators, who wish to keep their discontents alive; who care not for the professed objects of Catholic desire, but look to the ulterior purposes of mischief; to separation and revolution. If this is so, we can only defeat the evil intentions of such men in two ways: either by correcting their disposition or by taking away their means. The former is beyond human power; let us avail ourselves of the latter. Let us remove those circumstances which, operating upon the feelings of the Catholics, render them fit instruments in the hands of agitators for the promotion of such dangerous designs. I am inclined to believe that there are those who have ulterior views and designs.

"Of those who are the most clamorous for concession there are some, I do believe, who would be much disappointed if that concession were granted. And next to the gratification which I should feel in tranquillizing a loyal and high-minded people by the introduction of that equality of right without which there can be no reciprocal liking and confidence, is that of disappointing the guilty hopes of those who delight, not in tranquillity and comfort, but in grievances and remonstrances; who use their sincere and warm-hearted countrymen as screens to their own ambitious purposes, and who consider a state of turbulence and discontent as best suited to the ends which they have in view. That state it may be their wish to prolong, but so much the rather is it our interest and our duty to terminate as speedily as possible."

O'Connell was the "arch-agitator," and with ulterior views or designs; but what these designs were we have already learned from his words quoted a moment ago. He agitated but for liberty, real liberty; and he was earnest, sincere and true. The father and liberator of his country, sacrificing for her his private resources, his professional emoluments, his personal comfort and repose, he stands in history with a Christian, though Catholic name and character, which, in their beauty, lustre, glory, are unsurpassed.

Mankind are not agreed as to whether O'Connell was a statesman. Two opinions certainly are entertained with regard to this subject. Some claim that if he is to be regarded as a statesman at all he does not deserve to be placed in the first class. Others claim that he is not only to be given place among the first statesmen of the world, but that he is entitled to conspicuous place among the most prominent even of this class.

In estimating O'Connell's character as a statesman, as in all such cases, very much depends upon our conception and definition of statesmanship. If we mean by statesman, a mere politician, one connected with party, seeking mere party ends, and through party personal and selfish aggrandizement; if we mean by statesman one conversant only with the affairs of his own country and government, and interested solely in the progress and prosperity of his own people, even to the neglect or damage of other and possibly higher, though interests of foreign nations; if by statesman we mean a partisan, self-seeking, narrow, illiberal in his views and judgment with respect to state affairs, individual and national obligation and duty in this regard; if by statesmanship we mean the qualities or functions of the mere politician, the partisan, then O'Connell was not a statesman—he did not cultivate statesmanship. He had no party. He was not a partisan. He had to learn no party tactics. He was schooled in no party drill. The Irish people composed his party. It was their welfare he sought. He was solicitous to adopt, develop and sustain those methods, measures and means conducing to this end. Nor did he seek to advance and establish the welfare of his own country without due regard to the claims and rights of others. He accepted and applied to national, as well as individual life, the Christian maxim: "What we demand for ourselves, that concede." If, on the other hand, we mean by statesman one acquainted with state-craft, one conversant with its learning and philosophy as found in national experience and achievement, who, while valuing organization for important state and popular objects, is committed to no party; one who does not seek selfish promotion or emolument thereby, who, while understanding and insisting upon the just demands of his own country, concedes all that can be fairly and properly demanded of his own, we must pronounce O'Connell a statesman, and give him high rank, too, among the foremost statesmen of the world.

When O'Connell entered professional life there existed the strongest reasons for avoiding politics, and he seems rather to have been borne by the influence and pressure of a great occasion, when others hesitated and faltered, into the course and current of his subsequent life. His son and biographer says:

"No lawyer could then hope to rise in his profession unless willing to be the parasite and slave of the government, and it was not even safe, in Ireland at least, for Protestant or Catholic, but especially for the latter, to be found in opposition.

"For these and other reasons the leading members of Mr. O'Connell's family and circle of friends were very much indisposed to his putting himself forward in any public struggle, and he was himself, of course, fully aware of the disadvantages and dangers he must incur by so doing. But he could not be silent when he saw the legislative independence of his country about to be annihilated, and when it had become clear that the Minister sought to implicate the Catholics of Ireland in his crime. Overtures had already been made in private to some of their nominal leaders, and rumor said that they had not been unfavorably received, timidity, credulity or corruption, jointly or separately, operating to produce this result. There could not, indeed, be a doubt that the great bulk of the Catholic body felt as Irishmen should on this occasion, and abhorred the idea of the Union; but they were

entirely unaccustomed to acting in concert or coming forward
in their aggregate character. Some one was wanted to show
them the way. . Their 'natural leaders,' as the phrase went,
hung back, or were inclined to acquiescence in the proposed
measure. The Minister's designs against the good repute
and independence of the Catholic body seemed about to be
consummated, when just at the critical moment Daniel O'Connell stepped forward."

Seventy-five years ago, on the 13th of January, 1799, O'Connell delivered a speech at the Royal Exchange, Dublin, in
connection with which he introduced a series of resolutions,
the first and last of which embody and define, in few words,
his political philosophy. These resolutions read as follows :

"*Resolved*, That we are of opinion that the proposed incor-
porate union of the Legislature of Great Britain and Ireland
is, in fact, an extinction of the liberty of this country, which
would be reduced to the abject condition of a province sur-
rendered to the mercy of the minister and legislature of
another country, to be bound by their absolute will, and taxed
at their pleasure by laws, in the making of which this country would have no efficient participation whatever.

"*Resolved*, That, having heretofore determined not to come
forward any more in the distinct character of Catholics, but to
consider our claims and our cause, not as those of a sect, but
involved in the general fate of our country, we now think it
right, notwithstanding such determination, to publish the
present resolutions in order to undeceive our fellow-subjects
who may have been led to believe, by a false representation,
that we are capable of giving any concurrence whatsoever to
so foul and fatal a project, to assure them we are incapable of
sacrificing our common country to either pique or pretension;
and that we are of opinion that this deadly attack upon the
nation is the great call of nature, of country and posterity
upon Irishmen of all descriptions and persuasions, to every
constitutional and legal resistance; and that we sacredly
pledge ourselves to persevere in obedience to that call as long
as we have life."

The words of these resolutions, the wise, just and liberal

sentiments which they contain, remind one of the eloquent and sagacious utterances of the leading American statesmen of our Revolutionary times.

James Otis, one of the first and foremost champions of freedom and popular government, concentrating and voicing the judgment of these statesmen, declares that "government springs from the necessities of nature, and have an everlasting foundation in the unchangeable will of God. The first principle and great end of government being to provide for the best good of all people, this can only be done by a supreme legislature and executive ultimately in the people or the whole community, where God has placed it. The right of every man to his life, his liberty, no created being can rightfully contest. They are rights derived from the Author of Nature; inherent, inalienable and indefeasible by any law, compacts, contracts, covenants or stipulations which man can devise. God made all men naturally equal."

As a statesman O'Connell labored to establish the unity, independence, and freedom of Ireland. To this end he would emancipate every inhabitant, and perpetuate freedom of conscience; he would annul the Legislative Union between England and Ireland, and give to Ireland her own constitution and the rights it guaranteed, through her own government. In considering his long and persistent labors in behalf of his country, the sacrifices which he made, the sufferings and trials which he endured, his imprisonment and triumphant release therefrom, his double election from Clare, his entry and brilliant career in the Imperial Parliament, his matchless and eloquent addresses before the congregated thousands who gathered at Dublin, Ennis, Tara and other places made classic by his presence and utterances, we accept as fit and truthful when he says:

"I have already devoted all the faculties of my soul to

the pursuit of the liberties of my country; and humble as my capabilities are, I had already given them all to my native land.

"Alas! the gift was small, but it included certainly purity of design, sincerity of intention, perseverance of exertion, contempt of personal danger, neglect of personal advantage, and, finally, incorruptible integrity and truth."

And those other words which he uttered after accepting the plate tendered him on behalf of the Catholic people of Ireland, when, continuing, he said:

"For myself I need not tell you that, in the struggle for the liberties of Ireland, every peril, personal or political, is to me a source of pleasure and gratification. * * * I have heretofore loved my country for herself. I am now her bribed servant, and no other master can possibly tempt me to neglect, forsake, or betray her interests."

O'Connell claimed and demanded "home rule" for Ireland; the repeal of the act of union, and the restoration of the situation of 1782-1800, when Ireland had her separate and independent Parliament. And it will prove a difficult task for the opposers of such restoration to show why independent home government, wisely and firmly established under a just constitution, would not prove of the greatest benefit to the Irish, bringing them national peace, union and prosperity. Such government, judiciously administered, can prove no source of confusion, can generate no feelings of malcontent among the people.

If we in our States may enjoy self-government, independent as to all matters pertaining to State sovereignty, without confusion and with the largest good order and happiness, why may not Ireland with her home Parliament? Popular government is worth so much, is so desirable, is so calculated—if we may judge from national experience, our own especially—to work and support popular good that we

F

demand for Ireland and the Irish people this inestimable blessing. It would seem that Americans could do no less, no other thing. I know that the colored American, so lately made free, lifted from chattelhood to the dignity of manhood, citizenship, political responsibility and official duty, in the ardor and enthusiasm inspired by his new life of freedom, makes haste to extend his hand of sympathy and encouragement to the struggling son of Ireland, whose soul, catching the accents, the deathless, eloquent voice of O'Connell, would throw off its chains and assert its natural, inherent right of self-government. The colored American is too sensible of his debt of gratitude to O'Connell and the great leaders of the Irish people to be unsympathetic or indifferent to Ireland's conditions and struggles.

Before this audience, at this time, when popular conviction is so distinct and pronounced, as far as government by every nation for itself and in its own interest is concerned, I need not say that the enunciation and advocacy of this measure discover the wisdom of commanding and genuine statesmanship. And its establishment in Ireland, I believe, is the only thing that will bring conciliation and cordiality to Catholics and Protestants, securing justice, peace, prosperity and happiness to all the people.

History gives O'Connell yet another and not less interesting and pleasing character. I refer now to him as an abolitionist, occupying a deservedly conspicuous place by Clarkson, Wilberforce, Buxton, Brougham, Macaulay, Sturge, and others who compose the brilliant group of Great Britain's leading abolitionists. It has been well said that the "tribute which Great Britain has paid to the genius of humanity by her efforts and sacrifices for the abolition of the African slave trade and Negro slavery, is the aspect in which she delights to be contemplated by other nations.

If this be true we may not forget on this occasion what she owes to the noble sons of Ireland, whose eloquent words go so far to complete the beautiful testimony which she has borne on this subject. We may not forget the words of Curran; here I may emphasize those of O'Connell. More than half a century ago the former declared in words familiar to us:

"I speak in the spirit of our constitution, which makes liberty commensurate with and inseparable from our soil; which proclaims, even to the stranger and the sojourner, the moment he sets his foot upon our native earth, that the ground he treads is holy and consecrated by the genius of universal emancipation; no matter in what language his doom may have been pronounced; no matter what complexion, incompatible with freedom, an Indian or an African sun may have burnt upon him; no matter in what disastrous battle his liberty may have been cloven down; no matter with what solemnities he may have been devoted on the altar of slavery, the first moment he touches our sacred soil the altar and the god sink together in the dust; his soul walks abroad in her own majesty; his body swells beyond the measure of his chains that burst around him, and he stands redeemed, regenerated and disenthralled by the irresistible genius of universal emancipation."

In 1830, a year memorable as the one in which the friends of the abolition movement urged and demanded immediate, as opposed to gradual emancipation, O'Connell uttered these noble and grateful words:

"I am for speedy, immediate abolition. I care not what caste, creed or color slavery may assume, I am for its total, its instant abolition. Whether it be personal or political, mental or corporal, intellectual or spiritual, I am for its immediate abolition. I enter into no compromise with slavery; I am for justice in the name of humanity, and according to the law of the living God."

The utterance of such sentiments, made with force, eloquence and power, was well calculated, not only to change, reform and settle the popular judgment of Great Britain and the West India Islands, where slavery existed, against that institution, but, since the utterance was made by O'Connell, an orator of rare, royal power, a statesman of consummate ability, commanding by his address the attention of senates as well as the people of all civilized lands, its influence was felt especially and appreciated in our own country, encouraging, strengthening and sustaining the noble band of American abolitionists in their warfare upon a despotism black and cruel as death. O'Connell was not content, however, with the indirect, though inevitable effect, produced by his utterances on this subject upon the American people. He knew, too, how large the number of Irishmen was—sons of his own native land, Catholics, with church relationships in Ireland, which had been incorporated into our body politic, and become responsible in a good measure for the character of our nation as regarded by mankind. He therefore bore a direct and earnest and uncompromising and positive testimony against our enslavement of the Negro, and the proscription, the feeling of caste, which it generated and fostered. We remember his address to the Irish Repeal Association, of Cincinnati, Ohio, accompanying the Pope's allocution of slavery and the slave trade. Addressing the association, he commences by saying :

"We have read with the deepest affliction, not unmixed with some surprise and much indignation, your detailed and anxious vindication of the most hideous crime that has ever stained humanity—the slavery of men of color in the United States of America. We are lost in utter amazement at the perversion of mind and depravity of heart which your address evinces. How can the generous, the charitable, the humane, the noble emotions of the Irish heart have become extinct among you ? How can your nature be so totally changed as that you should become the apologists and defenders of that execrable system which makes man the property of his fellow-man, destroys the foundation of all moral and social virtues, condemns to ignorance, immorality and irreligion, millions of our fellow-creatures; renders the slave hopeless of relief, and perpetuates oppression by law, and in the name of what you call a constitution?

"It was not in Ireland you learned this cruelty. Your mothers are gentle, kind and humane. Their bosoms overflow with the honey of human charity. Your sisters are probably many of them still among us, and participate in all that is good and benevolent in sentiment and action. How, then, can you have become so depraved? How can your souls have become stained with a darkness blacker than the Negro's skin? You say you have no pecuniary interest in Negro slavery.

"Would that you had, for it might be some palliation of your crime! But, alas! you have inflicted upon us the horror of beholding you the volunteer advocates of despotism in its most frightful state; of slavery in its most loathsome and unrelenting form."

The association had made in its address this statement: "The very odor of the Negro is almost insufferable to the white, and, however much humanity may lament it, we make no rash declaration when we say the two races cannot exist together on equal terms under our Government and our institutions." He replies: "In the first place, as to the odor of the Negroes, we are quite aware that they have not as yet come to use much of the ottar-of-roses or eau-de-cologne. * * * But it is indeed deplorable that you should use a ludicrous assertion of that description as one of the inducements to prevent the abolition of slavery. The Negroes would certainly smell at least as sweet when free as they do now being slaves."

Continuing, he asks: "Have you enough of the genuine Irishman among you to ask what it is we require you to do? It is this:

"First, we call upon you in the sacred name of humanity

never again to volunteer on behalf of the oppressor, nor even for self-interest to vindicate the hideous crime of personal slavery.

"Secondly, we ask you to assist in every way you can in promoting the education of the free man of color, and in discountenancing the foolish feeling of selfishness, of that criminal selfishness, which makes the white man treat the man of color as a degraded or inferior being.

"Thirdly, we ask you to assist in obtaining for the free men of color the full benefit of all the rights and franchises of a freeman in whatever State he may inhabit.

"Fourthly, we ask you to exert yourselves in endeavoring to procure for the man of color in every case the benefit of trial by jury, and especially where a man, insisting that he is a freeman, is claimed to be a slave.

"Fifthly, we ask you to exert yourselves in every possible way to induce slave-owners to emancipate as many slaves as possible. * * *

"Sixthly, we ask you to exert yourselves in all the ways you possibly can to put an end to the internal slave-trade of the States. * * *

"Seventhly, we ask you to use every exertion in your power to procure the abolition of slavery by the Congress in the District of Columbia.

"Eighthly, we ask you to use your best exertions to compel the Congress to receive and read the petitions of the wretched Negroes, and above all the petitions of their white advocates.

"Ninthly, we ask you never to cease your efforts until the crime of which Lord Morpeth has accused the Irish in America, 'of being the worst enemies of the men of color,' shall be atoned for and blotted out and effaced forever."

He dwells then upon the duty of the Catholics and of the Catholic clergy, holding that "the Catholic clergy may endure, but they assuredly do not encourage the slave-owners. We have, indeed, heard it said that some Catholic clergymen have slaves of their own, but it is added and we are assured positively that no Irish Catholic clergyman is a slave-owner.

At all events, every Catholic knows how distinctly slave-holding, and especially slave-trading, is condemned by the Catholic church. That most eminent man, His Holiness, the present Pope, has, by an allocution published throughout the world, condemned all dealing and traffic in slaves. Nothing can be more distinct nor more powerful than the Pope's denunciation of that most abominable crime. Yet it subsists, in a more abominable form than His Holiness could possibly describe, in the traffic which still exists in the sale of slaves from one State of America to another. What, then, are we to think of you, Irish Catholics, who send us an elaborate vindication of slavery without the slightest censure of that hateful crime—a crime which the Pope has so completely condemned—namely, the diabolical raising of slaves for sale, and selling them to other States?"

He adds: "We conclude by conjuring you, and all other Irishmen in America, in the name of your fatherland, in the name of humanity, in the name of the God of mercy and charity, we conjure you, Irishmen and descendants of Irishmen, to abandon forever all defence of the hideous Negro slavery system. Let it no more be said that your feelings are made so obtuse by the air of America that you cannot feel, as Catholics and Christians ought to feel, this truth, the plain truth, that one man cannot have any property in another man. There is not one of you who does not recognize that principle in his own person; yet we perceive, and this agonizes us almost to madness, that you, boasting an Irish descent, should, without the instigation of any pecuniary or interested motive, but out of the sheer and single love of wickedness and crime, come forward as the volunteer defenders of the most degrading species of human slavery."

O'Connell's opposition to slavery was positive, stern, uncompromising, allowing no excuse or palliation. He refused even to take the hand of an American who was not opposed to the institution. Robert Purvis, Esq., one of the most distinguished colored Americans, an old abolitionist of consistent and useful record, wrote me a letter on the 14th instant, from which I take these words:

"It was my good fortune, while in England, to meet Ireland's great liberator, Daniel O'Connell. The interview occurred at the House of Commons. Upon being introduced to him as an American gentleman, he declined taking my hand. Whereupon my friend, John Scoble, Esq., (to whom I was indebted for the introduction), upon seeing this, immediately said: 'Mr. Purvis is an abolitionist, and is also identified with the oppressed race of the United States.' Mr. O'Connell instantly advanced toward me, and taking my hand in his, shook it warmly, saying: 'I will never take the hand of an American, nor should any honest man in this country do so, unless assured that he is opposed to the accursed system of chattel slavery.'"

The words of the address of O'Connell referred to, written in 1843, sound even now as wise counsel, earnest, paternal exhortation to the Irish citizens of America, being unmindful of the past, solicitous only for the future, to unite with the once enslaved and disfranchised colored American, to-day a fellow-citizen and a voter, in cordial, fraternal and patriotic purpose, and endeavor to put our Government and laws in harmony with that doctrine of our Declaration, the equality of rights for all before the law, upon which we have formed and built our political fabric as upon the rock. It is well if such purposes animate the heart of the Irishman; if these classes, so similar in past experience of oppression and suffering, so alike in duty and destiny, under American law, unite in such endeavor.

My opinion of O'Connell as an orator is sufficiently indicated already. It will be conceded that the world has seen few abler, more skillful and powerful popular orators than he. John Randolph called him the finest orator in Europe. Possessing rare native vigor of mind, its powers disciplined by complete education ; his memory filled with varied and large knowledge of men and things; his imagination buoy-ant and elastic; his logic, his humor, his invective, his sarcasm abundant, and trained, musical voice, with the power and manner of an actor, he was irresistible, and, in many respects, incomparable. An American writer says of him that "every chord of the human bosom lay open to his touch, and he played upon its passions and emotions with a master's hand. He could subdue his hearers to tears by his pathos, or toss them with laughter by his humor. His imagination could bear them to a giddy height on its elastic wing, or he could enchain their judgment by the strong links of his logic. He could blanch their cheeks as he painted before their eyes some atrocity red with blood, or he could make them hold their sides as he related some broad Irish ancedote fresh from Cork."

O'Connell was indeed an orator of wondrous, marvelous power, and it all he dedicated to truth, freedom and justice. It is as the defender of the Catholics of Ireland—demanding for them in forum, Parliament, or in popular assembly emancipation and freedom of conscience; as the advocate and expounder of propositions of governmental reform in the interest of his countrymen; as the champion of British and American abolitionism, insisting upon liberty and equal rights for the Negro, that his oratorical power appears in its most resplendent character, dazzling our vision.

But I must conclude. Such, too briefly and imperfectly described, are the qualities of character, the transcendant powers and the beneficent achievements of him who stands in history a figure of light, full-orbed and radiant, the best type and representative of the Irish name, the benefactor of mankind.

In my youth I read and was moved and deeply impressed by the words with which I conclude may address. Henry B. Stanton, Esq., dwelling upon the fact that a demand was made finally that the National Repeal Association repudiate the non-resistant doctrine of O'Connell, says:

"The alienation of large numbers of his friends overtaking him when his powers were impaired by years of exhausting toil broke the spirit of the old man, undermined his constitution, and compelled him to repair to the continent to resuscitate his waning health and drooping heart. But he left the field of action too late. His energies rapidly declined; death overtook him while on his weary pilgrimage; his eye saw the sun for the last time in a foreign sky, and he slept his final sleep far from the land which gave him birth, and from that ocean by whose side his cradle was rocked. The stroke that felled him to the earth sent a pang through many a heart in every country where humanity has a dwelling-place; for his sympathies, like his reputation, were world wide. He had delivered his own countrymen from the bonds of ecclesiastical tyranny, and had pleaded for the victims of a hellish traffic on the shores of Africa, for the swarthy surfs of British cupidity on the banks of the Ganges, for the persecuted Jews of ancient Damascus, and for the stricken slaves in the isles of the Carribbean Sea and in the distant States of America."

Requiescat in pace! Let him rest in peace! His name is immortal—the priceless, enduring heritage of mankind.

CITIZENSHIP AND THE BALLOT.

THE RELATIONS OF THE COLORED AMERICAN TO THE GOVERNMENT AND ITS DUTY TO HIM—A COLORED AMERICAN THE FIRST HERO OF THE REVOLUTIONARY WAR.*

In the broad and far-reaching track of slavery across this country, we witness a grand desolation of civil and political rights. Every class in the American population can enter its complaint that it has been shorn of many rights and privileges, by reason of its existence. But none can utter that long, loud, lamentable complaint, making the ear to tingle and the heart to bleed, that can be uttered by the colored American, the immediate victim of its barbarous torture. As a slave he has been denied himself, his wife, his children, and his earnings. And when emancipated his freedom has been, in some sense, a mockery, because he has been deprived of those civil and political rights and powers which render enfranchised manhood valuable and its dignities a blessing.

The colored man is not content when given simple emancipation. That certainly is his due, at once and without condition ; but he demands much more than that: he demands absolute legal equality. He claims the right to bring a suit in any and all the courts of the country, to be a wit-

*Address delivered before the Colored Men's Convention of Indiana, in Masonic Hall, at Indianapolis, October 25, 1865.

ness of competent character therein, to make contracts, under seal or otherwise, to acquire, hold, and transmit property, to be liable to none other than the common and usual punishment for offences committed by him, to have the benefit of trial by a jury of his peers, to acquire and enjoy without hindrance education and its blessings, to enjoy the free exercise of religious worship, and to be subjected by law to no other restraints and qualifications, with regard to personal rights, than such as are imposed upon others. All this he claims. In some States all this is conceded to him. There is one thing more, however, he demands; he demands it at the hands of the nation and in all the States. It is the free and untrammelled use of the ballot. Shall he have it ?

Never was there a more fitting time to consider, discuss, and decide this question. Since the outbreak of the terrible rebellion, the colored American has had another and better introduction to the American people. They are beginning to regard him with greater favor, and their old stubborn prejudices are beginning to soften. Indeed, in some States they have already entered upon the work of repealing those legislative malformations known as Black Laws. Once in the path of justice and of duty, it is easy for us to pursue it till we reach the glorious goal.

It becomes our duty in this connection to consider and refute, if possible, the chief objections urged against Negro suffrage.

In the first place, it is urged, with an air of very great confidence, that none other than a white man can, or ought to be, an elector. Hence it is that in well-nigh all the States in which persons of African descent are denied the elective franchise, you will find in their organic laws language like the following :

"Every *white* male citizen of the United States, of the

age of twenty-one years, who shall have been a resident of the State one year next preceding the election, and of the county, township, or ward in which he resides such time as may be prescribed by law, shall have the qualifications of an elector and be entitled to vote at all elections."

What is meant by the word white as here used? The courts have not left us without an answer to this question. For the courts of Ohio, from whose constitution these words are quoted, both under the constitution of 1802 and the constitution of 1851, have given a full consideration to the word "white" and settled its definition for all time in the light of what they please to call well-established legal principles. They furnish us in their definition this very unique and remarkable classification of the people, to wit, the black, the mulatto, and the white; and they hold "that all men nearer white than black, or of the grade between the mulatto and the white are white, and entitled to vote as white male citizens." This certainly gives breadth and comprehension to the word "white," and makes all persons except blacks and mulattoes "white." Let one more drop of Anglo-Saxon blood than Negro course your veins and you are at once endowed with the requisite qualifications of an elector.

On this point let full justice be done the court. Let it speak for itself. In the case of Parker Jeffries *vs.* John Ankeny and others, at the December term of the court in banc, this doctrine was held, in the following words: "In the constitution and laws on this subject there were enumerated three descriptions of persons, whites, blacks, and mulattoes, upon the last two of which disabilities rested; that the mulatto was the middle term between the extremes, or the offspring of a white and a black; that all nearer white than black or of the grade between the mulattoes and the whites were entitled to enjoy every political and social privilege of the white citizen; that no other rule could be adopted so intelligible and so practicable as this, and that further refinements would lead to inconvenience and no good result." This is the law of Ohio to-day.

In 1859, when the Legislature of Ohio was within Democratic control, "an act to prescribe the duties of judges of elections in certain cases and preserve the purity of elections," was passed, the first section of which reads as follows: "That the judge or judges of any election held under the authority of any of the laws of this State, shall reject the vote of any person offering to vote at such election and claiming to be a white male citizen of the United States whenever it shall appear to such judge or judges that the person so offering to vote has a distinct and visible admixture of African blood." This statute, however, has been pronounced unconstitutional by the Supreme Court, in the celebrated case of Anderson *vs.* Millikin and others, as reported in the eleventh of the Ohio State Reports, and the old doctrine on this subject reaffirmed.

Upon what principles of humanity, justice, and law is this doctrine founded ? And upon what principles of logic or law are such complexional discriminations made ? This color theory of the elective franchise finds no sanction in the affirmations of reason, or in the dictates of common sense. Nor is any sanction given it in the organic law of our nation. The Declaration of Independence announces the doctrine, "that all men are created equal," and the Constitution. in which no word "white" is found, provides "that Congress shall guarantee to each State a republican form of government," and "that the citizens of each State shall be entitled to all the privileges and immunities of the citizens of the several States." Democracy, too, which is the soul of law, and but another name for justice itself, "conceding nothing but what it demands, and demanding nothing but what it concedes," guarding the rights of the humble as well as the exalted, and protecting the rights of the black man as well as the rights of the white man, scouts it as absurd and unjust, inconsistent and irrational.

It is true that the opinion obtains to a very great extent among all classes of our people that the Constitution of the United States, either by the direct use of the word "white," or by some phraseology equivalent thereto, does, and was intended to exclude colored men from every right and privilege of a legal and political character under it. Hence the gibberish jargon "that our government is a white man's government." This notion, however, is forever refuted by these masculine and truthful words of one of the justices of our national Supreme Court. He says:

"It has been often asserted that the Constitution was made exclusively by and for the white race. It has already been shown that in five of the thirteen original States colored persons then possessed the elective franchise, and were among those by whom the Constitution was ordained and established. If so, it is not true, in point of fact, that the Constitution was made exclusively *by* the white race. And that it was made exclusively *for* the white race is, in my opinion, not only an assumption not warranted by anything in the Constitution, but contradicted by its open declaration, that it was ordained and established by the people of the United States, for themselves and their posterity; and, as free colored persons were then citizens of at least five States, and so in every sense part of the people of the United States, they were among those for whom and whose posterity the Constitution was ordained and established."

On what ground, then, does the white man claim to be a voter? And on what argument can he predicate his monopoly of the voting privilege? Does he claim it as an inherent and natural right, peculiar to himself? Does he claim it on the ground of peculiarity of origin? Does he demand it on the basis of peculiar conventional regulation? What are the peculiar legal or political characteristics that distinguish him to the exclusion of his black fellow-countryman as a citizen of the United States and a voter? Blind prejudice can make answer to these questions with great readiness. It would say, *he is white.* But what is the answer of wisdom, logic, and law? They would say, the color of a man's skin is no criterion or measure of his rights.

This fact will be fully recognized by our courts when they come to make that definition of citizenship, and the rights and powers of a citizen, which, while it excludes the elements of white and black, but contains all the essential qualities that distinguish the citizen, will challenge criticism and defy refutation. It is to be hoped that the Supreme Court of the nation will have occasion to give us this definition very soon. We certainly need it. It ought to be given, in justice to the colored American, and that the whole people of the country may learn from some authoritative source who constitute the citizens of the land, and upon what their rights and powers depend.

This objection to the black man's voting is wholly physical and external. He is *black*, and therefore he shall not vote.

It is as if all the men who have black hair and black beards, being in the majority and having the power, should decide that they alone are voters, and that no man having light hair and sandy beard shall vote; or, as if all the men of large noses in the land banding themselves together, should decide that they alone are voters, and that no man having a small nose shall vote. One might well ask, where is the justice of this procedure? Men of light hair and sandy beards might resist with propriety the decision of the black-hair and black-beard gentry. And who would say that the small-nose men had no

right to utter powerful anathemas against the men of large
nasal proportions, who had committed this unnatural outrage.
These supposed cases sufficiently illustrate and refute this.
objection.

It is also urged, by way of objection to our use of the ballot, " that we are an ignorant and degraded class, and would
not use the elective franchise in an intelligent and manly manner if we had it."

This objection, like all others of similar character, is to be
met with firmness and candor. It is not to be forgotten in
this connection, that we have served as slaves in this country
for more than two hundred years, and that during these many
years of our servitude few indeed have been the rays of light
that have streaked the darkness of our existence. Nor is it to
be forgotten that the nominally free among us have been
haunted by a prejudice more terrible than that which pursued the Cagots of Spain and France. This pro slavery public
sentiment has been well-nigh omnipotent, as omnipresent. It
has entered every cranny and crevice of American society. It
has closed against us the school, the college, the law, and the
theological seminary. It has hindered our progress in politics,
religion, literature, and the arts.

Notwithstanding all this, we have made surprising advancement in all things that pertain to a well-ordered and
dignified life. Though uttered frequently, it may be, in
unclassic and inelegant English, we have always been able
to give the reason for our political as well as our religious
faith.

We have grown among us authors and orators, doctors and
lawyers; we have established newspapers and periodicals;
we have founded churches and erected schools; we have
furnished our pulpits with ministers and our school rooms.
with teachers of our own complexion.

G

We have held large State and national conventions, conducting our business with accuracy and precision, according to the rules by which ordinary deliberative assemblies are governed. The leading men of these gatherings, in handling the great subjects of interest to the American people at large, as well as the topics pertaining more especially to our own welfare, have made exhibitions of a very correct and thorough understanding of our national history, the genius of our institutions and the philosophy of our politics. Indeed the newspapers and periodicals of this and foreign countries on such occasions have made handsome and flattering mention of their displays of learning, eloquence, and power.

It may not be inappropriate to offer here the opinion of Hon. Samuel Galloway on this very point, given as long ago as 1849. In speaking of our condition and progress he said :

"Now they (the colored people) have many and well-conducted schools; they have teachers of respectable intellectual and moral qualifications; there are many who command general respect and confidence for integrity and intelligence; questions of general and proper interest have become with them topics of discussion and conversation; in a few words, the intellectual and moral tone of their being is ameliorated."

But it may be said that such words, if true, can only have application to the colored men of the North. This, however, cannot be so, for it must be well understood by all conversant with the history and character of the colored people of this country, North and South, that very many of our most sober, industrious, and thrifty men come from the South; indeed it will not be denied that seven-eighths of our mechanics, gun-smiths, blacksmiths, brick and stone masons, carpenters, cabinet-makers, plasterers, and painters come from the Southern section of the land. This is said not in praise of slavery and slave-holding institutions, but in spite of them. This statement only testifies to the energy, the enterprise, the purpose and genius of the colored American.

On this point the history of our country will furnish us no inconsiderable evidence, for if it can be shown that in the past, when opportunity was given us, we wielded the ballot with intelligence and conscientiousness, who can say, after many years of progress in all substantial and valuable attainments, that we are not now able to vote in a skillful and conscientious manner.

It will be remembered that persons of African descent, under our old confederation, were voting citizens of the United States, and voted in at least five States of the Union at the time of the adoption of our national Constitution. With regard to this matter, Justice Curtis, formerly of the United States Supreme Court, in his dissenting opinion in the famous Dred-Scott case uses these words : " Of this there can be no doubt. At the time of the ratification of the articles of confederation all free native-born inhabitants of the States of New Hampshire, Massachusetts, New York, New Jersey, and North Carolina, though descended from African slaves, were not only citizens of those States, but such of them as had the necessary qualifications possessed the franchise of electors on equal terms with other citizens." And he might have added that when the United States Constitution was framed colored men voted also in Pennsylvania, Connecticut, Rhode Island, Delaware, and Tennessee. Indeed they voted in a majority of the States, and in very many of the Northern States they have continued to vote to this day.

In this connection the manly and vigorous words of North Carolina's ablest and most distinguished jurist are of special value. The Hon. William Gaston, of the supreme court of

North Carolina, in pronouncing the opinion of that court in the case of the State *vs.* Manuel, makes use of these brave utterances:

"According to the laws of this State (North Carolina) all the human beings within it, who are not slaves, fall within one of two classes. Whatever distinctions may have existed in the Roman laws between citizens and free inhabitants, they are unknown to our institutions. Before our Revolution, all free persons born within the dominions of the King of Great Britain, whatever their color or complexion, were native-born British subjects—those born out of his allegiance were aliens. Slavery did not exist in England, but it did in the British Colonies. Slaves were not, in legal parlance, persons, but property. The moment the incapacity, the disqualification of slavery was removed, they became persons, and were then either British subjects or not British subjects, according as they were or were not born within the allegiance of the British King. Upon the Revolution no other change took place in the laws of North Carolina than was consequent on the transition from a colony dependent on a European King to a free and sovereign State—slaves remained slaves, British subjects in North Carolina became North Carolina freemen, foreigners, until made members of the State, remained aliens, slaves manumitted here became freemen; and, therefore, if born within North Carolina are citizens of North Carolina, and all free persons born within the State are born citizens of the State. The Constitution extended the elective franchise to every freeman who had arrived at the age of twenty-one, and paid a public tax, and it is a matter of universal notoriety that, under it, free persons, without regard to color, claimed and exercised the franchise until it was taken from freemen of color a few years since by our amended Constitution."

In none of these States, in which we have been allowed the use of the ballot, have we betrayed the confidence or the trust reposed in us. No flattering promises, no false statements of designing politicians, no offers of money or strong potations of liquor have been used by partisans with any degree of success in our case. We have constantly sought out the party and the candidates that would conserve and perpetuate American liberty and free institutions. No mere party shibboleth has ever had weight with us. Our training, secured in a life of oppression; our experience, gathered from contact with the instruments of torture and despotism, wed us to the party of freedom and free principles.

Touching the capability and sincerity with which the right of suffrage is exercised by the colored men of New York, the Hon. Wm. H. Seward, now occupying the first position in the Cabinet of President Johnson, holds the views presented in the following letter :

WASHINGTON, *May* 16*th*, 1850.

DEAR SIR : Your letter of the 6th inst. has been received. I reply to it cheerfully and with pleasure.

It is my deliberate opinion, founded upon careful observation, that the right of suffrage is exercised by no citizen of New York more conscientiously, or more sincerely, or with more beneficial results to society, than it is by the electors of African descent. I sincerely hope that the franchise will before long be extended, as it justly ought, to this race who of all others need it most.

I am, very respectfully, your obedient servant,

WM. H. SEWARD.

This objection, however, if it possesses any real significance, and if urged with any degree of sincerity and candor covers entirely too much ground. For under it, what becomes of the ignorant and degraded white American, and what of the newly-naturalized foreigner, whose untutored mind fails to read and understand the meaning of American politics?

Leaving these objections, then, we come with sobriety and earnestness to the question : Upon what ground does the colored American plant his claims to the elective franchise?

As far as the native-born inhabitants of the country are concerned, we have no faith in the opinion that the right of suffrage is, in any sense to be regarded simply as conventional. We hold that it is an inseparable and essential element of self-government; and none, certainly, on reflection, will question this position. Without the privilege of saying who shall make our laws, what they shall be, and who shall execute them, there can be no self-government. This was the sentiment of the Fathers of the Republic; and upon this foundation-principle, as upon enduring granite, they established the free institutions of the land. This right is not created by constitutions simply, nor is it uncreated by them. Its existence does not depend upon the texture of man's hair, the conformation of his countenance, or the color of his skin. It is a constituent element of manhood; and it stands prominent among the chief duties of civil society to sustain and guard it.

But are we men, and are we so related to the American Government that it owes us any obligation of protection in the exercise of this right? The declaration that we are men requires no amplification or illustration. The anti-slavery movement of this country has progressed too far, and the character and achievements of the colored American stand now too prominently before the world for his manhood to be doubted. Nor is it any denial of his manhood that his fellows, overcoming him by brute force, have enslaved and outraged him; for this notion was forever blasted when Terence, clad in chains, rushed out upon the Amphitheater of Rome, thrilling the vast concourse there assembled, by the announcement of the masculine and nervous sentiment: "*Homo sum : atque nihil humani a me alienum puto.*"

Our relation to the Government will be seen at once,

when it is remembered, in the first place, that we are native-born inhabitants and therefore citizens. That nativity gives citizenship is a doctrine fully recognized by American law and American usage. Its existence, as far as our country is concerned, dates back to the very beginning of the Government. Chancellor Kent gives it full indorsement in these terms : " Citizens, under our Constitution and laws, mean free inhabitants, born within the United States or' naturalized by the laws of Congress. If a slave born in the United States be manumitted or otherwise legally discharged' from bondage, or if a black man be born within the United' States, and born free, he becomes thenceforward a citizen."'

But when we urge our citizenship as a reason why we should' be allowed to vote, we are very gravely informed that voting and holding office are not essential to citizenship. It is said,. women are citizens, and so are minors, but they are neither allowed to vote nor hold office. Why put us in the category and condition of women and minors? Qualified by age, residence, and general attainments, our position is now one of men, and we demand this right *prima facie* as such. There may be inge-' nuity in this ambidexterity, but certainly no reason. It is but a crude and inconsistent dogma, injected into American law and American politics by slavery. Its true character, however, becomes more apparent as we progress.

Our relation to the Government and its duty toward us will be more fully apprehended when we call to mind the fact that we are, and always have been, taxpayers. Nor is the amount of tax we pay to be regarded as trivial and of small account. In proportion to our number, we pay a very handsome and considerable sum. In the State of Ohio, in which, according to the census of 1860, the colored men number only 36,673, over ten millions of dollars are held by them, subject to taxation. In the city of Cincinnati alone they are owners of nearly two million of dollars' worth of personal property and real estate. In the farming districts of the State—in Gallia, Jackson, Pike, Ross, Highland, Franklin, Clark, Shelby, and Mercer counties—the colored men are owners of large farms, which, in many instances, are well stocked and cultivated according to the most approved methods of agriculture. But the taxes paid by the colored men of Ohio are small, compared with those paid by the same class in the larger and more densely populated States. The taxes of the colored men of the States of New York, Pennsylvania, and Louisiana swell to large, indeed, enormous proportions.

These tax burdens, too, we have met most cheerfully. Never have we excused ourselves, and never have we been excused from them on account of our color or our race. Even when, after payment of them, denial has been made us of any advantage accruing therefrom, on account of our color, they have been levied and paid to the entire satisfaction of the Government.

It will not be denied that taxation and protection are correlative terms. If the Government taxes a man it owes him protection. Nor can it be justly denied that he who meets the burden imposed by the Government, who pays its taxes, who supplies it with the materials of life and development, should have a voice in the enactment and execution of the laws according to which its taxes are imposed, collected, and expended. Taxation, protection, and representation we hold, therefore, to be inseparable, constituting at once the bond of union and the bond of obligation between the Government and the citizen.

It is to be borne in mind, also, that we have not only promptly met our obligations as taxpayers, but we have behaved ourselves, at all times and under all circumstances, as earnest and devoted patriots.

Indeed, we love this country. We love it as our native country, although it has been the land of our sore oppression. Its Constitution and the free institutions, which are its natural outgrowth, are objects of our fondest affection. The evidences of this affection are found scattered through the history of the country, as it records the heroic deeds of the colored American in our revolutionary struggles, the war of 1812, and the bloody battles of our late stupendous rebellion.

Always on the side of the Government, always struggling for the maintenance of law and order, we have rallied at the call of the country, bringing her our strong arms, our indomitable courage, and our unswerving loyalty.

To our own conduct in this respect our statesmen, orators, and generals have borne their testimony in the most eulogistic terms. Over the gallant conduct of the colored soldiers of the Revolution the glowing periods of Eustis and Pinckney cast a halo of immortal beauty, while their brilliant achievements on Lake Erie and at New Orleans are immortalized in the eloquent sentences of Drake and Jackson.

Says Governor Eustis, of Massachusetts, in a speech delivered in Congress, December 12, 1820:

"At the commencement of the Revolutionary War, there were found in the Middle and Northern States many blacks and other people of color capable of bearing arms, a part of them free, the greater part slaves. The freemen entered our ranks with the whites. The time of those who were slaves was purchased by the States, and they were induced to enter the service in consequence of a law, by which, on condition of their serving in the ranks during the war, they were made freemen. In Rhode Island, where their numbers were more considerable, they were formed, under the same considerations, into a regiment commanded by white officers, and it is required in justice to them to add that they discharged their duty with zeal and fidelity. The gallant defence of Red Bank, in which this black regiment bore a part, is among the proofs of their valor.

"Among the traits that distinguish this regiment was their devotion to their officers; when their brave Colonel Greene was afterwards cut down and mortally wounded, the sabres of the enemy reached his body only through the limbs of his faithful guard of blacks, who hovered over him, and protected him, every one of whom was killed, and whom he was not ashamed to call his children. The services of this description of men in the navy is also well known."

The Hon. Charles Pinkney, of South Carolina, when addressing the House of Representatives of the United States on the same occasion, also said:

"It is a most remarkable fact that, notwithstanding, in the course of the Revolution, the Southern States were completely overrun by the British, and that every negro in them had an opportunity of leaving his owner, few did. They were then, and still are, as valuable a part of our population to the Union as any other equal number of inhabitants. They were in numerous instances the pioneers, and, in all, the laborers of your armies. To their hands were owing the erection of the greatest part of the fortifications raised for the protection of our country. some of which, particularly Fort Moultrie, gave at that early period of the inexperiences and untried valor of our citizens, immortality to American arms, and in the Northern States numerous bodies of them were enrolled into and fought, by the side of the whites, the battles of the Revolution."

In the constitutional convention of New York held in 1821, Dr. Drake, the delegate from Delaware County, said:

"In your late war they (the colored people of New York) contributed largely to some of your most splendid victories. On Lakes Erie and Champlain, when your fleets triumphed over a foe superior in numbers and engines of death, they were manned in a large proportion with men of color. And in this very house, in the fall of 1814, a bill passed, receiving the approbation of all branches of your Government, authorizing the Government to accept the services of a corps of 2,000 free people of color. Sir, these were times which tried men's souls. In these times it was no sporting matter to bear arms. These were times when a man shouldered his musket he did not know but he bared his bosom to receive a death wound ere he laid it aside; in these times these people were found as ready and as willing to volunteer in your service as any other. They were not compelled to go. They were not drafted. No! , Your pride had placed them beyond your compulsory power. But there was no necessity for its exercise; they were volunteers; yes, they were volunteers to defend that country from the inroads and ravages of a ruthless and vindictive foe, which had treated them with insult, degradation, and slavery."

The hero of New Orleans, Gen Andrew Jackson, addressed his colored troops in these complimentary and matchless words:

"Soldiers! When on the banks of the Mobile I called you to take up arms, inviting you to partake the perils and glory of your *white fellow citizens,* I expected much from you; for I was not ignorant that you possessed qualities most formidable to an invading enemy. I knew with what fortitude you could endure hunger and thirst, and all the fatigues of a campaign. I knew well how *you loved your native country,* and that you as well as ourselves had to defend what *man* holds most dear—his parents, wife, children, and property. *You have done more than I expected.* In addition to the previous qualities I before knew you to possess, I found among you a noble enthusiasm which leads to the performance of great things.

"Soldiers! The President of the United States shall hear how praiseworthy was your conduct in the hour of danger, and the representatives of the American people will give you the praise your exploits entitle you to. Your general anticipates them in applauding your noble ardor.

"The enemy approaches, his vessels cover our lakes, our brave citizens are united and all contention has ceased among them. Their only dispute is, who shall win the prize of valor, or who the most glory, its noblest reward."

That the blood of loyal fathers courses the veins of loyal sons is manifest from the fact that the only loyal class in our population is that furnished by the colored American. He has conceded to others the monopoly of treason. No traitor encased in *ebony* has been found in all the land. Those who boast of *ivory* encasings furnish the traitors. Davis and Stephens, Vallandingham and Pendleton, together with all the lesser bodies that reflect their treason, claim any other than a Negro origin. We are glad of it. We lay no claim to these men. They may be learned, able, and eloquent, but with hearts surcharged with treason their learning, ability and eloquence are not to be prized as the common sense and sound judgment of a loyal man, however black, whose soul is obedient to the commands of liberty and patriotism. When, at the commencement of the present rebellion, we proffered the Government our services, and the President, the governors of the various States, and the chief commanders of our army rejected them, informing us that this was a "white man's war," our ardor and enthusiasm abated not a single tittle. We were patient. We did not run to the enemy. We gave him no aid. With us he found no comfort. At length the time came when our learned statesmen, our sagacious politicians, and our earnest generals discovered that the rebellion was of such proportions, its spirit so malignant and obstinate, that "military necessity," if not justice, demanded that the colored American have a place as a soldier in the mighty contest which has been waged for the maintenance of liberty, free principles, and democratic institutions. We were then called to the service; and that our response has been manful is proved by the fact that nothwithstanding we were at first denied equal pay, the usual allowance for clothing, and every opportunity for promotion beyond the rank of a non-commissioned officer, we have already given to the service over two hundred thousand stalwart, brave, and gallant men. And since entering the service the colored soldier has been truly heroic. You will seek in vain among the soldiers of any land, ancient or modern, for exhibitions of greater endurance, more undaunted courage, and more enthusiastic devotion than he has displayed. His behavior at Port Hudson, at Milliken's Bend, at Nashville, at Petersburg, at Suffolk, at New Market Heights, at Fort Wagner and Olustee, not to mention many other places at which the colored soldier played a conspicuous part, covers him with imperishable glory. It has been especially fortunate, too, for this country that the colored American has been so earnestly patriotic and loyal. For divided as the country has been, the South arrayed against the Government, and thousands of disaffected persons in the North indirectly giving sympathy and aid to the rebellion, the colored American has been, by reason of his numbers and Spartan qualities as a soldier, a power aiding greatly in bringing victory to the arms of the Government.

With regard to our numbers, our strength, and the value of our loyalty to the Government, the judicious and truthful statements of Robert Dale Owen in a letter addressed to the 'Hon. Salmon P. Chase, on the conditions of lasting peace, and founded upon the facts and figures of 1860, are comprehensive and clear. He says:

"By the census of 1860 the number of white males between the ages of 18 and 45 is, in the loyal States, about four millions, and in the disloyal States about one million three hundred thousand; a little upwards of three to one. The disproportion seems overwhelmingly great. But this calculation, as a basis of military strength, is wholly fallacious, for it includes persons of one color only. Out of the above four millions the North has to provide soldiers and (with inconsiderable exceptions, not usually extending to field labor) laborers also. But of the three millions and a half of slaves owned in the rebel States, about two millions may be estimated as laborers. Allow three hundred thousand of these as employed in domestic services and other occupations followed by women among us, and we have seventeen hundred thousand plantation hands, male and female, each one of which counts against a Northern laborer on farm or in workshop. Then of that portion of population whence soldiers and out-door laborers and mechanics must chiefly be taken, the Northern States have four millions and the Southern States three millions. Supposing the Negroes all loyal to their masters, it follows that the true proportions of strength available in this war—that is, of all soldiers to fight and laborers to support the nation while fighting—may fairly enough be taken at three in the South to four in the North. Under the supposition of a South united, without regard to color, in an effort for recognition, shall we obtain peace by subduing her? If history teach truth we shall not. Never, since the world began, did nine millions of people band together, resolutely inspired by the one idea of achieving their independence, yet fail to obtain it. It is not a century since one-third of the number successfully defied Great Britain. But let us suppose the Negroes of the South loyal to the Union instead of to their masters, how stands the matter then? In that case, it is not to a united people, but to a Confederacy divided against itself, that we are opposed; the masters on one side, the laborers, exceeding them in number, on the other. Suppose the services of these laborers transferred to us, what will then be the proportion on either side of forces available, directly and indirectly, for military purposes? As about five and three-fourths to one and one-third; in other words, nearly as nine to two. Such a wholesale transfer is, of course, impossible in practice. But in so far as the transfer is possible, and shall occur, we approach the above results."

But, indeed, our transfer has been, as a class, a wholesale one. It has been so all along the past. It is so to-day; if not in bodily presence, certainly in spirit and aspiration.

And it is a source of special pride and pleasure that we are able to announce the fact that this has been so from the very beginning of the American Government. For if history be true he who on the second day of October, 1750, was advertised in the Boston *Gazette* or *Weekly Journal* as a runaway slave, fell twenty years afterwards in the Boston massacre, March 5th, 1770, in "the first act of the drama of the American Revolution," a hero and a martyr. Crispus Attucks, a mulatto slave, was the first American that fell giving his life and blood in defense of his country. His bold and daring conduct stirred the hearts and nerved the arms of his comrades, whom John Adams describes in his plea in defense of the soldiers who shot him, as a "motley rabble of saucy boys, Negroes and mulattoes, Irish Teagues and outlandish jack tars." Be it so. God takes the weak things of the world to confound the mighty. And Attucks and Gray, Caldwell, Maverick and Car, were the first offerings of the country deemed worthy to be made against "the encroachments of arbitrary power."

As the first hero of the Revolutionary War was a black man, may we not indulge the hope and prayer that the last hero of our present struggle may be one of the dark-hued sons of American toil. And when we rear that monument in the midst of the Mississippi Valley, which shall perpetuate the glory of our present victorious achievements, a monument of grander and loftier proportions than Bunker Hill monument, may we not inscribe his name upon its granite sides in golden characters.

We claim the elective franchise in the name of our manhood, our nativity, and our citizenship, in the name of the doctrine that taxation, protection, and representation are naturally inseparable, and in the name of that loyalty under the promptings of which we have performed for the country and the Government, in the army and the navy, such brave and manly deeds. We claim it, too, because we are intelligent men, men of sufficient intelligence to wield it conscientiously and with good results to the State.

In making our claim in the light of these considerations we come with no new and unusual theories, in the name of no false and fanatical conceptions of right and law. Our claim is based upon principles which, when applied to any and all other classes of the people, are recognized as just and democratic.

In addition to these all-sufficient reasons in favor of our claim we cannot fail to mention a consideration that must sooner or later result favorably to us from political necessity. Our arms are victorious; the revolted States are now to be reconstructed in accordance with the fundamental principles of the Constitution and the anti-slavery policy of the Government. As the Government has, for the last four years, needed loyal and earnest men to handle the musket in war, so it to-day needs men of the same character to wield the ballot in sustaining its principles. The ballot is no less potent than has been the musket. From what source can these loyal and earnest voters be had? The white men of the seceding States have almost all shown themselves unfaithful to the Government; not more than one-fourth of them have remained heartily true to the Union. This faithful and honorable minority will not be able by its votes to sustain the policy of the Government. The other part of the white population has been conquered, it is true, but not converted. Their submission is only that of restive and malignant rebels—sullen acquiescence, while they are actuated by no other purpose than to hinder and, if possible, prevent the establishment of the great principles that underlie our governmental policy. What more could be expected of men whose souls have been embittered by their sad experiences in the effort to establish their independence, and who have been educated by the teachings of slavery and the false social influence it engenders to hate the Government and despise the free principles it seeks to establish in the subjugated States. But one course will be left the Government. It cannot import voters. They must certainly be residents of the States in which they vote. Its only course will be to put the ballot in the hands of the Negro, who, in all the history of the past, has given incontestible evidence of his devotion to the Union of the States founded on the Constitution and freedom. Thus, as military necessity brought us emancipation and arms, political necessity may yet bring us enfranchisement and the ballot. Touching this point, one of the ablest and most profound thinkers of our country utters the following pregnant words on the question :

"Do we need the aid of the Negro as a loyal citizen? They (all thoughtful men) will admit it to be one of the great questions of the day, whether (leaving the abstract right or wrong of the case untouched) we can prudently or safely for our own sakes withhold from the freedman his political rights, and thus leave disfranchised, at a critical juncture in our history, a loyal half of a disaffected population. They will ask themselves whether, as we have found need of the Negro as a soldier to aid in quelling the rebellion we do not require his assistance as pressingly in the character of a loyal citizen in reconstructing on a permanently peaceful and orderly basis the insurrectionary States."

This is a fit theme for the consideration and reflection of our wise men. Upon it we need not dwell at length in this connection. The future will bring us its golden promise.

The path of duty with regard to us is plain to the American people. Justice and magnanimity, expediency and self-interest indicate but one course. Shall those who are

Π

natives to the soil, who fight the battles of the country, who pledge to its cause their property and their sacred honor be longer denied the exercise of the ballot?   It ought not, it cannot be.   The great events that are coming to pass in this nation, the crumbling of slavery and the dissipation of prejudice, give prophecy of a different result.   God and destiny are on our side, and it becomes the colored American to prepare himself at once for the complete investure of legal equality.

BISHOP RICHARD ALLEN.

THE MONUMENT TO HIS MEMORY — THE FIRST MONUMENT EVER ERECTED BY THE COLORED RACE IN AMERICA.

[The following address was reported in the Philadelphia *Press* of December 18, 1876, with these editorial comments by Hon. J. W. Forney, the editor:

Professor John M. Langston, LL.D., pronounced a discourse last evening at the Bethel African Methodist Church, in this city, printed at length in the *Press* this morning, which will attract and deserves unusual attention. It is the work of a scholar and a statesman, and, as such, will be read with profit by thoughtful men. The colored people have made marvellous strides since they began to be paid for their labor and to vote their opinions. They have elevated themselves even as they enriched their prostrated and lately pauperized oppressors. As they lifted themselves out of a brutalizing slavery, they lifted their pardoned persecutors out of hopeless poverty. Such a race can neither be bought nor safely intimidated. They will rise in defiance of all obstacles. Professor Langston is one proof of the inevitable fulfilment of this prophecy ; and his words last night showed how he means they shall labor to make it sure. Let them honor such a leader as their apostle, by steadily raising themselves to the high level of his great gifts, and by emulating his own remarkable and exemplary career.

The 22d day of last September had been fixed by those having charge of the enterprise as the time when there should be erected in Fairmount Park a monument in honor of Bishop Richard Allen. Dr. Daniel A. Payne had been invited to unveil the monument, and Professor John M. Langston to deliver the address. Because of an unfortunate railroad accident, in which the material of the monument was badly broken, the exercises did not take place in September. But last evening they came off at the Bethel A. M. E Church, corner of Sixth and Lombard streets, in this city. The Professor delivered it to over two thousand persons, by special request. Elder R. E. Wayman, the pastor, opened the services with appropriate religious exercises, and Dr. H. M. Turner, publisher of the *Christian Recorder* of this city, in a few well-chosen remarks introduced the orator. Professor Langston asked his hearers to imagine themselves on the 22d day of last September in Fairmount Park, in the presence of the monument.]

If one were asked what most peculiarly distinguishes Anglo-Saxon civilization, he must answer : individual and

popular achievement as connected with civil and religious
liberty. The Magna Charta, the Declaration of Independence, the Proclamation of Emancipation, are not only muni-
ments of our freedom, but in a peculiar sense monuments,
which at once attest and commemorate the struggles, the
sacrifices, and the triumphs made and achieved in its behalf. Many triumphs of free thought as regards the enunciation of new theologic and ecclesiastical truth distinguish
the history of the Church. In most instances these have
cost protracted struggle as well as large sacrifice. Associated with the triumphs of freedom in the Church or State,
there are names of distinguished men who, under Providence, have been permitted to stimulate, direct, define, and
record public feeling and judgment with regard thereto, as
well as to include and enforce lessons of struggle and sacrifice indispensable to earnest and protracted endeavor.
Not more in the jubilant spirit inspired by the triumphs,
than the docile, earnest one impressed by the teachings of
the struggles and sacrifices indicated, we meet to-day to
honor the name and to perpetuate the memory of a representative Christian hero in the erection of this monument.
We cannot be unmindful of the great event which renders
this day memorable; nor may we pass without making special and definite allusion to it. Fourteen years ago, one
year six months eighteen days after his inauguration as
President of the United States, Abraham Lincoln issued his
preliminary proclamation of emancipation. It contains
among others these words :

"That on the first day of January, in the year of our Lord
one thousand eight hundred and sixty-three, all persons held
as slaves within any State, or designated part of a State, the
people whereof shall then be in rebellion against the United
States, shall be thenceforward and forever free; and the
Executive Government of the United States, including the

military and naval authorities thereof, will recognize and maintain the freedom of such persons, and will do no act or acts to repress such persons, or any of them, in any efforts they may make for their actual freedom.

"That the Executive will, on the first day of January aforesaid, by proclamation, designate the States and parts of States, if any, in which the people thereof, respectively, shall then be in rebellion against the United States; and the fact that any State, or the people thereof, shall on that day be in good faith represented in the Congress of the United States by members chosen thereto at elections wherein a majority of the qualified voters of the State shall have participated, shall, in the absence of strong countervailing testimony, be deemed conclusive evidence that such State, and the people thereof, are not then in rebellion against the United States."

One hundred days had elapsed when, on the first day of January, 1863, the President issued, as promised, his proclamation designating the States and parts of States then in rebellion, and wherein " all slaves were declared to be free." In this proclamation occur these famous passages :

" Now, therefore, I, Abraham Lincoln, President of the United States, by virtue of the power in me vested as commander-in-chief of the army and navy of the United States, in time of actual armed rebellion against the authority and Government of the United States, and as a fit and necessary war measure for suppressing said rebellion, do, on this first day of January, in the year of our Lord one thousand eight hundred and sixty-three, and in accordance with my purpose so to do, publicly proclaimed for the full period of one hundred days from the day first above mentioned, order and designate, as the States and parts of States wherein the people thereof respectively are this day in rebellion against the United States, the following, to wit : Arkansas, Texas, Louisiana, (except the parishes of St. Bernard, Plaquemines, Jefferson, St. John, St. Charles, St. James, Ascension, Assumption, Terre Bonne, Lafourche, Ste. Marie, St. Martin, and Orleans, including the city of New Orleans,) Mississippi,

Alabama, Florida, Georgia, South Carolina, North Carolina, and Virginia, except the forty-eight counties designated as West Virginia, and also the counties of Berkeley, Accomac, Northampton, Elizabeth City, York, Princess Ann, and Norfolk, (including the cities of Norfolk and Portsmouth,) and which excepted parts are for the present left precisely as if this proclamation were not issued. And by virtue of the power and for the purposes aforesaid, I do order and declare that all persons held as slaves within said designated States or parts of States are, and henceforward shall be, free; and that the Executive Government of the United States, including the military and naval authorities thereof, will recognize and maintain the freedom of said persons. And upon this act, sincerely believed to be an act of justice, warranted by the Constitution upon military necessity, I invoke the considerate judgment of mankind and the gracious favor of Almighty God."

Although two years and a half of sanguinary struggle intervened before our emancipation as a war measure was determined by the victory of our loyal army, we very properly regard the 22d day of September, 1862, as the dawn of that glad day of freedom whose full-orbed sun poured its resplendent rays, in noon-tide glory, upon our enfranchised millions, when the thirteenth amendment of the Constitution was ratified, and our emancipation established in the organic law of the nation. *Esto perpetua!* Every consideration of fitness, whether we have regard to the person whom we would honor, or the event which marks it, induces us to select this day before all others of the year for these exercises. Here we bring, in our thoughts, the emancipator of our race face to face with one of that race, who, by a bold and fearless self-assertion, demonstrated its moral power—its fitness for freedom as shown in independent, manly thought, endeavor, and achievement. Here we associate the name of Allen with that of Lincoln, whose act in striking the shackles from the limbs of four millions of slaves is largely justified by the conduct of one who is indeed a type and representative of his race.

This day's enterprise, however, is new. For the first time in its history, certainly for the first time in this country, our race erects a monument to the memory of one of its own number. Two hundred and forty-five years of enslavement ill prepares our people for incurring the outlay connected with such work, while our leading men have been denied those opportunities and responsibilities which, developing character and purpose, make large personal achievement and personal distinction possible. The erection of monuments, like the purchase of pictures and statuary, implies not only the cultivation of taste, but the possession of means beyond the pressure of daily want. It implies more ; the due appreciation of such special achievement, tending to advance the good of society, in some important and exalted sense, with which the name of the person, whose services are commemorated, is associated and identified.

We have neither failed in the past ten years of our freedom to become conversant with our more prominent men, to admire their moral heroism in many cases, their manly conduct in the midst of the most discouraging circumstances, nor to economize our means in such manner as to be able to make this offering in honor of high personal worth. No apology may be justly asked of us for what we now do, nor do we volunteer such. All nations, all races of men delight to honor their mighty dead, and we are not, and would not be, in our feelings or acts an exception to this rule.

Richard Allen was born in Philadelphia, on the 14th day of February, 1760, sixteen years before the Declaration of American Independence. In his early childhood he was carried to the State of Delaware, where he was held a slave until he reached his majority, or thereabout, when at the suggestion of his owner he bought himself, paying sixty pounds of gold and silver. Of his owner he says: "He was what the world calls a good mas'er. He was more like a father to his slaves than anything else. He was a very tender, humane man." Of his own condition as a slave he says: "I had it often impressed upon my mind that I should one day enjoy my freedom, for slavery is a bitter pill, notwithstanding we had a good master. But when we would think that our day's work was never done, that after our master's death we were liable to be sold to the highest bidder, as he was much in debt, my troubles were increased, and I was often brought to weep between the porch and altar. But I have reason to bless my dear Lord that a door was opened unexpectedly for me to buy my time and enjoy my liberty."

Allen, though born to the condition and lot of a slave, was not insensible to those things which pertain to freedom and equal rights. Sensitive enough by nature to the claims of justice and humanity, as he grew in years, enlarging and improving his knowledge, his mind and soul were aroused and moved by the stirring deeds and matchless utterances of the revolutionary period through which he lived. Under the influence of the great thoughts, the lofty aspirations, and the noble purposes, which produced the social commotions of his time and made the Declaration of Independence a moral possibility, he pleaded the cause of the enslaved in words which impressed and moved at once the slave and the slaveholder, for he addressed each. He opens and concludes his address to the latter in these truthful and forcible words:

"The judicious part of mankind will think it unreasonable that a superior good conduct is looked for from our race by those who stigmatize us as men whose baseness is incurable, and may, therefore, be held in a state of servitude that a merciful man would not doom a beast to; yet you try what you can to prevent our rising from a state of barbarism you represent us to be in; but we can tell you from a degree of experience that a black man, although reduced to the most abject state human nature is capable of, short of real madness, can think, reflect, and feel injuries, although it may not be with the same degree of keen resentment and revenge that you who have been, and are, our oppressors would manifest if reduced to the pitiable condition of a slave. We believe if you would try the experiment of taking a few black children, and cultivate their minds with the same care, and let them have the same prospect in view as to living in the world as you would wish for your own children, you would find upon the trial they were not inferior in mental endowments. I do not wish to make you angry, but to excite your attention, to consider how hateful slavery is in the sight of that God who hath destroyed kings and princes for their oppression of the poor slaves. Pharaoh and his princes, with the posterity of King Saul, were destroyed by the Protector and Avenger of slaves. Would you not suppose the Israelites to be utterly unfit for freedom, and that it was impossible for them to obtain any degree of excellence? Their history shows how slavery had debased their spirits. Men must be wilfully blind and extremely partial that cannot see the contrary effects of liberty and slavery upon the mind of man; I truly confess' the vile habits often acquired in a state of servitude are not easily thrown off; the example of the Israelites shows how, with all that Moses could do to reclaim them from it, they still continued in their habits more or less, and why will you look for better from us? Why will you look for grapes from thorns, or figs from thistles? It is in our posterity enjoying the same privileges with your own that you ought to look for better things. When you are pleaded with, do not you reply as Pharaoh did, 'Wherefore do ye, Moses and Aaron, let the people from their work? Behold, the people of the land now are many, and you make them rest from their burdens.' We wish you to consider that God himself was the first pleader of the slaves."

Concluding, he says: "Will you, because you have reduced us to the unhappy condition our color is in, plead our incapacity for freedom and our contented condition under oppression as a sufficient cause for keeping us under the grievous yoke? I have shown the cause; I will also show why they appear contented as they can in your sight, but the dreadful insurrections they have made when opportunity afforded are enough to convince a reasonable man that great uneasiness and not contentment is the inhabitant of their hearts. God himself hath pleaded their cause. He hath from time to time raised up instruments for that purpose, sometimes mean and contemptible in your sight. At other times He hath used such as it hath pleased Him, with whom you have not thought it beneath your dignity to contend. They have been convinced of their error, condemned their former conduct, and become zealous advocates for the cause of those whom you will not suffer to plead for themselves."

His address to the former (the slave) is full of wise Christian sentiment and counsel. It is brief, and I present it in full. He says: "Feeling an engagement of mind for your welfare, I address you with an affectionate sympathy, having been a slave and as desirous of freedom as any of you; yet the bands of bondage were so strong that no way appeared for my release. Yet at times a hope arose in my heart that a way would open for it; and when my mind was mercifully visited with the feeling of the love of God, then these hopes increased, and a confidence arose that He would make way for my enlargement; and as a patient waiting was necessary, I was sometimes favored with it; at other times I was very impatient. Then the prospect of liberty almost vanished away, and I was in darkness and perplexity. I mention my experience to you, that your hearts may not sink at the discouraging prospects you may have, and that you may

put your trust in God, who sees your condition; and as a
merciful father pitieth his children, so doth God pity
them that love Him; and as your hearts are inclined to
serve God you will feel an affectionate regard toward your
masters and mistresses, so called, and the whole family in
which you live. This will be seen by them, and tend to promote your liberty especially with such as have feeling masters.
And if they are otherwise, you will have the favor and love
of God dwelling in your hearts, which you will value more
than anything else; which will be a consolation in the worst
condition you can be in, and no master can deprive you of it;
and as life is short and uncertain, and the chief end of our
having a being in this world is to be prepared for a better, I
wish you to think of this more than anything else; then you
will have a view of that freedom which the sons of God enjoy; and if the troubles of your condition end with your lives
you will be admitted to the freedom which God hath prepared
for those of all colors that love him.   Here the power of the
most cruel master ends, and all sorrow and tears are wiped
away. To you who are favored with freedom, let your conduct
manifest your gratitude toward the compassionate masters who
have set you free; and let no rancor or ill-will lodge in your
breast for any bad treatment you may have received from
any.   If you do, you transgress against God, who will not
hold you guiltless.   He would not suffer it even in his be-
loved people Israel, and do you think he will allow it unto
us?   Many of the white people have been instruments in the
hands of God for our good; even such as have held us in captivity are now pleading our cause with earnestness and zeal,
and I am sorry to say that too many think more of the evil
than of the good they have received, and instead of taking
the advice of their friends turn from it with indifference.
Much depends upon us for the help of our color—more than

many are aware. If we are lazy and idle, the enemies of freedom plead it as a cause why we ought not to be free, and say we are better in a state of servitude, and that giving us our liberty would be an injury to us; and by such conduct we strengthen the bonds of oppression, and keep many in bondage who are more worthy than ourselves. I entreat you to consider the obligations we lie under to help forward the cause of freedom. We who know how bitter the cup is of which the slave hath to drink, O how ought we to feel for those who yet remain in bondage. Will even our friends excuse—will God pardon us for the part we act in making strong the hands of the enemies of our color?"

His gratitude to those who, by word or deed, sought the deliverance and elevation of his race is beautifully expressed in "a short address to the friends of him who hath no helper." "I feel," he says, "an inexpressible gratitude towards you who have engaged in the cause of the African race. You have wrought a deliverance for many from more than Egyptian bondage; your labors are unremitted for their complete redemption from the cruel subjection they are in. You feel our affliction; you sympathize with us in our heart-rending distress, when the husband is separated from the wife and the parents from the children, who are never more to meet in this world. The tear of sensibility trickles from your eye to see the sufferings that keep us from increasing. Your righteous indignation is aroused at the means taken to supply the place of the murdered babe. You see our race more effectually destroyed than was in Pharaoh's power to effect upon Israel's sons; you blow the trumpet against the mighty evil; you make the tyrants tremble; you strive to raise the slave to the dignity of a man; you take our children by the hand to lead them in the path of virtue by your care of our education; you are not afraid to call the most abject of our race brethren, children of one Father, who hath made of one blood all the nations of the earth. You ask for this, nothing for yourselves, nothing but what is worthy the cause you are engaged in; nothing but that we would be friends to ourselves, and not strengthen the bands of oppression by an evil conduct when led out of the house of bondage. May He who hath arisen to plead our cause, and engaged you as volunteers in the service, add to your numbers until the princes shall come forth from Egypt, and Ethiopia shall stretch out her hands unto God."

While such utterances show the spirit of the man, his anxiety for the freedom and elevation of his race, his disposition and purpose to labor to accomplish such end, the high moral and religious ground upon which he made his demand, the Christian earnestness which gave life to his faith and sustained him in his labors and sacrifices, they distinguish him as an early and prominent laborer in the cause of our emancipation. In this work indeed he seems not to have built upon another's foundation, and we do no man injustice by writing high up towards the very top of the list, among the names of the early abolition worthies of the Revolutionary period of our country, the name of Richard Allen. Herein he certainly stands a representative character.

If a sad experience of slave life, a close identification of oppression and suffering with the slave, gave edge to Allen's advocacy of impartial freedom, his treatment by his Christian brethren of the Methodist Episcopal Church, a member of which he became upon his conversion, must have intensified his purpose, as he left that church to build one where freedom should find a home and beneath whose fostering and protecting care free principles should grow and expand in the full amplitude of their nature. To describe the treatment which he and his associates received I adopt his own language. He says: "A number of us usually attended St. George's Church, in Fourth street, in Philadelphia, and when the colored people began to get numerous in attending the church, they moved us from the seats we usually sat on and placed us around the wall, and one Sabbath morning we went to church, and the sexton stood at the door and told us to go in the gallery. He told us to go and we would see where to sit. We expected to take the seats over the ones we formerly occupied below, not knowing any better. We took those seats. Meeting had begun and they were nearly done singing, and just as we got to the seats the elder said, 'Let us pray.' We had not been long upon our knees before I heard considerable scuffling and low talking. I raised my head up and saw one of the trustees, H—— M——, having hold of Rev. Absalom H. Jones, pulling him up off his knees and saying, 'You must get up; you must not kneel here.' Mr. Jones replied, 'Wait until prayer is over.' Mr. H—— M—— said, 'No; you must get up now or I will call for aid and force you away.' Mr. Jones said, 'Wait until prayer is over, and I will get up and trouble you no more.' With that he beckoned to one of the other trustees, L—— S——, to come to his assistance. He came and went to William White to pull him up. By that time prayer was over and we all went out of the church in a body, and they were no more plagued with us in the church. This raised a great excitement and inquiry among the citizens, insomuch that I believe they were ashamed of their conduct. But my dear Lord was with us, and we were filled with fresh vigor to get a house erected to worship God in."

The conduct of these church officers we condemn with our whole being. The conduct of Allen and his associates we applaud as natural, manly, and noble. As we have read the history of this transaction, it has seemed very much as if the African Methodist Episcopal Church was, in an important and special sense, the organized Christian protest of the colored American against unjust, inhuman, and cruel complexional discriminations, and the illiberal and unchristian treatment founded thereon, accorded those against whom such discriminations are made. Certainly the founder of the church, its foremost minister for many years, and its first bishop, did not fail to leave posterity the example of wise Christian demeanor in this matter. In meeting and overcoming the opposition made to the establishment of the new church, its founder acted with great wisdom and sagacity. Occupying our position, standing at the point where, after sixty years have elapsed since its organization, we may look upon the results already accomplished through its agency; may estimate the value of its property, now reaching millions of dollars; the number of its members, counted by hundreds of thousands; the number of its ministers, found in a thousand pulpits and itinerating every part of the country; the number of its bishops, no longer one, but six, distinguished largely as well for their learning as their piety, may estimate in some suitable manner its achievements in behalf of popular education, virtue and religion. We can, and do, bear cheerful testimony to the correctness of this statement. These are all valuable results, and they cannot be too highly prized.

There is another result secured in the establishment of this church, however, which deserves special mention. At the time of its organization one great want, perhaps the greatest want, of the colored American was opportunity to be himself, to think his own thought, express his own conviction, make his own utterance, test his own powers, cultivate self-reliance, and thus, in the exercise of the faculties of his own soul, trust and achieve. The *sense* of responsibility is indispensable to this end, and where there is no pressure of obligation connected with duty and opportunity this end is never reached. The moral law which binds here is fixed even more unalterably than that of the Medes and Persians. The opportunity, the responsibility, and the obligation of which I speak, were the gifts, rare and precious, essential to individual as well as national development and strength, furnished in this new ecclesiastical organization. And were defence needed for Allen's course in leaving one and founding another Methodist Church, we find it especially in the consideration here presented. As the founder of this church Allen proved himself the benefactor of his race.

The life of Richard Allen, as a minister and bishop, is full of interest, and may be studied by the Christian scholar with large profit. Without scholarly attainment or culture, relying, as far as learning went, upon the simpler rudiments of knowledge, he trusted his native sense, illuminated by the Spirit which never failed him, even in the most trying hour. The disposition which he cultivated was that of the genuine Christian. He labored, he preached, he presided in his conference with that judicious, considerate, and cultured demeanor which, while it adds a charm to Christian character at all times, is the fittest adornment of exalted and dignified position. He always entertained an intelligent appreciation of education, and favored its thorough and general spread among the people. As the people became educated, as they cultivated virtue and religion, he hoped and believed that the colored American, by displaying his capabilities and powers, would command the respect of all fair-minded persons. Possessing solid, rather than brilliant and dazzling powers of mind, and hence properly classed among the thinkers of logical, mental bias, Bishop

Allen was, nevertheless, a pulpit orator, whose style was marked by a tender and lively sensibility, a vigorous and vivid imagination, a deep and moving pathos. The power of his eloquence was demonstrated in the effect produced upon the multitudes moved and converted through his preaching before and after his election to the bishopric. Sometime during the year 1784 he preached for several weeks in Radnor. His congregation was composed mainly of white persons; few colored people lived in the neighborhood. In connection with his labors here this beautiful testimony is borne: "Some said: 'This man must be a man of God; we never heard such preaching before.'"

The secret of his power is revealed in the words, "This man must be a man of God." He was strong in his earnest and abiding faith in his Heavenly Father, upon whose ability and purpose to fulfill his promises he relied with the confidence of a child. His sermons, his addresses, all his writings confirm this opinion.

A thorough and careful study of the character of Bishop Allen will convince us that he possessed all the qualities of mind which distinguish real greatness. He was intelligent, docile, sagacious, judicious, earnest, patient, industrious, self-reliant and yet self-sacrificing, fearless, humane, conscientious and just, while he was always tenacious of his own convictions and opinions. Dr. Daniel A. Payne, honored this day in unveiling his monument, speaking of Bishop Allen, presents his estimate of him in the following words:

"Though not learned, he was intelligent; though not brilliant, he was solid; a man of correct judgment, a far-sighted churchman, he was modest without timidity, and brave without rashness. A lover of liberty, civil and religious, he became its hero, and felt himself highly honored and

I

sincerely happy in doing and suffering to secure the blessings of ecclesiastical liberty for his despised and insulted race.   Black men, the world over, will yet do homage to his noble character, and white men, too, when they shall have learned to look upon men * * * from the summit of Calvary."

This day's proceedings make good, in some degree, the prophecy of these last words.   Possessing such qualities of character, a minister of excellent name and influence, the founder of a great and growing church, its first bishop, inaugurating and shaping its discipline and government, his name may be enrolled, without disparagement to any concerned, in close association with those of Wesley, the founder of the Methodist Episcopal Church; Asbury, the first bishop of that church, and Whitfield, the evangelist, men whose eloquence and labors mankind can never forget nor fail to appreciate.

Of the integrity and habits of industry cultivated by Richard Allen special mention must be made; otherwise, one fails to do him justice.   He was a man of vigorous native integrity, and in his pursuit, even as a slave, of an honorable and conscientious course of life, he stimulated and strengthened this noble trait of character.   He was careful of his good name, and was wont to guard it with vigor and decision.   In his "Narrative" of the conduct of the colored people of Philadelphia, who in 1793 did so much to assist the whites during a terrible malady which then prevailed, he not only showed himself able in defending his race against unjust and false censure, but demonstrated a deep appreciation of his own uprightness.   In this extremity of the people he was behind no one in arduous and fatiguing labors, nursing the sick, caring for and burying the dead.   And this he did at no small pecuniary loss to himself.   Of this he makes no complaint.   He complains only of partial and censorious treatment of the blacks, who were charged with "having taken advantage of the distressed situation of the people;" and in the most forcible manner, by inevitable inference, presents in a single question the rule which should govern us in our dealings with all classes. Admitting that some of the blacks may have dealt in an improper way with the sick and distressed, but asserting that many whites were also guilty, he asks: "Is it a greater crime for a black to pilfer than for a white to privateer?"

He was an industrious man. His habits of industry had been contracted in slavery; and after he had entered upon the labors of the ministry, but before the African Methodist Episcopal Church had been organized, his necessities were frequently such that he had to intermit those labors by other of a manual sort to supply his necessary wants.

In speaking of his custom in this regard he says: "My usual method was, when I would get bare of clothes, to stop traveling and go to work, so that no man could say I was chargeable to the Connexion. My hands administered to my necessities." The cultivation of such habits of industry, together with a prudent economy, distinguished his entire life, and enabled him, after meeting those demands which are inseparable from our domestic relations and educating his children, to leave to his family a considerable estate. A generous and worthy testimony is borne to Richard Allen as a husband and a father, and in such relations his life and conduct furnish valuable and praiseworthy examples.

In concluding, I may congratulate you, my friends, upon what we here witness. This occurrence is alike honorable to us and to him whose virtues we celebrate. We are permitted, in this centennial year of the nation, on this memorable day of our emancipation, in this beautiful and consecrated spot, to inaugurate and dedicate a monument to one whose name and deeds we seek to honor and perpetuate. The character of Richard Allen is now historical and representative. In his deeds, no less than his name and lineage, the colored American of every class must feel a deep interest, as well as a special and just pride. · His race, his enslavement, his struggles, endear him to us; but his deeds, his achievements excite and command the highest admiration and praise of our souls. This day we inscribe his name upon yon marble shaft, and, while we treasure it in our affections, commit it to the sacred keeping of posterity.

EQUALITY BEFORE THE LAW.

THE TREATMENT OF THE AMERICAN MAN OF COLOR BEFORE AND SINCE THE ADOPTION OF THE THIRTEENTH AMENDMENT.*

[The Oberlin Weekly *News* thus describes the reception of the following oration: Prof. Langs'on held the unbroken attention of his audience to the close. He was frequently interrupted by applause, and when he concluded, the expressions of approval were loud and protracted. Oberlin has long regarded him with special affection and respect, and has watched his gradual but steady advancement in position and fame with feelings of pride and satisfaction. He has risen by sheer ability and work to the position he now occupies. Standing, as he does, at the head of Howard University, and in the foremost rank among the orators of the country, he is doing more, perhaps, than any other man in shaping the character and destiny of the colored race in the United States. The citizens of Oberlin, many of whom have known him from boyhood, rejoice in his past success and trust him for the future. He is now just in the prime of life, and greater things yet may be reasonably expected from him.]

MR. PRESIDENT AND FRIENDS: I thank you for the invitation which brings me before you at this time, to address you upon this most interesting occasion. I am not unmindful of the fact that I stand in the presence of instructors, eminently distinguished for the work which they have done in the cause of truth and humanity. Oberlin was a pioneer in the labor of abolition. It is foremost in the work of bringing about equality of the Negro before the law. Thirty years ago, on the first day of last March, it was my good fortune, a boy seeking an education, to see Oberlin for the first time. Here I discovered at once that I breathed a new

---

* Delivered at Oberlin, May 17, 1874, on the Anniversary of the adoption of the 15th Amendment of the United States Constitution.

atmosphere. Though poor, and a colored boy, I found no distinction made against me in your hotel, in your institution of learning, in your family circle. I come here to-day with a heart full of gratitude, to say to you, in this public way, that I not only thank you for what you did for me individually, but for what you did for the cause whose success makes this day the colored American a citizen sustained in all the rights, privileges, and immunities of American citizenship by law.

As our country advances in civilization, prosperity and happiness, cultivating things which appertain to literature, science, and law, may your Oberlin, as in the past, so in all the future, go forward, cultivating a noble, patriotic, Christian leadership. In the name of the Negro, so largely blest and benefitted by your institution, I bid you a hearty God-speed.

Mr. President: Within less than a quarter of a century, within the last fifteen years, the colored American has been raised from the condition of four-footed beasts and creeping things to the level of enfranchised manhood. Within this period the slave oligarchy of the land has been overthrown, and the nation itself emancipated from its barbarous rule. The compromise measures of 1850, including the Fugitive Slave law, together with the whole body of law enacted in the interest of slavery, then accepted as finalities, and the power of leading political parties pledged to their maintenance, have, with those parties, been utterly nullified and destroyed. In their stead we have a purified constitution and legislation no longer construed and enforced to sanction and support inhumanity and crime, but to sustain and perpetuate the freedom and the rights of us all.

Indeed, two nations have been born in a day. For in the death of slavery, and through the change indicated, the colored American has been spoken into the new life of liberty and law; while now, other and better purposes, aspirations and feelings, have possessed and moved the soul of his fellow-countrymen. The moral atmosphere of the land is no longer that of slavery and hate; as far as the late slave, even, is concerned, it is largely that of freedom and fraternal appreciation.

Not forgetting the struggle and sacrifice of the people, the matchless courage and endurance of our soldiery, necessary to the salvation of the Government and Union, our freedom and that reconstruction of sentiment and law essential to their support, it is eminently proper that we all leave our ordinary callings this day, to join in cordial commemoration of our emancipation, the triumph of a movement whose comprehensive results profit and bless without discrimination as to color or race.

Hon. Benjamin F. Butler, on the 4th day of July last, in addressing his fellow-citizens of Massachusetts, at Framingham, used the following language, as I conceive, with propriety and truth:

"But another and, it may not be too much to say, greater event has arisen within this generation. The rebellion sought to undo all that '76 had done, and to dissolve the nation then born, and to set aside the Declaration that all men are created equal, with certain inalienable rights, among which are life, liberty and the pursuit of happiness. The war that ensued in suppressing this treasonable design, demanded so much greater effort, so much more terrible sacrifice, and has imprinted itself upon the people with so much more sharpness and freshness, that we of the present, and still more they of the coming generation, almost forgetting '76, will remember '61 and '65, and the wrongs inflicted upon our fathers by King George and his ministers will be obliterated by the remembrance of the Proclamation of Emancipation, the assassination of the President, the restoration of the Union, and the reconstruction of the country in one united, and as we fondly trust, never to be dissevered nation."

The laws of a nation are no more the indices of its public sentiment and its civilization, than of its promise of progress toward the permanent establishment of freedom and equal rights. The histories of the empires of the past, no less than the nations of the present, bear testimony to the truthfulness of this statement. Because this is so, her laws, no less than her literature and science, constitute the glory of a nation, and render her influence lasting. This is particularly illustrated in the case of Rome, immortalized, certainly, not less by her laws than her letters or her arms. Hence the sages, the jurists, and the statesmen of all ages, since Justinian, have dwelt with delight and admiration upon the excellences and beauties of Roman jurisprudence. Of the civil law Chancellor Kent eloquently says: "It was created and matured on the banks of the Tiber, by the successive wisdom of Roman statesmen, magistrates and sages; and after governing the greatest people in the ancient world for the space of thirteen or fourteen centuries, and undergoing extraordinary vicissitudes after the fall of the Western Empire, it was revived, admired and studied in northern Europe, on account of the variety and excellence of its general principles. It is now taught and obeyed not only in France, Spain, Germany, Holland, and Scotland, but in the islands of the Indian Ocean and on the banks of the Mississippi and the St. Lawrence. So true, it seems, are the words of d'Augesseau, that "the grand destinies of Rome are not yet accomplished; she reigns throughout the world by her reason, after having ceased to reign by her authority." And the reason through which she here reigns, is the reason of the law.

It is no more interesting to the patriot than to the philanthropist to trace the changes which have been made during the last decade in our legislation and law. Nor is there anything in these changes to cause regret or fear to the wise and sagacious lawyer or statesman. This is particularly true since, in the changes made, we essay no novel experiments in legislation and law, but such as are justified by principles drawn from the fountains of our jurisprudence, the Roman civil and the common law. It has been truthfully stated that the common law has made no distinction on account of race or color. None is now made in England or in any other Christian country of Europe. Nor is there any such distinction made, to my knowledge, in the whole body of the Roman civil law.

Among the changes that have been wrought in the law of our country, in the order of importance and dignity, I would mention, first, that slavery abolished, not by State but national enactment, can never again in the history of our country be justified or defended on the ground that it is a municipal institution, the creature of State law. Henceforth, as our emancipation has been decreed by national declaration, our freedom is shielded and protected by the strong arm of national law. Go where we may, now, like the atmosphere about us, law protects us in our locomotion, our utterance, and our pursuit of happiness. And to this leading and fundamental fact of the law the people and the various States of the Union are adjusting themselves with grace and wisdom. It would be difficult to find a sane man in our country who would seriously advocate the abrogation of the 13th amendment to the Constitution.

In our emancipation it is fixed by law that the place where we are born is *ipso facto* our country; and this gives us a domicile, a home. As in slavery we had no self-ownership, nor interest in anything external to ourselves, so we were without country and legal settlement. While slavery existed, even the free colored American was in no better condition; and hence exhortations, prompted in many instances by considerations of philanthropy and good-will, were not infrequently made to him to leave his native land, to seek residence and home elsewhere, in distant and inhospitable regions. These exhortations did not always pass unheeded; for eventually a national organization was formed, having for its sole purpose the transportation to Africa of such colored men as might desire to leave the land of their birth to find settlement in that country. And through the influence of the African Colonization Society not a few, even, of our most energetic, enterprising, industrious and able colored men, not to mention thousands of the humbler class, have been carried abroad.

It may be that, in the providence of God, these persons, self-expatriated, may have been instrumental in building up a respectable and promising government in Liberia, and that those who have supported the Colonization Society have been philanthropically disposed, both as regards the class transported and the native African. It is still true, however, that the emancipated American has hitherto been driven or compelled to consent to expatriation because denied legal home and settlement in the land of his nativity. Expatriation is no longer thus compelled ; for it is now settled in the law, with respect to the colored, as well as all other native-born Americans, that the country of his birth, even this beautiful and goodly land, is his country. Nothing, therefore, appertaining to it, its rich and inexhaustible resources, its industry and commerce, its education and religion, its law and Government, the glory and perpetuity of its free institutions and Union, can be without lively and permanent interest to him, as to all others who, either by birth or adoption, legitimately claim it as their country.

With emancipation, then, comes also that which is dearer to the true patriot than life itself: country and home. And this doctrine of the law, in the broad and comprehensive application explained, is now accepted without serious objection by leading jurists and statesmen.

The law has also forever determined, and to our advantage, that nativity, without any regard to nationality or complexion, settles, absolutely, the question of citizenship. One can hardly understand how citizenship, predicated upon birth, could have ever found place among the vexed questions of the law; certainly American law. We have only to read, however, the official opinions given by leading and representative American lawyers, in slaveholding times, to gain full knowledge to the existence of this fact. According to these opinions our color, race and degradation, all or either, rendered the colored American incapable of being or becoming a citizen of the United States. As early as November 7th, 1821, during the official term of President Monroe, the Hon. William Wirt, of Virginia, then acting as Attorney-General of the United States, in answer to the question propounded by the Secretary of the Treasury, "whether free persons of color are, in Virginia, citizens of the United States within the intent and meaning of the acts regulating foreign and coasting trade, so as to be qualified to command vessels," replied, saying among other things : "Free Negroes and mulattoes can satisfy the requisitions of age and residence as well as the white man; and if nativity, residence and allegiance combined (without the rights and privileges of a white man) are sufficient to make him a citizen of the United States, in the sense of the Constitution, then free Negroes and mulattoes are eligible to those high offices," (of President, Senator or Representative,) "and may command the purse and sword of the nation." After able and elaborate argument to show that nativity in the case of the colored American does not give citizenship, according to the meaning of the Constitution of the United States, Mr. Wirt concludes his opinion in these words: "Upon the whole, I am of the opinion that free persons of color, in Virginia, are not citizens of the United States, within the intent and meaning of the acts regulating foreign and coasting trade, so as to be qualified to command vessels."

This subject was further discussed in 1843, when the Hon. John C. Spencer, then Secretary of the Treasury, submitted to Hon. H. S. Legare, Attorney-General of the United States, in behalf of the Commissioner of the General Land Office, with request that his opinion be given thereon, "whether a free man of color, in the case presented, can be admitted to the privileges of a pre-emptioner under the act of September 4, 1841." In answering this question, Mr. Legare held: "It is not necessary, in my view of the matter, to discuss the question how far a free man of color may be a citizen in the highest sense of that word that is, one who enjoys in the fullest manner all the *jura civitatis* under the Constitution of the United States. It is the plain meaning of the act to give the right of pre-emption to all denizens; any foreigner who had filed his declaration of intention to become a citizen is rendered at once capable of holding land." Continuing, he says: "Now, free people of color are not aliens; they enjoy universally (while there has been no express statutory provision to the contrary) the rights of denizens."

This opinion of the learned Attorney-General, while it admits the free man of color to the privileges of a pre-emptioner under the act mentioned, places him legally in a nondescript condition, erroneously assuming, as we clearly undertake to say, that there are degrees and grades of American citizenship. These opinions accord well with the *dicta* of the Dred-Scott decision, of which we have lively remembrance.

But a change was wrought in the feeling and conviction of our country, as indicated in the election of Abraham Lincoln President of the United States. On the 22d day of September, 1862, he issued his preliminary Emancipation Proclamation. On the 29th day of the following November Salmon P. Chase, then Secretary of the Treasury, propounded to Edward Bates, then Attorney-General, the same question in substance which had been put in 1821 to William Wirt, viz.: "Are colored men citizens of the United States, and therefore competent to command American vessels?" The reasoning and the conclusion reached by Edward Bates were entirely different from that of his predecessor, William Wirt. Nor does Edward Bates leave the colored American in the anomalous condition of a "denizen." In his masterly and exhaustive opinion, creditable alike to his ability and learning, his patriotism and philanthropy, he maintains that "free men of color, if born in the United States, are citizens of the United States; and, if otherwise qualified, are competent, according to the acts of Congress, to be masters of vessels engaged in the coasting trade. In the course of his argument he says:

1. "In every civilized country the individual is born to duties and rights, the duty of allegiance and the right to protection, and these are correlative obligations, the one the price of the other, and they constitute the all-sufficient bond of union between the individual and his country, and the country he is born in is *prima facie* his country.

2. "And our Constitution, in speaking of natural-born citizens, uses no affirmative language to make them such, but only recognizes and reaffirms the universal principle, common to all nations and as old as political society, that the people born in the country do constitute the nation, and, as individuals, are natural members of the body politic.

3. "In twe United States it is too late to deny the political rights and obligations conferred and imposed by nativity; for our laws do not pretend to create or enact them, but do assume and recognize them as things known to all men, because pre-existent and natural, and, therefore, things of which the laws must take cognizance.

4. "It is strenuously insisted by some that 'persons of color,' though born in the country, are not capable of being citizens of the United States. As far as the Constitution is concerned, this is a naked assumption, for the Constitution contains not one word upon the subject.

5. "There are some who, abandoning the untenable objection of color, still contend that no person descended from Negroes of the African race can be a citizen of the United States. Here the objection is not color but race only. * * * * The Constitution certainly does not forbid it, but is silent about race as it is about color.

6. "But it is said that African Negroes are a degraded race, and that all who are tainted with that degradation are forever disqualified for the functions of citizenship. I can hardly comprehend the thought of the absolute incompatibility of degradation and citizenship; I thought that they often went together.

7. "Our nationality was created and our political government exists by written law, and inasmuch as that law does not exclude persons of that descent, and as its terms are manifestly broad enough to include them, it follows, inevitably, that such persons born in the country must be citizens unless the fact of African descent be so incompatible with the fact of citizenship that the two cannot exist together."

When it is recollected that these broad propositions with regard to citizenship predicated upon nativity, and in the case of free colored men, were enunciated prior to the first day of January, 1863, before emancipation, before even the 13th amendment of the Constitution was adopted; when the law stood precisely as it was, when Wirt and Legare gave their opinions, it must be conceded that Bates was not only thoroughly read in the law, but bold and sagacious. For these propositions have all passed, through the 14th amendment, into the Constitution of the United States, and are sustained by a wise and well-defined public judgment.

With freedom decreed by law, citizenship sanctioned and sustained thereby, the duty of allegiance on the one part, and the right of protection on the other recognized and enforced, even if considerations of political necessity had not intervened, the gift of the ballot to the colored American could not have long been delayed. The 15th amendment is the logical and legal consequences of the 13th and 14th amendments of the Constitution. Considerations of political necessity, as indicated, no doubt hastened the adoption of this amendment. But in the progress of legal development in our country, consequent upon the triumph of the abolition movement, its coming was inevitable. And, therefore, as its legal necessity, as well as political, is recognized and admitted, opposition to it has well-nigh disappeared. Indeed, so far from there being anything like general and organized opposition to the exercise of political powers by the enfranchised American, the people accept it as a fit and natural fact.

Great as the change has been with regard to the legal status of the colored American, in his freedom, his enfranchisement, and the exercise of political powers, he is not yet given the full exercise and enjoyment of all the rights which appertain by law to American citizenship. Such as are still denied him are withheld on the plea that their recognition would result in social equality, and his demand for them is met by considerations derived from individual and domestic opposition. Such reasoning is no more destitute of logic than law. While I hold that opinion sound which does not accept mere prejudice and caprice instead of the promptings of nature, guided by cultivated taste and wise judgment as the true basis of social recognition; and believing, too, that in a Christian community, social recognition may justly be pronounced a duty, I would not deal in this discussion with matters of society. I would justify the claim of the colored American to complete equality of rights and privileges upon well considered and accepted principles of law.

As showing the condition and treatment of the colored citizens of this country, anterior to the introduction of the Civil Rights Bill, so called, into the United States Senate, by the late Hon. Charles Sumner, I ask your attention to the following words from a letter written by him:

"I wish a bill carefully drawn, supplementary to the existing Civil Rights Law, by which all citizens shall be protected in equal rights:—

"1. On railroads, steamboats and public conveyances, being public carriers.

"2. At all houses in the nature of 'inns.'

"3. All licensed houses of public amusement.

"4. At all common schools.

"Can you do this? I would follow as much as possible the language of the existing Civil Rights Law, and make the new bill supplementary."

It will be seen from this very clear and definite statement of the Senator, that in his judgment, in spite of and contrary to common law rules applied in the case, certainly of all others, and recognized as fully settled, the colored citizen was denied those accommodations, facilities, advantages and privileges, furnished ordinarily by common carriers, inn keepers, at public places of amusement and common schools ; and which are so indispensable to rational and useful enjoyment of life, that without them citizenship itself loses much of its value, and liberty seems little more than a name.

The judicial axiom, "*omnes homines æquales sunt,*" is said to have been given the world by the jurisconsults of the Antonine era. From the Roman, the French people inherited this legal sentiment; and, through the learning, the wisdom and patriotism of Thomas Jefferson and his Revolutionary compatriots, it was made the chief corner-stone of jurisprudence and politics. In considering the injustice done the colored American in denying him common school advantages, on general and equal terms with all others, impartial treatment in the conveyances of common carriers, by sea and land, and the enjoyment of the usual accommodations afforded travelers at public inns, and in vindicating his claim to the same, it is well to bear in mind this fundamental and immutable principle upon which the fathers built, and in the light of which our law ought to be construed and enforced. This observation has especial significance as regards the obligations and liabilities of common carriers and inn-keepers; for from the civil law we have borrowed those principles largely which have controlling force in respect to these subjects. It is manifest, in view of this statement, that the law with regard to these topics is neither novel nor unsettled; and when the colored American asks its due enforcement in his behalf, he makes no unnatural and strange demand.

Denied, generally, equal school advantages, the colored citizen demands them in the name of that equality of rights and privileges which is the vital element of American law. Equal in freedom, sustained by law; equal in citizenship, defined and supported by the law; equal in the exercise of political powers, regulated and sanctioned by law; by what refinement of reasoning, or tenet of law, can the denial of common school and other educational advantages be justified? To answer, that so readeth the statute, is only to drive us back of the letter to the reasonableness, the soul of the law, in the name of which we would, as we do, demand the repeal of that enactment which is not only not law, but contrary to its simplest requirements. It may be true that that which

J

ought to be law is not always so written ; but, in this matter, that only ought to remain upon the statute book, to be enforced as to citizens and voters, which is law in the truest and best sense.

Without dwelling upon the advantages of a thorough common school education, I will content myself by offering several considerations against the proscriptive, and in favor of the common school. A common school should be one to which all citizens may send their children, not by favor, but by right. It is established and supported by the Government; its criterion is a public foundation ; and one citizen has as rightful claim upon its privileges and advantages as any other. The money set apart to its organization and support, whatever the sources whence it is drawn, whether from taxation or appropriation, having been dedicated to the public use, belongs as much to one as to another citizen ; and no principle of law can be adduced to justify any arbitrary classification which excludes the child of any citizen or class of citizens from equal enjoyment of the advantages purchased by such fund, it being the common property of every citizen equally, by reason of its public dedication.

Schools which tend to separate the children of the country in their feelings, aspirations and purposes, which foster and perpetuate sentiments of caste, hatred, and ill-will, which breed a sense of degradation on the one part and of superiority on the other, which beget clannish notions rather than teach and impress an omnipresent and living principle and faith that we are all Americans, in no wise realize our ideal of common schools, while they are contrary to the spirit of our laws and institutions.

Two separate school systems, tolerating discriminations in favor of one class against another, inflating on the one part, degrading on the other; two separate school systems,

I say, tolerating such state of feeling and sentiment on the part of the classes instructed respectively in accordance therewith, cannot educate these classes to live harmoniously together, meeting the responsibilities and discharging the duties imposed by a common government in the interest of a common country.

The object of the common school is two-fold. In the first place it should bring to every child, especially the poor child, a reasonable degree of elementary education. In the second place it should furnish a common education, one similar and equal to all pupils attending it. Thus furnished, our sons enter upon business or professional walks with an equal start in life. Such education the Government owes to all classes of the people.

The obligations and liabilities of the common carrier of passengers can, in no sense, be made dependent upon the nationality or color of those with whom he deals. He may not, according to law, answer his engagements to one class and justify non-performance or neglect as to another by considerations drawn from race. His contract is originally and fundamentally with the entire community, and with all its members he is held to equal and impartial obligation. On this subject the rules of law are definite, clear, and satisfactory. These rules may be stated concisely as follows : It is the duty of the common carrier of passengers to receive all persons applying and who do not refuse to obey any reasonable regulations imposed, who are not guilty of gross and vulgar habits of conduct, whose characters are not doubtful, dissolute or suspicious or unequivocally bad, and whose object in seeking conveyance is not to interfere with the interests or patronage of the carrier so as to make his business less lucrative.

And, in the second place, common carriers may not impose upon passengers oppressive and grossly unreasonable orders and regulations. Were there doubt in regard to the obligation of common carriers as indicated, the authorities are abundant and might be quoted at large. Here, however, I need not make quotations. The only question which can arise as between myself and any intelligent lawyer, is as to whether the regulation made by common carriers of passengers generally in this country, by which white passengers and colored ones are separated on steamboats, railroad cars, and stage coaches, greatly to the disadvantage, inconvenience, and dissatisfaction of the latter class, is reasonable. As to this question, I leave such lawyer to the books and his own conscience. We have advanced so far on this subject, in thought, feeling, and purpose, that the day cannot be distant when there will be found among us no one to justify such regulations by common carriers, and when they will be made to adjust themselves, in their orders and regulations with regard thereto. to the rules of the common law. The grievance of the citizen in this particular is neither imaginary nor sentimental. His experience of sadness and pain attests its reality, and the awakening sense of the people generally, as discovered in their expressions, the decisions of several of our courts, and the recent legislation of a few States, shows that this particular discrimination, inequitable as it is illegal, cannot long be tolerated in any section of our country,

The law with regard to inn-keepers is not less explict and rigid. They are not allowed to accommodate or refuse to accommodate wayfaring persons according to their own foolish prejudices or the senseless and cruel hatred of their guests.

Their duties are defined in the following language, the very words of the law:

"Inns were allowed for the benefit of travelers, who have

certain privileges whilst they are in their journeys, and are in a more peculiar manner protected by law.

"If one who keeps a common inn refuses to receive a traveler as a guest into his house, or to find him victuals or lodging upon his tendering a reasonable price for the same, the inn-keeper is liable to render damages in an action at the suit of the party grieved, and may also be indicted and fined at the suit of the King.

"An inn-keeper is not, if he has suitable room, at liberty to refuse to receive a guest who is ready and able to pay him a suitable compensation. On the contrary, he is bound to receive him, and if, upon false pretences, he refuses, he is liable to an action."

These are doctrines as old as the common law itself; indeed, older, for they come down to us from Gaius and Papinian. All discriminations made, therefore, by the keepers of public houses in the nature of inns, to the disadvantage of the colored citizen, and contrary to the usual treatment accorded travelers, is not only wrong morally, but utterly illegal. To this judgment the public mind must soon come.

Had I the time, and were it not too great a trespass upon your patience, I should be glad to speak of the injustice and illegality, as well as inhumanity, of our exclusion, in some localities, from jury, public places of learning and amusement, the church and the cemetery. I will only say, however, (and in this statement I claim the instincts, not less than the well-formed judgment of mankind, in our behalf,) that such exclusion at least seems remarkable, and is difficult of defense upon any considerations of humanity, law, or Christianity. Such exclusion is the more remarkable and indefensible since we are fellow-citizens, wielding like political powers, eligible to the same high official positions, responsible to the same degree and in the same manner for the discharge of the duties they impose; interested in the progress and civilization of a common country, and anxious, like all others, that its destiny· be glorious and matchless. It is strange, indeed, that the colored American may find place in the Senate, but it is denied access and welcome to the public place of learning, the theatre, the church and the graveyard, upon terms accorded to all others.

But, Mr. President and friends, it ill becomes us to complain; we may not tarry to find fault. The change in public sentiment, the reform in our national legislation and jurisprudence, which we this day commemorate, transcendent and admirable, augurs and guarantees to all American citizens complete equality before the law, in the protection and enjoyment of all those rights and privileges which pertain to manhood, enfranchised and dignified. To us the 13th amendment of our Constitution, abolishing slavery and perpetuating freedom; the 14th amendment establishing citizenship and prohibiting the enactment of any law which shall abridge the privileges or immunities of citizens of the United States, or which shall deny the equal protection of the laws to all American citizens; and the 15th amendment, which declares that the RIGHT of citizens of the United States to vote shall not be denied or abridged by the United States or by any State, on account of race, color, or previous condition of servitude, are national utterances which not only recognize, but sustain and perpetuate our freedom and rights.

To the colored American, more than to all others, the language of these amendments is not vain. To use the language of the late Hon. Charles Sumner, "within the sphere of their influence no person can be *created*, no person can be *born*, with civil or political privileges not enjoyed equally by all his fellow-citizens; nor can any institution be established recognizing distinction of birth. Here is the great charter of every human being, drawing vital breath upon this soil, whatever may be his condition and whoever may be his parents. He may be poor, weak, humble or black; he may be of Caucasian, Jewish, Indian or Ethiopian race; he may be of French, German, English or Irish extraction; but before the Constitution all these distinctions disappear. He is not poor, weak, humble or black; nor is he Caucasian, Jew, Indian or Ethiopian; nor is he French, German, English or Irish—he is a *man*, the equal of all his fellow-men. He is one of the children of the State, which like an impartial parent, regards all its offspring with an equal care. To some it may justly allot higher duties according to higher capacities; but it welcomes all to its equal hospitable board. The State, imitating the Divine Justice, is no respecter of persons."

With freedom established in our own country, and equality before the law promised in early Federal, if not State legislation, we may well consider our duty with regard to the abolition of slavery, the establishment of freedom and free institutions upon the American continent, especially in the island of the seas, where slavery is maintained by despotic Spanish rule, and where the people declaring slavery abolished, and appealing to the civilized world for sympathy and justification of their course, have staked all upon "the dread arbitrament of war." There can be no peace on our continent, there can be no harmony among its people till slavery is everywhere abolished and freedom established and protected by law; the people themselves, making for themselves, and supporting their own government. Every nation, whether its home be an island or upon a continent, if oppressed, ought to have, like our own, a "new birth of freedom," and its "government of the people, by the people, and for the people," shall prove at once its strength and support.

Our sympathies especially go out towards the struggling patriots of Cuba. We would see the "Queen of the Antilles" free from Spanish rule; her slaves all freemen, and herself advancing in her freedom, across the way of national greatness and renown. Or if her million and a half inhabitants, with their thousands of rich and fertile fields, are unable to support national independence and unity, let her not look for protection from, or annexation to, a country and government despotic and oppressive in its policy. By its proximity to our shores, by the ties of blood which connect its population and ours; by the examples presented in our Revolutionary conflict, when France furnished succor and aid to our struggling but heroic fathers; by the lessons and examples of international law and history; by all the pledges made by our nation in favor of freedom and equal rights, the oppressed and suffering people of Cuba may justly expect, demand our sympathies and support in their struggle for freedom and independence. Especially let the colored American realize that where battle is made against despotism and oppression, wherever humanity struggles for national existence and recognition, there his sympathies should be felt, his word and succor inspiriting, encouraging and supporting. To-day let us send our word of sympathy to the struggling thousands of Cuba, among whom, as well as among the people of Porto Rico, we hope soon to see slavery, indeed, abolished, free institutions firmly established, and good order, prosperity and happiness secured. This accomplished, our continent is dedicated to freedom and free institutions; and the nations which compose its population will enjoy sure promise of national greatness and glory. Freedom and free institutions should be as broad as our continent. Among no nation here should there be found any enslaved or oppressed. "Compromises between right and wrong, under pretence of expediency," should disappear forever; our house should be no longer divided against itself; a new corner-stone should be built into the edifice of our national, continental liberty, and those who " guard and support the structure," should accept, in all its comprehensiveness, the sentiment that all men are created equal, and that governments are established among men to defend and protect their inalienable rights to life, liberty, and the pursuit of happiness.

EULOGY ON CHARLES SUMNER.

THE GREAT CHAMPION OF EQUAL RIGHTS FOR
THE COLORED AMERICAN — HIS CHARACTER AS
SCHOLAR AND ORATOR, AUTHOR AND LAWYER,
REFORMER, STATESMAN AND MAN.*

MR. PRESIDENT, LADIES AND GENTLEMEN OF HOWARD
UNIVERSITY SENATE: I am not insensible of, nor do I fail to
appreciate, the honor you have done me by your invitation
to pronounce a eulogy on the late Hon. Charles Sumner.
Nor am I insensible of the responsibility which I assume in
undertaking this task. Impelled, however, by sentiments of
gratitude to, and admiration for, the subject of my address,
and supported by the assurance of your sympathy, I go forward, I trust, with wise and reasonable confidence.

When Charles Sumner died a great man passed through
the gateway of death to his place in history. Henceforth his
name is to be associated in the minds of men with the great
and illustrious of mankind—with the names of Wilberforce,
O'Connell, Washington, Chase, and Lincoln. Nor is the
place to be assigned him, even in this galaxy of the departed
worthies, any other than one prominent and conspicuous.

His achievements mark and distinguish the present as the
most memorable epoch of our national history; and as these
achievements are recalled and considered, in their moral significance, in the ages to come, the grandeur and glory of his

* Delivered in Howard University, Washington 'D. C., on Friday, April 24,
1874.

name and services must ever increase. Indeed, he has passed from life, its struggles, its sacrifices, its defeats, to immortality, its reward, its crown.

Many-sided is the person upon whose character we now dwell ; so distinguished for variety of brilliant and command-ing qualities, that one may not hope, in a brief address, to do more than refer to a few of his more prominent and distin-guishing characteristics. It shall be my purpose to speak of him as scholar and orator, author and lawyer, reformer, statesman and man.

In addition to his native ability, there were three things which contributed to make Mr. Sumner a profound and com-plete scholar : his early domestic advantages, his location within the reach of the best schools and institutions of learn-ing of his country, and the rare privilege of association with the best scholars and professional men of his own and other countries, from the earliest young manhood through life. He neither failed to appreciate nor cultivate these opportunities. It is impossible to estimate the effect of such influences upon the scholarship, the achievements, and the eminence of Lord Bacon. It is equally impossible to measure, adequately, their effect upon the character of Charles Sumner. While he was not especially distinguished in mathematical study, nor the natural sciences, he was profoundly read in the classics, ancient and modern, of his own and foreign tongues; and cultivating, as he did, a linguistic knowledge, he was led a natural and easy route to the study and mastery of meta-physical, moral, theological and legal science. His efforts demonstrate his profound learning in all these particulars and show him the master of large, various, and complete culture.

The fame of his scholarship is not confined to his own country, nor to the people who cultivate with us the English tongue; for his writings are translated into the German, the French, and other modern languages; and wherever read, his reputation as a scholar is established. Abroad he is regarded above all others as the scholar of our country. Certainly, no one among our prominent public men is comparable with him in this respect.

There is much in the character of Charles Sumner as a scholar that makes it proper to class him with the great scholars of England—Bacon and Burke. Like both, he was distinguished for untiring industry, variety of acquirement, and efficient use of knowledge with pen and tongue. His learning may not have been as profound and scientific as that of Bacon; it was like that of Burke, comprehensive and various. Without the selfish ambition of Bacon, he cultivated largely the virtue to which the broad fields of literature and learning supply abundant and healthful nourishment; and, like Burke, goes down to posterity distinguished for solid, scholarly integrity.

The great orators of our own and other countries are divided into two classes. The one is distinguished both f r matter and manner of delivery, while the other is more especially distinguished for the matter presented. The one class cultivate more particularly the extemporaneous habit of address; the other make the most thorough preparation, writing and even delivering their addresses from manuscript or memory. Of the first class, as well as the second, our country has produced rare and eminent representatives. To the first class belonged Clay and Webster; to the second, Seward and Sumner. As an orator, Charles Sumner was distinguished for his scholarly habit of thought and expression. While he cultivated in composition and style the chief graces of the rhetorician, he by no means neglected the weighty and effective qualities of the logician. His addresses abound in learning of a moral, metaphysical, theological, legal, historical, and classical character. The more elaborate ones are indeed orations, read with the interest and profit with which one reads profound and learned dissertations. They are models ; and the time may come when, like the great speeches of the great Greek orator, his will be treated and studied as the best productions of their class in literature.

In ardor, imagination, occasional and exceptional power, Mr. Sumner was by no means as distinguished as Chatham, Burke and Henry. In his palmy days, however, with his noble presence, manly and dignified bearing, his delivery was commanding and impressive. Few persons in any age or country have had such opportunity to make display of rhetorical power as Mr. Sumner. The subject upon which he made his great speeches was one challenging at once the sympathy, admiration and acceptance of the hearer, whether he addressed senates or popular assemblies. It was peculiarly his privilege to champion and defend the cause of an enslaved and outraged people, at a time and in a manner which made him a marked man at home and abroad, aroused against him the fury of the mob and the blood-thirsty purpose of those who defended the slave oligarchy in Congress, and gave him not only the Senate and his own countrymen as auditors, but the civilized world. This fact is not to be omitted in estimating his power as an orator. Here he was not only sustained, but strengthened and developed. His audience was such as no orator had ever before. Herein he will have no successor.

The writings of Mr. Sumner, distinguished as well for their rich and attractive style, their perspicuous and fluent diction, their learned and historic illustration, their beautiful and striking antithesis, their natural and lucid method as the principles, the sentiments, the maxims, explained and enforced in appropriate and impressive manner, must, like·

those of Webster, take high rank in the classics of our literature.   In the classification of his writings, they are
placed with those of the great masters, Bacon and Burke,
and with the prose writings of Milton.   The ability and
learning of Milton, Bacon and Burke are no more impressed
upon their writings than those of Sumner upon his; nor are
the subjects considered by them treated with greater skill,
power, and effect.   The writings of each largely reflect the
advanced thought, public conviction, and the moral, religious
and political wants of his time, and they are, therefore, interesting and valuable historically, as well as because of their
intrinsic merit.   Historically, the writings of Sumner will
prove to be of the largest value : for it will not be denied
that his elaborate addresses, which have to do with the anti-
slavery movement, while they contain accurate and generous
sentiments with regard to justice, freedom, and law—being
emphatic, too, even as the writings of the Hebrew masters,
as to the change and reformation to take place in popular
judgment and purpose—mark, as no other writings, the successive eras of the progress of this movement toward consummation. With his writings in this regard, no book as yet
written, no history of the American anti-slavery movement,
is comparable.   For this, if for no other consideration, literary or moral, these addresses are invaluable, and will
always be studied with the liveliest interest.   Our interest
in this movement, its trials, its sacrifices, martyrdoms, defeats, but final glorious triumphs, can never fail; and so long
as it animates our hearts, the words of its most gifted advocate will be read with undiminished pleasure.   His writings,
though mainly, are by no means entirely confined to anti-
slavery subjects.   Moral and political topics, those of law,
municipal and international finance, and literature, are
treated by him with learning and grace.   His works are vol-

uminous and comprehensive, though as yet unfinished. They are no more distinguished for the variety of their subject-matter, however, than the ability, learning, and wisdom displayed in the treatment.

As a writer, Mr. Sumner is remarkable rather for talent than genius; for industry discovered in mastering learning than originality in invention ; a scholarly and fearless presentation and vindication of self-evident and fundamental principles and truths. His writings, speeches, letters and addresses, preserved and published according to his original plan, in ten beautiful volumes, will always be read, studied and admired by the student and scholar of this and other lands, as rich and valuable contributions to literature.

In native ability, in training and general accomplishment, if confined to the court and juridical labors, Mr. Sumner would have made one of our most eminent and successful lawyers. Called early, however, from the court to the cultivation of letters, and thence to the duties of Senator and political leader, his reading and thoughts were given necessarily to those broader and more inviting branches of the law, which have to do with national and international interests. His reputation, therefore, is not that of a technical lawyer; and, yet he has been both an efficient teacher and practitioner. He is rather distinguished for his comprehensive and accurate knowledge of the fundamental principles and rules of constitutional and international law, and in connection with his duties as a Senator and in his addresses to the people, he furnishes evidence of his commanding ability in this regard.

Where the technical lawyer is ordinarily weak, halting, hesitating, doubting, because he finds no rule or precedent, he was bold, fearless and aggressive, feeling assured that his advocacy of a particular measure or line of policy would be at last accepted by the Government and people, because sanctioned by reason and the spirit of the law. Hence he always occupied advanced positions upon subjects of national concernment; and while he aroused, he informed and directed public conviction. As to our present reconstruction upon the basis of equal freedom, in defence of all those principles of law and morals which constitute its foundation and justification, he not only demonstrated large ability, but large understanding of constitutional law and its application.

I may not pass, unnoticed, in this connection, Mr. Sumner's celebrated argument before the Supreme Court of Massachusetts, in the case of Sarah J. Roberts. While this argument, like all of his speeches, is full of generous and just sentiments, replete with learning, it is chiefly remarkable for its clear enunciation, for the first time in our judicial legislative history, of the doctrine of "Equality before the law," and for its bold advocacy of equal and impartial common-school privileges for colored children. Speaking of this argument, he once said: "Upon it I am willing to go down to posterity." His admirers and friends have nothing to fear as to the verdict of posterity with regard to the merits and conclusion of this argument.

To one conversant with the writings of Mr. Sumner, or who, enjoying personal acquaintanceship with him, has listened to his matchless words upon the various topics of the law, the universality and exhaustiveness of his attainments seem remarkable. The ethics of the law he understood and cultivated with sincerity and wisdom. He was profoundly read in its biography, and entertained the liveliest appreciation of, and admiration for, the eminent members and ornaments of the bar.

Mr. Sumner entertained for Judge Story especially the

first writer on American constitutional law, his friend and instructor, the highest respect and admiration; and we may quote his own words here as not only expressive of this respect and admiration, but as confirmatory of the opinion attributed to him with regard to the eminent members of his profession. He says, speaking of Judge Story : "In genius for the law, in the exceeding usefulness of his career, in the blended character of judge and author, he cannot yield to our time-honored master, Lord Coke; in suavity of manner and silver-tongued eloquence, he may compare with Lord Mansfield, while in depth, accuracy, and variety of judicial learning, he surpassed him far; if he yields to Lord Stowell in elegance of diction, he exceeds even his excellence in curious explorations of the foundations of that jurisdiction which they administered in common, and in the development of those great principles of public law, whose just determination helps to preserve the peace of nations; and even in the peculiar field illustrated by the long career of Eldon, we find him a familiar worker, with Eldon's profusion of learning, and without the perplexity of his doubts. There are many who regard the judicial character of the late Chief-Justice Marshall as unapproachable. I revere his name, and have read his judgments, which seem like 'pure reason,' with admiration and gratitude, but I cannot disguise that even these noble memorials must yield in juridical character, learning, acuteness, fervor, variety of topics, as they are far inferior in amount to those of our friend. There is still spared to us a renowned judge, at this moment the unquestioned living head of American jurisprudence, with no rival near the throne —Chancellor Kent—whose judgments and works always inspired the warmest eulogy of the departed, and whose character as a jurist furnishes the fittest parallel to his own in the annals of our law."

K

The name of Charles Sumner deserves a conspicuous place among the illustrious names of the American bar. There we enroll it. By his learning, varied and profound, his achievements (if not at the bar, in the line of the profession,) lasting and valuable, his devotion to the profession, earnest and manly, he establishes his claim to such distinction.

His education, his learning, his associations, as well as his magnificent native endowment, fitted him for the arduous and trying labors to which he was called in the United States Senate. Here he was to accept and perform the double duty of reformer and statesman. His senatorial record testified how well and bravely, even to martyrdom, he discharged the duty thus imposed; and a grateful and free nation holds in lasting remembrance his noble deeds. In his own words: "Law-givers are among the greatest and most God-like characters. They are reformers of nations; they are builders of human society."

Whether we call to mind his efforts at the Boston bar in behalf of the colored youth; his earnest testimony in favor of equal rights, borne in his refusal to deliver a lecture before a lyceum of New Bedford, because distinction was made against colored persons on account of their complexion; his clear and manly utterances against slavery, from 1845 to the time he took his seat in the Senate; or his numerous able and eloquent speeches made in the Senate and before the people, from this time till Kansas was saved to freedom, the Fugitive-Slave Law repealed, the rebellion suppressed, slavery abolished, the Southern States reconstructed, the Constitution amended, the ballot given to the colored American, his protection in the enjoyment of civil rights established, and the proposition made to enact a supplementary Civil Rights Bill, to secure full equality before the law, we can but conclude that he has shown himself the reformer of the nation, the builder of American society upon a better and a firmer foundation of justice and freedom. In his disinterestedness, courage, labors, devotion, energy, sufferings without complaint, and success without inflation, resentment or abatement of purpose and zeal, he has certainly shown himself even God-like.

As a reformer and statesman, his mighty powers were confluent; and his life in this double character was as majestic, beautiful, and irresistible as the stream. Here he found the amplest opportunity to make conspicuous and commanding display of his peculiar qualities of character; his native and acquired abilities, his conscientiousness, his moral courage, his devotion, his enthusiasm, and his determination to compromise in no manner or form with the iniquity and curse of despotism. What though it cost cruel censure and abuse by opponents, sometimes even the stinging criticism instead of the commendation of friends; conscious of rectitude, keenly appreciating his duty to the enslaved and his country, settled in his purpose to discharge this duty, there was no struggle too great, no labor too arduous for him; like Paul, he was ready and willing to die daily for the truth.

His character as a reformer was in no sense narrow. Like his character as a statesman, it was formed after the pattern of the broadest and most beautiful characters of history. Before he entered upon public life, before he came even to the bar, he had read with enthusiastic admiration the writings of the noble men whose triumphs in reform make glorious the history of the race, and whose lives are justly reckoned benefactions. But more than this, Mr. Sumner had enjoyed intimate association with the able and ardent reformers of his own and other countries, and by such association he had been inspired and largely fitted for the struggles which awaited him in life. To a noble nature, an intellect of superior power, reason, conscience, imagination, sensibility and will, thoroughly educated, alive and reliable; to these masculine and vigorous powers of his soul he had added that wisdom and ardor, courage and devotion, which such contact would naturally inspire and support. From these sources were poured into the esteem of his great soul waters clear and pure, which, while they increased its volume and current, bore up his purpose and courage, as the Tiber the noble Horatius; while he through trial, struggle and suffering, passed to victory and applause.

Entering the Senate with the slave oligarchy the master of the land, American liberty itself tottering upon the brink of its ruin; free thought, free speech, freedom of locomotion well-nigh gone; with the executive, legislative and judicial departments of the Government under its control; our State legislation and policy largely inspired and directed in its interest; our most learned and influential men in pulpit and congressional place, engaging themselves, not in the stern and valorous work of meeting and overpowering this common enemy, but in devising plans of compromise and reconciliation, he engaged with the nerve and spirit of a gladiator in what proved to him personally, and to the nation, more than a moral conflict, whose weapons are logic, truth and law. He, the flower and glory of our younger Senators, as if to teach that American liberty itself must die, was made, in open day, and in the Senate, the victim and martyr of slaveholding madness and hate. Subsequently the nation was made to pour out its treasure, and make its costliest offering—its bravest and most beautiful and loving sons—to save, through blood and struggle, its priceless inheritance of union, government and liberty. From this baptism of blood grateful to Mr. Sumner, our leader in the beginning, and the last of our great Senators permitted to remain in the Senate to perfect the work of our national reconstruction, our nation goes forth upon its mission of civilization and freedom, not unmindful of him to whom so much is due, and to whom she gives, in the affections of her great heart, the chief place among the worthies whose names and deeds adorn—cover with the brightest glory, our reconstruction in freedom.

Macaulay, in dwelling upon the labors of Milton, says: "His public conduct was such as was to be expected from a man of a spirit so high and an intellect so powerful. He lived at one of the most memorable eras in the history of mankind, at the very crisis of the great conflict between Oromasdes and Arimanes : liberty and despotism, reason and prejudice. That great battle was fought for no single generation, for no single land. The destinies of the human race were staked on the same cast with the freedom of the English people. Then were first proclaimed those mighty principles, which have since worked their way into the depths of the American forests, which have roused Greece from the slavery and degradation of two thousand years, and which from one end of Europe to the other have kindled unquenchable fire in the hearts of the oppressed, and loosed the knees of the oppressors with a strange and unwonted fear. Of these principles, then struggling for their infant existence, Milton was the most devoted and eloquent literary champion."

When these principles, struggling not for their "infant existence," not against kingly power, but for more matured life and broader and more far-reaching influence, against slaveholding insolence and usurpation; under other circumstances, at a different time, in the midst of more advanced civilization; when the "American forests" had been changed into the homes of intelligent millions; when America itself.

in its government and law, its name and power, had become to enthralled and struggling nations the promise and shield of liberty and Christian progress, Charles Sumner, with indus-try and wisdom, by pen and tongue, proved himself not only a bold and daring, but sagacious and successful champion of the cause of emancipation; the cause not only of the slave, and of his countrymen, but of civilization itself. Nor will the civilized world find it either disagreeable or difficult to express suitably, and perpetuate its gratitude and appre-ciation of his arduous and effective labors. His words, ad-dressed to Webster in his appeal to him to be true to free-dom, mankind will now apply to Mr. Sumner himself; for he was true and fearless, where Webster, faltering and fail-ing, lost the high encomium proffered him.

"The aged shall bear witness of you," said Mr. Sumner. "The young shall kindle with rapture as they repeat the name of Webster, and the large company of the ransomed shall teach their children, and children's children to the latest generation to call you blessed, while all shall award you another title, not to be forgotten in earth or heaven—'De-fender of Humanity.'"

As a statesman, simply, without regard to his character of reformer, Mr. Sumner, by reason of his display of large learning, wisdom, and ability, in connection with the affairs of State, must always occupy a prominent and conspicuous place in the estimation of mankind. In intellectual quali-ties and accomplishments, the peer of Webster and Clay, he was, in fixedness and elevation of purpose, conscientious-ness and integrity, their superior. The master of the stand-ard works on constitutional and international law; by taste and choice the student of that branch of history and biog-raphy which furnishes and illustrates the soundest philoso-phy of statesmanship; conversant not more with the lives and teachings of the statesmen of America than those of Britain, France, Germany, Italy, and the countries of more different antiquity, he entered upon official life with preparation for service such as no other of his countrymen ever possessed. His public career, covering a period of twenty-three years in the United States Senate, considered and estimated in the light of and according to the usual and ordinary tests of statesmanship, shows him the prince of our Senators.

But history will accord him a higher honor, even, than this. In his case the reformer is linked and intertwined with the statesman; and while he shall be known as the American Senator, chiefly honored by his associates of the august body of which he was a member, as well as by his countrymen, he was yet not heedless of the sufferings of his fellowmen, nor insensible to the duty enjoined by justice; and, henceforth the world accords him the title—"Defender of Humanity."

It is to be regretted, as well for personal as other reasons, that the last and crowning measure proposed and advocated by Mr. Sumner did not receive legislative sanction and popular acceptance before his death. We may wisely enough congratulate ourselves and fellow-citizens, however, that he was spared to bring forward and explain, with such fulness of statement and force of argument, his "Supplementary Civil Rights Bill;" and now there does not remain the least doubt as to its passage. It is surprising that a measure so accordant with justice and the fundamental teachings of the common law, so harmonious with the principles of our Constitution, and so justified and supported by considerations of sound public policy, was not at once incorporated into our municipal code.

His last day in the Senate was made memorable by the

announcement, through his distinguished colleague, that his native State, the commonwealth which he loved so dearly, and whose faithful and laborious representative he had been so long, had reconsidered and revoked the resolution of censure two years before passed upon him.   This was the last business to which he gave attention in the Senate; and all certainly rejoice that his eyes were not closed till after this action of his State had relieved and gladdened his heart.

Of magnificent bodily proportions, commanding appearance, imperial bearing, and imposing presence, Mr. Sumner excited and attracted the admiration of all who saw him. He possessed the most vigorous and powerful qualities of intellect, the sternest constitutional integrity, and the largest endurance.   From no selfish ambition did he strive to secure the fullest development and culture of his large capacities and powers; but in the free and unstinted bestowal of his services to advance the welfare of society, discovered the most exalted spirit of benevolence.   In what he refused to do, no less than in what he did, in private life not less than in public, in the less formal addresses which he delivered to committees and others waiting upon him in his beautiful home, no less than in his addresses in the Senate or before the people, his opinions, convictions, and counsel were supported by what he deemed reasonable and proper.   There is no fact connected with his private life which more fully illustrates his keen sense of propriety and purity of character than his refusal to do the least thing, to make any effort whatever to secure either the nomination or election to the United States Senate.   To the same purpose is the fact that he never expended a single cent, directly or indirectly, to secure political advancement.   His preferment, like his greatness, depended upon nothing adventitious; upon no chicanery, intrigue, or corruption.   He was promoted upon his ability and fitness; and when he came to the Senate, as the successor of the foremost of New England's statesmen, it was found that Massachusetts had lost nothing in his election, either in dignity or ability.

His conscientiousness and integrity, like his powers of mind, grew more resplendent as his labors became more arduous and trying, even up to the end of his life. And now that he is gone, we are reminded of a striking parallel in Jewish history. The Hebrew prophet and judge, after anointing Saul king, justified his own integrity before Israel in these words : " Behold here I am; witness against me before the Lord, and before His anointed; whose ox have I taken; or whose ass have I taken; or whom have I defrauded; whom have I oppressed ; or of whose hand have I received any bribe to blind mine eyes therewith, and I will restore it you." And they said : "Thou hast not defrauded us, nor oppressed us, neither hast thou taken ought of any man's hand."

Such testimony and commendation, beautiful and emphatic, the American people bear to the integrity and purity of the departed Senator. He had no sordid view of public duty or official life. His native sense of honor, his purity and elevation of character, were, in connection with the public service, exemplified in the most pleasing and admirable manner.

Whether Mr. Sumner conversed with Emerson or advised some humble colored youth where and how to educate himself, related his own experience or dwelt upon that of others, discussed in his own, or a foreign tongue, matters of national or international interest, he displayed neither vanity nor ostentation; his conduct was marked always in private by sobriety and dignity of demeanor, simplicity and humility. To those who needed and sought his counsel, he was by no means inaccessible. And the number of young colored persons who have had their wavering purposes and sinking spirits strengthened and fired for duty and struggle by his tender, encouraging, and eloquent words, is not small. His services to the colored race, great in other, have not been by any means insignificant in this direction. The very last service of this kind done by him was in behalf of a young colored gentleman, now a student of the law department of Howard University.

It is proper to state, too, that from no other single individual, unconnected with the faculty of that department, has it received more valuable service than from Mr. Sumner. Through his influence Ralph Waldo Emerson delivered to the students of the law department an address which carried the name of Howard University far around the world. He himself, before that time, had delivered the first address ever presented to a class of young colored lawyers in our country, at the first commencement connected with the department. In this address he uses these memorable words, pregnant with wisdom and sound counsel : "I do not doubt that every denial of equal rights, whether in the school-room, the jury-box, the public hotel, the steamboat, or the public conveyance, by land or water, is contrary to the fundamental principles of republican government, and therefore to the Constitution itself, which should be corrected by the courts, if not by Congress. See to it that this is done. The Constitution does not contain the word ' white ; ' who can insert it in the law ? Insist than the common school, where the child is prepared for the duties of manhood, shall know no discrimination unknown to the Constitution. ⁄ Insist, also, that the public conveyances and public hotels, owing their existence to law, shall know no discrimination unknown to the Constitution, so that the Senator and the Representative in Congress, who is the peer of all at the national capital, shall not be insulted and degraded on the way to his public duties. Insist upon equal rights everywhere; make others insist upon them.

Insist that our institutions shall be brought into perfect harmony with the promises of the Declaration of Independence, which is grand for its universality. I hold you to this allegiance : first, by the race from which you are sprung; and secondly, by the profession which you now espouse."

The mistakes of Senator Sumner, if such he made, were such as only a great man would make. His faults, as well as his virtues, demonstrate the strength of his character. His faults, however, pale in the brightness and glory of the many virtues which distinguish his private and public conduct. No bigot in religion, he was poised and fixed in his religious moorings, by faith in Christian truth, so that, in his last hour, in the midst of intensest pain, without anxiety or perturbation, he could assure his attendants, " I will soon be at rest." To his rest he has gone, bearing with him the richest and rarest honors and distinctions, as scholar and orator, author and lawyer, reformer, statesman and man. His purposes, plans and labors, were commensurate with the limits of his country, the wants and highest good of the people, the requirements and behests of truth. If he espoused especially the cause and claims of the colored American, to liberty and equality before the law, it was not that he might serve a class simply. He pleaded the Negro's cause, not more in the interest of the Negro than in that of the whole people. He would elevate, purify, and sustain in the whole people the best conviction and the wisest purpose, that their highest and lasting good might be attained and preserved. We are all, therefore, his debtors; and his name and fame, like his words and deeds, are left to the keeping of no particular class—not even to his countrymen. Mankind will claim him as a benefactor and ornament of the race, and the monument which perpetuates his name, in grand proportions, beauty of design and grace, shall be built upon enduring, historical foundations.

OUR PATRIOT DEAD.

THE NOBLE SPIRITS WHO DIED TO SAVE THE UNION AND PERPETUATE THE FREEDOM OF THE REPUBLIC.*

COMRADES: This day our nation does honor to her noble dead. Turning aside from our ordinary employments, it is fit that our fathers and mothers, our brothers and sisters, the young man and maiden, the white and the black, should gather in the cemeteries where our dead heroes slumber, there to express sorrow and gratitude, while we honor their memory and magnify their heroism.

In the war of the Rebellion—a war so costly to our nation in treasure and precious blood—no discrimination was made finally as to those who were called and rushed with life to the defence of our country and its Union, with regard to nationality or complexion. Nor did age excuse itself. The hoary-headed father and the tender youth heard alike and heeded, in thousands of instances, the bugle call to arms. Nor did woman excuse herself, for if not clad in the uniform of the soldier, and performing the rougher and more dangerous toils of field life, she made herself "The Good Angel of the Hospital," and was not less interested in the defeats or victories that distinguished the cause of the Government than her sterner brother.

In our National Cemeteries commingle the ashes of all

---

* An oration delivered at the National Cemetery, Hampton, Virginia, May 30, 1873.

the noble men who *dared* and *died* in our late war, sacrificing life in a manly and honorable discharge of duty—dying
in answer to the demands of intelligent patriotism; and now
from the battlements of their heavenly abodes they witness
and approve our humble efforts to express our profound
gratitude, our deep sorrow as well as our cordial admiration
and lasting remembrance of those who thus died for the
honor, the liberty of the country and the perpetuity of the
Government.

With no regard, therefore, to nationality, without consideration of age or sex, only glorying in the fact of our citizenship, let the spirit of this occasion enthuse and possess
our hearts and souls; and going hence let it be with a new
devotion to our free institutions, our liberty and our religion,
determined, as our dead brothers have done, to consecrate
all, even life itself, to their conservation and maintenance.

Gathered in this sacred place, in the midst of these tender
and hallowed associations, before many of the class once owners, before many of the class once slaves, in the presence of
many persons formerly residents of the North, in the presence
of fellow Americans lately engaged in a deadly conflict, on
the one part struggling to maintain the Government, on the
other to overthrow it, and upon its ruins to establish another,
I am admonished, now, in the days of our victory and the
assurance of long life—indeed immortality to the Government—that we can and ought to inculcate and practice not
less the faith and hope than the charity so beautifully described in the words of St. Paul, " Charity suffereth long,
and is kind; charity envieth not; charity vaunteth not itself,
is not puffed up, doth not behave itself unseemly, seeketh not
her own, is not easily provoked, thinketh no evil; rejoiceth
not in iniquity, but rejoiceth in the truth; beareth all things,
believeth all things, hopeth all things, endureth all things."

In the words I utter this day such charity I would cultivate. For though at the cost even of our noblest and truest men, having been victorious, as noble victors always do, we can well afford to cultivate the largest magnanimity, and while we do not alienate, draw and attach to the Government, in the strongest and most lasting affection, those who but yesterday we met upon the field of bloodiest conflict. But it is only as this charitable disposition and conduct are earnestly and intelligently reciprocated that such desirable result can be wisely expected. It is to be hoped that such reciprocation will be thoroughly and generally shown by all classes of the people.

In order to appreciate duly the blessings wrought through the death of our fallen heroes we may be permitted to particularize somewhat.

And first, through the victories which their struggles, their sufferings, their self-denial and their death brought to the country, we enjoy and hope to perpetuate NATIONAL UNITY. Before the war of the Rebellion our nation was divided in its great overshadowing purpose, its judgment, and affection. The people of the North, under the influence of free principles and their devotion to the sentiment of liberty and equality, emancipated their slaves, and sought to establish through the State and the Federal Government, as far as the same could be done constitutionally, free institutions. Hence they opposed the spread of slavery; they denied its legal existence in the Territories. To all this the people of the South were opposed; and here we find the source of our division—a division not superficial, but fundamental, affecting law, politics, religion, education, industry, commerce—indeed, every interest, State and national, adversely. Divided thus in our purpose, our judgment, and affection, it was not strange that eventually our differences culminated in a sectional, deadly war. We have now only to rejoice that coming out of this war with victory crowning the endeavors of the Government, and with slavery, the cause of this division, utterly overthrown, we are one people, not only in nationality, in territory and Government, but in purpose, as we trust, in judgment and affection.

To-day the forty millions of our population are united in the purpose to conserve and maintain American liberty. All accept without difference of opinion the doctrine that freedom and the exercise of political power legally belong to every American, and our hearts are aglow with the single sentiment of earnest and abiding love for such liberty and freedom. In the progress of our national existence and institutions we have reached that period when we may confidently and wisely adopt the words of our eloquent Webster:

"While the Union lasts, we have high, exciting, gratifying prospects spread out before us, for us and our children. Beyond that I seek not to penetrate the veil. God grant that in my day, at least, that curtain may not rise! God grant that on my vision never may be opened what lies beyond! When my eyes shall be turned to behold, for the last time, the sun in heaven, may I not see him shining on the broken and dishonored fragments of a once glorious Union ; on States dissevered, discordant, belligerent; on a land rent by civil feuds, or drenched, it may be, in fraternal blood! Let their last feeble and lingering glance rather behold the gorgeous ensign of the Republic, now known and honored throughout the earth, still full high advanced, its armies and trophies streaming in their original lustre, not a stripe erased or polluted, not a single star obscured, bearing for its motto no such miserable interrogatory as ' What is all this worth ?' nor those other words of delusion and folly, ' Liberty first and Union afterwards ;' but everywhere, spread all over, in characters of living light, blazing on all its ample folds as they float over the sea and over the land, and in every wind under the whole heavens, that other sentiment, dear to every true American heart : ' Liberty and Union, now and forever, one and inseparable!' "

Our orator had not rightly estimated the influence of slavery, the unyielding purpose of the friends of freedom against its encroachments, when he gave utterances to those matchless words. But the struggle has come; the legions of freedom and slavery have met; the desperate fight is over; freedom has again won a glorious victory, and henceforth in our regenerated country there can be no national strife; Americans will not again imbue their hands in each other's blood, in a treasonable attempt to overthrow the Government and dismember the Union.

I am not unmindful of considerations of a material character, commercial and otherwise, which might be urged in favor of the importance and permanence of our Union.

These, however, now as well as those of a moral and political character, the latter especially, conspire to make our Union lasting.

Our Union is assured mainly, however, in the unity of our national convictions our patriotic sentiments.

But national unity would not only be impossible, it would be largely valueless without national freedom; for, as the poet has said, "'Tis liberty that gives to life its lustre and perfume."

Our freedom does not mean simple emancipation, mere release of body, self-ownership or freedom of locomotion. It is all of these, but far more beside. It is the enjoyment of free thought, free speech, citizenship, the ballot; but above all the opportunity to rise and achieve, thereby becoming great and influential among our countrymen, to cultivate all those things which pertain to dignified life, and the highest interest of our country. That we may rightly estimate this great blessing that the noble men whose graves we would this day cover with the sweetest flowers died to bring to our countrymen, we must recollect that just anterior to the war there was no freedom, no free thought, no free speech, no freedom of locomotion enjoyed in full measure by the American people. Indeed American liberty itself had well-nigh gone, "glimmering through the dream of things that were, a school boy's tale, the wonder of an hour." But to-day the sun in the heavens is not more bright and glorious, its light and heat more lovely and life-giving than the sun of liberty in our moral sky, which, shining with a new heat and a new lustre, is to us the source of our civil and political life and happiness, in which we delight ourselves and fear no molestation.

Liberty, however, is nothing more than license, a thing of caprice, without present or permanent value, without *Law* as its shield and protection; and we should emphasize the important and valuable blessing brought us through the war, in which so many of our sons, brothers, and fathers fell—the equal and all protecting law, beyond whose care we cannot go, however distant, or devious, or hidden our route.

Where the brave men slumber and sleep, who dying purchased for us liberty regulated and defended by law—

> " 'Tis holy ground.
> This spot where, in their graves,
> We place our country's braves,
> Who fell in freedom's holy cause,
> Fighting for liberties and laws ;
> Let tears abound."

But more than national unity, freedom and law regulating it, was given the nation through the bloody struggles of the rebellion. We were given a free Christianity, an unmuzzled and fearless clergy, and now we may hope that the day is not distant when such reform will have taken place in the country as to insure the practice of sound morality among all classes of the people and in all branches and departments of the Government. Thus the highest interests of the

L

people will be conserved, good order maintained, and civilization advanced. Indeed already we are realizing these pleasing and beneficial results. Accepting these benefits, brought us in the providence of our Heavenly Father, through the suffering and the death of those whom we this day honor, it is our duty to prove ourselves wise and faithful custodians thereof, and as far as possible make them of the largest advantage to ourselves and posterity. Indeed—

"Such graves as these are hallowed shrines,
    Shrines to no code or creed confined ;
The Delphian vales, the Palestines,
    The Meccas of the mind."

If what has already been said and indicated be true the dead whose memories we revere, and whose patriotic and heroic deeds we would celebrate, fought and fell to save and perpetuate our Government and free institutions, to save and reconsecrate and sanctify the doctrines of our Declaration and Constitution, to emancipate and introduce into the body-politic, as citizens and voters, office holders and equals, persons formerly held as slaves in our country. Therefore, to-day we are one nation, possessing a common country, enjoying our freedom, our liberty, and rights under the protection of a Government whose destiny we believe is high and glorious. But the life of our Government is only assured as the sentiment and purpose which brings us here to-day animate our souls, and stimulate and sustain our devotion to liberal principles.

The history of our country is distinguished for three leading wars, the Revolutionary War, the War of 1812, and the war of the late Rebellion. We would honor the dead of all these wars, for they were all waged in the interest of our country, to secure its independence, to maintain its interests and its liberties, the union and the majesty of the law. We would honor the memory of Washington ; we would suitably appreciate the achievements of Jackson ; we would not fail to hold in constant remembrance, and cherish with grateful hearts the masterly and noble efforts of the great leaders who gave victory to our arms in the fearful struggle of the Rebellion. Standing, as we do this day, in this cemetery, in the presence of more than five thousand graves, calling to mind, too, the thousands of other graves in the presence of which this day the American people assemble themselves to honor the dead, recollecting what sacrifices, what sufferings, what courage and Spartan heroism these noble dead endured and displayed, one would erect to their memory a monument, whose base should be broader than this vast cemetery, whose summit should pierce the very stars, and all over whose sides should be written, in characters never to be effaced, the history of their achievements, their valor, their fidelity and their patriotic devotion.

If such monument may not be erected, let our cemeteries, in which the patriotic dead of the war of the Rebellion slumber, be indeed national gardens, in which are grown from the ashes of the fallen those sentiments of patriotism, liberty, law and union, which should fire the heart and energize and nerve the purpose of the faithful and earnest American. The words of the poet are apt:

> "Here let them rest;
> And summer's heat and winter's cold
> Shall glow and freeze above the mold—
> A thousand years shall pass away—
> A nation still shall mourn this clay,
> Which now is blest."

OUR POLITICAL PARTIES.

THE REPUBLICAN AND DEMOCRATIC PARTIES COMPARED IN THEIR ADMINISTRATIONS OF THE GOVERNMENT.*

FELLOW-CITIZENS: The political parties of the country have held their conventions, defined their positions, and made and announced their nominations. The voters of the country are now called upon to make their choice. Choice here is free; and voters are only bound and restricted by those considerations of sound policy and patriotism which justly define and limit their obligation and duty. Perhaps never in the history of our country, a history distinguished in its more memorable parts for the establishment of free institutions, was there a time when the duty of the American voter, to consider well and wisely what vote to cast, what party to bring and support in power, was so imperative as in this centennial year of our national independence.

The earlier days of the Republic are distinguished for noble and heroic deeds, for self-denial and sacrifices made and performed in its behalf. Then our foe was a foreign and open one. Within the past fifteen years a domestic foe has with organized forces met the Government in deadly conflict, upon a bloody field; and vanquished, has, in fact, brought forth "works meet for repentance" as evidence of cordial acceptance of the new condition of affairs. This domestic

---

* A speech delivered in Saratoga, N. Y., April 1, 1876.

foe when defeated made its threat, relying upon one of the great political parties of the country for its support in carrying it out, that though whipped in the field, it would yet prove itself victor in politics. Shall the sacrifices of these latter days go for naught ? Have our brave men died in vain ? Are the burdens of the nation to prove no warning for our good ? Are the monuments of devastation and ruin casting their dark shadows over one section of our country to teach us no useful lessons of admonition? These questions are answered in the affirmative or negative, wisely or foolishly, as we sustain by our vote the one or the other party. But in considering and determining our duty as voters, we ought to rise above mere partisan devotion. We ought to remember that party is but a means, an instrument used to gain some special or general political end. The end sought, the results to be accomplished must be fully considered in determining the character of the party and our duty to support, or refuse to support it. The language of its declaration of principles, the past character of its nominees and their protestations of loyalty to past records, will not always suffice to satisfy us of its and their trustworthiness. We are required often to seek after the reputation of the party, and the probable associations, and party and individual obligations of the candidates after their election. And in discharging our duty in this regard, while we are fearless we should be impartial and just. Let us not make haste to condemn unduly, nor to accept without wise discrimination, the claim of any candidate or party.

With such feelings as I indicate, with a lively sense of our responsibility as American citizens and voters, where does duty lead us in the exercise of our suffrages, to the Democratic or the Republican party ?

In discussing this question there are two things we cannot

separate in our minds. Indeed we ought not to separate them. We cannot separate the party and its candidate ; and we cannot deny that the party being the larger and more important moral force, gives character and aim to its candidates, and not the candidates to the party. The party is the principal, the candidate the agents ; the latter the servants, the former the masters. These considerations should be emphasized, since the representatives and advocates of one of our political parties, conceding the bad eminence of their party, invite, with some degree of earnestness and eloquence, the attention of the people to the towering ability and good name of their chief candidate. They even call him "reformer ;" forgetting that when elected he can only accomplish, in his administration of the Government, those results, however able and excellent he may be, which his party and its leaders will allow. We have in our political history an interesting chapter, which illustrates with special force this subject and the judgment of the people with regard thereto. You will recollect that only so far back as 1872, in our last presidential campaign, the Democratic party, despairing of being able to find a candidate among its own leaders, though many of them were distinguished for learning and personal integrity, nominated an old, earnest abolitionist, a man distinguished as able, great and good, whose life is brilliant and beautiful in its triumphs, as their candidate for the Presidency. But Horace Greeley, supported by the intellectual giants of the Republic, Sumner and Schurz, in a strange and unnatural alliance with the Liberal Republican movement, was unable to impart to the Democratic party such good name and influ. ence as to induce the people to give it their confidence and support. Protracted and aggravated recreancy to principle, the obligations of patriotism and loyalty, the influence and warnings of party experiences in our own and other countries, are not soon forgotten nor easily forgiven. Nor do individual names, pouring by contrast floods of light upon party shortcomings, "sins of omission and commission," serve to eclipse and obscure them. No intelligent and honest American, in the light of Greeley's example, the elaborate and able addresses of Sumner, the learned and thrilling denunciations of Schurz, could in 1872 consent to vote the Democratic ticket. This party has made no change in doctrine or purpose as we are advised, and if we are to judge of its future by its past, of its probable course from the character of its chief men, North and South, from the character of the section of the country whence come its members and sympathy mainly, its principles as enunciated and expounded in the addresses of its orators, the significant insinuations and allusions to its past dignity and acts, we can but conclude that this party still stands *super vias antiquas.* Every American citizen, every individual intent upon justice and fair-dealing, intelligent and impartial in his judgment, will recognize the justness of the criterion here implied. Whatever the names of its candidates, whatever their past political relations, whatever their social position or their reputation as honorable, sincere, and upright men, the party, in principle, in purpose, and aim, is the same. What it has been and what it is, and what spirit animates it, we can determine from its opposition to those measures of reform—reform in the true and best sense, progress and advancement in all those things which pertain to national goodness and greatness—inaugurated and sustained by the Republican party whose nominations we meet to ratify.

On the 4th day of March, 1861, Abraham Lincoln, the first chief magistrate elected by the suffrages of the Republican voters of the country, took the oath of office prescribed by the Constitution and entered upon the administration of the Government. Quite sixteen years have elapsed since that time, and our country and Government have passed an ordeal of trial, our institutions a test and strain, such as the history of the world cannot parallel. During this entire period the Republican party has been in power and held justly responsible for the judicious and efficient conduct of the Government. During this period the achievements of the party have been in their character and scope magnificent and marvelous. These achievements very naturally group themselves under distinct designations.

First. Those which are in a moral and legal sense reformatory in their character. And here we may hang, as it were upon a chain of gold in glowing beauty, all those which pertain to the abolition of slavery, the reconstruction of the seceded States, and the protection therein against rebel hate and violence, of all loyal classes, white and black.

Secondly. Those acts which are war-like, having to do with that bloody and costly contest between the slave oligarchy and the Government, in which the former, after years of aggression and encroachment upon the rights of the people, was forever overthrown and the authority of the latter established, and is now honored in all sections of the country.

Thirdly. Our immense fiscal transactions, including the finances, the currency and the banking system of the Government.

Fourthly. Those which concern our internal improvements, the protection of immigrants, the encouragement of labor, and the advancement of education and science. The single great work of building the Pacific Railroad, the iron band which unites in a cordial and perpetual embrace the East and the West, must ever command the admiration and challenge the gratitude of the people.

Fifthly. Those efforts of the Government which concern our relations with foreign powers, especially the establishment of the peaceful method of arbitration for the settlement of international differences.

If we consider the obstructions, the hindrances overcome by the Government in seeking the accomplishment of such results, it will be found that, difficult as the task itself was, the chief source of difficulty was found in the persistent and sometimes cruel opposition of the Democratic party and its leaders. Their severe and exaggerating criticisms, their inimical comments, show the depth of their opposition and its pertinacity.

If the financial, the legal, the moral, the material and the industrial reforms of the Republican party are of value and deserve to be maintained, the Democratic party, if our judgment be correct, must not be brought as yet in power; for its success is their overthrow, and their overthrow a lasting damage to the country.

The country may be very justly felicitated upon the ability and efficiency with which the affairs of the Government generally have been administered by the party now in power; but we find cause of special congratulation in the fact that marked wisdom, integrity and success have characterized the collection and disbursement of the public funds. One has only to become conversant with the immense receipts and expenditures of the Government, made necessary largely by the suppression of the late rebellion, uaint himself with the thoroughness and promptness generally with which the revenues of all sorts are collected and the comparatively small loss connected with the expenditure thereof, to appreciate the statement just made. In illustration and enforcement of it, I adduce two facts, one showing how and to what extent the public debt has been reduced to the date named, and the other the loss upon the expenditures of the Government for the time mentioned. And first, the public debt had reached its highest figure June 30, 1866, when it amounted to $2,773,236,173.69. Since then the revenues of the nation have exceeded the expenditures, leaving a balance each year for the redemption of the public debt. From June 30, 1866, to June 30, 1875, the public debt has been reduced $599,711,641.74. This reduction has taken place in the face of reduced taxation. Under the acts of Congress dated July 13, 1866, March 2, 1867, February 3, 1868, March 1 and July 20, 1868, July 14, 1870, May 1 and June 6, 1872, the internal revenue taxation has been reduced from its highest point in 1866, $309,226,813.42, to $110,007,493.58, June 30, 1875. In this reduction of the public debt, and this descending scale of taxation, we have at a single glance the policy of the administration to maintain the public credit, and at the same time lighten the burdens of the people.

In a statement showing the receipts and disbursements of the Government from January 1, 1834, to June 30, 1875, exhibiting also the amount of defalcations and the ratio of losses per $1,000 to the aggregate received and disbursed, arranged in periods, as nearly as practicable, of four years each, and also in the periods prior and subsequent to June 30, 1861, prepared under the direction of the Secretary of the Treasury, it is shown that from July 1, 1861, to June 30, 1875, the gross total of receipts being $12,709,645,059.91, and the gross total of losses being $4,348,098.10, the loss on $1,000 was 34 cents, while the gross total of disbursements, exclusive of the post-office, being from July 1, 1861, to June 30, 1875, $12,566,892,569.53, and the gross total of losses $9,905,205.37, the loss on $1,000 was 78 cents.

From January 1, 1834, to June 30, 1861, the gross total

of receipts being $1,390,986,145.18, and the gross total of losses being $2,907,527.31, the loss on $1,000 was $2.09, while the gross total of disbursements, exclusive of the post-office, being from January 1, 1834, to June 30, 1861, $1,369,-977,502.52, and the gross total of losses being $12,361,722.91, the loss on $1,000 was $9.02.

Senator Anthony, on the 28th of last June, in remarks made by him to the Senate, makes this statement: "The losses on the $1,000 of disbursements were, in the administration of Jackson, $10.55; Van Buren, $21.15; Harrison, $10.37; Polk, $8.34; Taylor and Fillmore, $7.64; Pierce $5.86; Buchanan, nearly $6.98; Lincoln, $1.41; Johnson 48 cents; Grant, the first four years, 40 cents; the second four years, 26 cents—showing a constant decline, which is owing in a large degree to the improved manner of keeping the accounts; and this is due very largely to the committees on finance and appropriations, who have introduced legislation which has compelled much greater accuracy and responsibility. The average percentage of losses during this whole period on the disbursements is $1.59 on the thousand. I do not believe that the aggregate of any class of corporate or private business, banking, commercial, or any other kind, can show so small a percentage of loss as this, and it is gratifying that the percentage of loss is continually decreasing, coming down from $21.15 in the administration cf Van Buren, to an average of twenty-three cents on the thousand dollars, or only about one-sixtieth as much under the present administration. This is exclusive of the post-office, which administers its own revenue. In the post-office the loss has gone down from $11.18 on the $1,000, in Jackson's administration, and $26.19 in Van Buren's, to $1.59 for the first term of Grant, and $1.01 for the second, with an average of $3.51 for the whole period."

As expressive of my own feelings and opinions on this subject, I adopt the apt and forcible words of a writer, who says : " We have endeavored to show, by the statements submitted, the magnitude of the financial operations of the Government during fifteen years of Republican rule. They may be safely held up as being without a parallel in our history, if not in the history of nations. To carry on these operations through a long series of years, without infringing upon the constitutional rights of a single citizen, or without oppressing the industrial interests of the country, has required the highest degree of administrative and legislative talent, and the highest order of executive integrity. It should be borne in mind that these heavy financial responsibilities were forced upon the country by treasonable Democracy and that the part performed by the Republican party was simply the execution of an imperative duty which it owed to the Union, to freedom, to humanity and to the world's civilization. With these figures before us, with a clear remembrance of those terrible years of sacrifice and suffering, when the hopes of the nation centered in the courage and patriotism of the Republican party, with at least $150,000,000 of yearly expenditures to remind us of a party that betrayed the nation, and with a burdensome public debt, which a loyal people are nobly bearing, who that loves his country or wishes to see it continue in the paths of peace and prosperity can give his vote or influence to the support of a party that stands to-day as responsible for the Rebellion, as it did when its recognized head, James Buchanan, folded his arms and gave it the sanction of his official encouragement, by the admission that he had no power to coerce.

The executive, legislative and administrative ability, sagacity and efficiency of the Republican party are no more demonstrated in the wise conduct of our financial affairs than in the establishment of a national currency reliable, if fluctuating, abundant and of universal and uniform value throughout the country. Founded upon the integrity and credit of the nation our currency may be regarded as absolutely safe. And according to recent and reliable estimate its circulation *per capita* amounts to $18.33. It only remains to provide for the redemption in coin or its equivalent and our system of currency will be as wise and safe as any the ingenuity of man has devised. To the accomplishment of this result without shock or damage to our business interests, the Republican party is pledged as against Democratic inflation.

The charge that business stagnation in the country, the seeming paralysis of our great industries, is attributable to the character of our currency as unreliable and scarce finds no foundation in fact. Money was never so abundant and it is a thousand times more reliable than under the old State-bank system. According to reports made to the Comptroller of the Currency, May 12, 1876, the aggregate resources of 2,089 national banks amount to $1,793,306,002.78. And as we all understand, no matter how poorly a national bank may be managed, it may even fail, but no holder of its notes loses a single dollar, for its issues are secured by a deposit of United States bonds.

Our business depression must be accounted for upon some other hypothesis. It is largely, if not mainly, due to the two-fold cause : first the persistent and violent criticisms of many of the leaders of the Democratic party; and secondly, the fear that that party may come into power, and if so that it would upturn and revolutionize our system of currency. Such considerations, however absurb and baseless the criticisms may be, and however improbable it may be that the Democratic party will be given soon the control of the

Government, have the most disastrous effects upon business enterprises. How can this cause of evil be removed ? Not by putting in power the party responsible for its existence. Only by sustaining that party which has established this system, and now promises to improve it by making our currency redeemable in coin or its equivalent and at a day fixed and not distant.

Imperfect as any description of the achievements and triumphs of the Republican party may be, enough has been said to demonstrate its claim upon public sympathy and support. Its maintenance of the national credit, its defence and support of the national honor and the national integrity, entitle it specially to gratitude and the admiration of the country. This party has countenanced no executive, congressional or official acts which tarnish the good name of the nation.

The guaranty, therefore, that the promises and pledges of the Republican party will be kept and redeemed, if continued and sustained in power, is written in the plainest and boldest manner in the record of its past accomplishments.

But how about the Democratic party? It has a record, and its promises and pledges as presented in the St. Louis platform are manifold, being embodied in language which sounds much like the sonorous periods of a Fourth of July oration.

After the use of the word "reform" some fifteen times in the platform as applied to the administration of the Federal Government, the Union eleven years ago happily rescued from the danger of a corrupt centralism, a sound currency, the sum and mode of Federal taxation, the profligate waste of public lands, the omissions of the Republican Congress, and the errors of our treaties and our diplomacy, reform as a controlling issue of the election necessary in the civil, the higher grades of public service, and the declaration that the abuses, wrongs and crimes described—the product of sixteen years' ascendancy of the Republican party—create a necessity for reform, and that this can only be had by a peaceful revolution, the platform closes in these words : "We demand a change of system, a change of administration, a change of parties, that we may have a change of members and of men."

It becomes us to inquire and to know what such words mean before giving our support to the party using them. Their meaning is partially discovered in the opposition offered to the measure brought forward and adopted by the Republican party. It is more fully and clearly discovered in the light of past declarations of the party and one of its chief and more prominent leaders of former days.

On the 4th day of March, 1829, Andrew Jackson was inaugurated President of the United States, and in his inaugural address presented his purposes as to reform in these words : "The recent demonstration of the public sentiment inscribe on the list of executive duties, in characters too legible to be overlooked, the task of reform; which will require, particularly, the correction of those abuses that have brought the patronage of the Federal Government into conflict with the freedom of elections, and the counteraction of those causes which have disturbed the rightful course of appointment, and have placed or continued power in unfaithful or incompetent hands."

His removal from office for political reasons simply, may be characterized as wholesale with him—"To the victors belong the spoils"—and upon this principle he distributed official patronage. Hitherto the number of persons removed from office by his predecessors was small. Washington removed in eight years 9, one a defaulter; John Adams in four years 10, one a defaulter; Jefferson in eight years 39; Madison in eight years 9, of which 6 were for cause; John Quincy Adams in four years 2, both for cause.

Reform, then, in the light of Jackson's·example, as far as it is applied by Democrats to the civil service, means, it is to be feared, wholesale removal and appointment for mere political reasons.

Admitting that the party in power is responsible for the proper management of the Government, that it is wise and safe as a general rule to make selections for positions in the civil as well as the higher grades of public service when needed from its supporters, that such supporters have the first and more imperative claim to its official patronage, other things being equal, it must, nevertheless, be conceded that respect should be had always to the capacity, fidelity and honesty of the applicant or appointee. Party zeal, party services, party advancement should not be allowed to outweigh the more important considerations of qualification and fitness for the proper performance of public duty.

But a change of system, a change of parties, that we may have a change of men and members, is demanded. This demand is certainly fundamental; it is radical; and what it means is a matter of concern to every voter. Does it mean retrocession—that we are to go back to our national position and condition in 1861 when the Democratic party went out of power? Does it mean that new men and new members, with anti-republican views and purposes, according to other systems of political, financial, legal, economic and social philosophy, are to pronounce the works of the Republican party for the past sixteen years a failure, and attempt something new? Does it mean that Democratic as opposed to Republican reconstruction is to be tried? What else can

be its meaning? The Democratic party would write across
the sixteen years of Republican abministration of the Government the appalling word, Failure! How futile! How
insane the attempt! The work of the party is vital; its
results are too deeply appreciated by the people for such
attempt to succeed.

On reading the Democratic platform you will find what,
under the circumstances, is a most remarkable omission.
No protection is promised to the loyal citizens, white and
black, of the South. "The rapacity of carpet-bag tyrannies,"
as many other things, is denounced; no guaranty, however,
of protection to the loyal, even though not carpet-baggers,
can be found in their platform. Though this be considered
natural in the Democratic party, it is, while it pretends to
accept the Constitution with the amendments as a final settlement of the controversies which engendered civil war, very
remarkable. I think it may be deemed significant. Does
it not mean that as far as the party is concerned, if given
power, the loyal people of the South will be compelled to
look thereafter for protection to the several State governments under which they live?

As bearing on this subject the language of the platform
is full of meaning :

"Reform is necessary to rebuild and establish in the
hearts of the whole people the Union eleven years ago happily rescued from the danger of a corrupt centralism, which,
after inflicting upon ten States the rapacity of carpet-bag
tyrannies, has honeycombed the offices of the Federal Government itself with incapacity, waste and fraud."

No party is worthy of our support whose record is not
clear, whose voice is not positive as to the matter of protection to every American citizen at home and abroad; especially at home; for, if there is any place where the citizen
should realize that he is safe, free from fear of disturbance,

M.

as to life, property or freedom, it is within the limits of his own country and under the government to which he owes and pays his allegiance. Should the State fail to give such protection, it is the duty of the General Government to give it. If this be centralism—the centralism denounced by the Democratic platform—I denounce their denunciation of it, and proclaim it sound law.

If the Democratic party mean to accept heartily the amendments of the Constitution and the reconstruction of the seceded States in accordance therewith, it will, it must recognize the obligation of the Government to protect defenceless and inoffensive citizens against violence and abuse, certainly when the maltreatment becomes murder and the State government is either impotent, or in the hands of those who will not wield its power, to protect its citizens. The language of the amendments implies this obligation of the Federal Government; and if the reconstruction of the States is to be sustained, in its integrity, the pledge of such protection and its practical redemption are indispensable.

On this matter there can be no theorizing. It is one of immediate and pressing importance. It is feared that the canvass upon which we are now entering cannot be conducted to its close peaceably, and the loyal citizens of the South permitted to exercise fully their political powers. Shall such citizens be protected against threats and intimidations, bloodshed and murder? Our hearts sicken even now at the horrid disorders, crimes and murders so lately reported as occurring in Hamburg, South Carolina.

The utterance of the Republican party with regard to protection is clear and comprehensive. The third section of its platform reads as follows:

"The permanent pacification of the Southern section of the Union, the complete protection of all its citizens in the free enjoyment of all their rights, are duties to which the Republican party is sacredly pledged. The power to provide for the enforcement of the principles embodied in the recent constitutional amendments is vested by those amendments in the Congress of the United St ites, and we declare it to be the solemn obligation of the legislative and executive departments of the Government to put into immediate and vigorous exercise all their constitutional powers for removing any just causes of discontent on the part of any class, and securing to every American citizen complete liberty and exact equality in the exercise of all civil, political and public rights. To this end we imperatively demand a Congress and Chief Executive whose courage and fidelity to these duties shall not falter until these results are placed beyond dispute or recall."

As one reads the platform of the Democratic party, calling to mind its declarations of sentiments in 1852, and since that time, both by the things said, the peculiar language employed, and by the things omitted and the apparent reason for the omission, he can but conclude that the charge made by the Republican against the Democratic party when it uses the following words, is just:

"We charge the Democratic party as being the same in character and spirit as when it sympathized with treason, and with making its control of the House of Representatives the triumph and opportunity of the nation's recent foes; with reasserting and applauding in the national capitol the sentiments of unrepented rebellion; with sending Union soldiers to the rear; with deliberately proposing to repudiate the plighted faith of the Government; with being equally false and imbecile upon the overshadowing financial question; with thwarting the ends of justice by its partisan mismanagement and obstruction of investigation; with proving itself through the period of its ascendancy in the lower House of Congress utterly incompetent to administer the Government. We warn the country against trusting a party thus alike unworthy, recreant and incapable."

If what has been said of the Democratic party, what is

inferred from its present utterances in the light of its past, from suspicious omissions noticed in connection with the platform be true, it is hardly worth while to spend much time in considering the character of its candidates. Having determined the character of the party it is an easy matter to decide what the candidates must be, and what they must do.

Whether Governor Tilden is a good man or a bad one, able or weak, of large general and executive talent, of broad and varied official experience, his term of executive control as the Governor of New York marked by efficiency and success, are all matters of small account as compared with the questions what his party is and what it would do were it in power.

I would not disparage, I would not even speak lightly, certainly not disrespectfully of the Governor of our Empire State. I prefer to concede his ability and sincerity. He is therefore the more dangerous as the representative of the Democratic party in power. A man of less ability, of less skill and purpose, would do far less injury. Here I assume that the party controls its servants, commanding and compelling their obedience. Every consideration of candor and propriety leads us to believe also that the principles and policy of the Democratic party are fully and earnestly accepted by its candidates, and if elected such candidates will spare no reasonable effort to give effect to those principles— to have the policy of the party adopted in obedience to its desire and command.

All this is equally true of the candidates of the Republican party; and because the principles and the policy of this party are, as I believe, true and correct, and the highest interests of the country will be subserved by their adoption, I rejoice, as you must rejoice, that the party has put in nomination for President and Vice-President two able and good men. These men have not been slow in accepting their nominations and

in announcing their views in their letters of acceptance.
They are men well known, of large experience in public affairs, and perfectly conversant with all those things which
pertain to the wise, economical and efficient administration
of the National Government. In their letters of acceptance
their indorsement of the principles of the party is natural
and cordial; and their discussion respecting them, so comprehensive and masterly, displaying such familiarity with the
necessity of their application that no one can question their
conscientious approval of them. Indeed Governor Hayes, in
his letter, in brief, terse, yet elaborate terms, dwells with such
force and clearness upon the reform in the civil service, combatting the sentiment "to the victors belong the spoils," and
commending the rule that "honesty, capacity, and fidelity
constitute the only qualifications for office"—upon the resumption of specie payments, maintaining that "uncertainty,
inseparable from an irredeemable paper currency," can be
ended only by such resumption upon a constitutional amendment; "which shall place beyond all danger of sectarian control or interference " our public school system, claiming that
" the Republican party is pledged to secure such amendment;"
upon the condition of the South, asserting that what it
"most needs is 'peace,' and peace depends upon the supremacy
of law," and that the first necessity of the people there " is
an intelligent and honest administration of the Government
which will protect all classes of citizens in all their political
and private rights "—that no one can mistake his judgment
and purpose, and no one, not even an opponent, can fail to
appreciate and commend his earnestness and candor. If
elected we cannot doubt the course which he will pursue.

His record as a brave and gallant soldier and officer of
the Union army, as a Republican tried in the walks of congressional life, and as Governor of Ohio, to the last position

having been elected three times, and each time against the most formidable opposition; as a lawyer and scholar of considerable experience and honorable name, demonstrates his capacity, his fidelity and his honesty. Did we need additional evidence of his self-reliance, moral courage and determination, his purpose to discharge fully and wisely the promises and obligations of the party against all opposition, and his ability to conduct the administration of the Government with efficiency and success in the interest, in fact, of all the people and every section of the country, we have it in his letter. But if we study well his speeches, his messages written during his different administrations as governor of one of the greatest and most thrifty States of our Union, the principles accepted and advocated by him before the people in his several campaigns, and subsequently enforced as elements of sound State policy, we shall discover the secret of that power which, wielded by a master, showed its possessor more then a match for Pendleton, Thurman and Allen. In well-informed circles these are called great men. Why not, in the view of all he has done and is, call Hayes a great man? I will; and the people in their vote will very soon announce their judgment on this subject. No charge of corruption is made against our candidates. No man, however blinded by partisan feeling and prejudice, questions their integrity, Their public, like their private character, is free from stain or tarnish. They need, in this regard, no defence.

Attack, however, is made upon the present administration of the party. It is charged that it is inefficient, wasteful, corrupt, and oppressive. The fact that a prominent official connected therewith has been found perpetrating acts of malfeasance in office—others of lesser prominence have been tried, convicted, sentenced and are now undergoing the punishment of the law—while the charge of fraudulent pratices has been made against certain leading Republican Members of Congress, and others holding no official positions, or such as are altogether subordinate, are adduced as proof positive and sufficient that this statement is true. And, then, the conclusion is reached *per saltum*, that the Republican party should be driven from power and the Democratic party installed. But admitting that these statements and charges are true, are we prepared to say that the administration of the National Government should be given to the Democratic party? In view of what this party is and what it has been; in view of what it proposes to do, as well as what it proposes to leave undone, our answer must be no. Reforms needed in the administration, in the various branches of the Government, are much more likely to be made by the Republican party, without violence or damage to the country, in its financial, commercial, industrial, political, and general interests, in obedience to a healthy public sentiment, than through the opposing political organization ; for the very evils against which we would guard were introduced, fostered and sustained by that party.

It is due the present administration to state that it has, in no instance, when just complaint has been made, failed to take vigorous and positive steps against offenders—those breaking law or neglecting or violating official obligations. And this the administration has done in obedience to the comprehensive and poignant order of its chief, "Let no guilty person escape."

But the administration of President Grant is not legitimately on trial before the people; for he is not the nominee of the Republican party. If it were, it would need no special and laborious defense. Its record in the main compares favorably with any administration which has preceded it; while, in many respects, it is peculiar and matchless. . It will soon take its place in the history of the country, and an impartial posterity will render it that award of commendation, on the whole, to which its merits entitle it.

Already I have trespassed too greatly upon your patience, and I must conclude my remarks. In doing so I would remind you that the contest upon which we are entering is not one of personal or party success merely. It is one of deeper, broader, more far-reaching, important and dignified character. Treating individuals and parties now as of small consequence, excepting as they are used as means and instrumentalities to accomplish great ends of private and public goods, we are called upon as intelligent and earnest, patriotic and devoted citizens, to determine, each for himself, how votes, given for the Democratic or Republican party, will tend to sustain the Democratic or Republican party, will tend to sustain the dignity and power of the Government, conserve our free institutions, under the Constitution, within the Union. Each of us is held responsible to his own conscience, posterity and God for the wisdom, or folly, displayed in exercising our suffrage; the most sacred as it is the most valuable right which we possess on American soil. In such spirit I present and here I leave this subject.

PACIFIC RECONSTRUCTION.

THE OTHER PHASE OF RECONSTRUCTION—PACIFI-
CATION THE TRUE POLICY.*

FELLOW CITIZENS: The thoughtful and patriotic American, animated by other than partisan and sectional considerations and feelings, turns with delight from the contemplation of the belligerent to the pacific phase of reconstruction.

Four years of bloody contest, characterized by all the evils attendant in the most aggravated form upon a civil strife of gigantic proportions, and twelve years of effort at reconciliation and readjustment, marked by displays of cruel, unrestrained fury, controlled only by military power, bring us, in all earnestness of soul, to inquire: "Is there no method by which the problem of reconstruction may be satisfactorily solved in some peaceful manner?"

Rising above party considerations, seeming sectional interests, as well as individual aggrandizement, we should study well every lesson of history, every lesson suggested by the precepts of Christianity, every lesson taught in sound political philosophy, having reference to this problem, which of all others commands consideration and intelligent solution.

In this discussion we have to do with one of the important sections of our country; one divided into great States, populated by millions of people, peculiar not less in their present than in their former condition and relations.

---

* Speech delivered at Congregational Tabernacle, Jersey City, N J., April 17, 1877.

Sixteen years ago there were three distinct classes composing the population of the South ; the first, the slaveholding class, the lords of the land and the lash ; the next, the class known as the " poor whites," the under grade of Southern society ; and thirdly, the Negroes, slaves, chattels personal. The first class were not only the owners of the wealth, but they possessed the education and the intelligence, the social and political influence of their various communities. From this class came, as well the old political leaders, as the military chieftains, who led the rank and file of the Southern army in the late rebellion. From this class, too, came the purpose and the energy which at once originated and sustained the revolt against the Government, and the attempt to organize the Southern Confederacy. If any single class may be called the " master class " of the South, occupying commanding place, and wielding controlling influence in the politics of that section, that class is the one of which I now speak. Deprived by the war largely of its property, its numbers considerably reduced by the same cause, its compact and easily moved organization not a little impaired, disappearing from politics for several years during the earlier period of reconstruction, within the past two or three years it has rallied, reorganized, assumed again political control, and once more promises to dominate the entire section. Louisiana and South Carolina seem just now passing from Republican control to that of this particular class. The latest Republican Governors, more learned, more efficient, more distinguished for exalted elements of personal character and statesmanship, surrender to the more commanding political and moral power of this class. Chamberlain gives place to Hampton, and Packard, it is thought, must surrender to Nichols !

The poor whites, in the days of slavery, cherished no love for the class of which I have spoken, and the latter had even greater affection for the slave than for the poor white. But things have changed. The poor white, called to the army as a common soldier, was taught that the white men of the South, rich and poor, had a common cause, for which they were called to struggle, to suffer, and to die, if need were, against the encroachments of a usurping and tyrannical Federal Government. He was taught to admire, and to love even, that class which furnished the daring and dashing leader, who commanded those forces which went out to do battle gallantly in defence of this common cause. No poor white man of the South fails to-day to entertain and express high admiration for Lee, "Stonewall" Jackson, Johnston, and Hood. United, then, in admiration of their leaders, political and military, and devoted to a common cause, which they hold, if one may judge by their words and deeds, as dear as life, there is a bond of sympathy and union existing between them which is as firm and abiding as the cause which they love and would conserve. Thus far, neither the offers of peaceful reconstruction nor the menace of armed efforts at readjustment have, as yet, reached and subdued these classes, united in such common sympathy and purpose.

Of the Negroes, formerly slaves, loyal to the Government at all times and under the most trying circumstances, Republican, not only by instinct, but from considerations of self-preservation as well as patriotism, the loftiest words of commendation may be spoken without fear of overstatement in their behalf. Emancipated, made citizens, given civil rights, and political powers, and the opportunity to rise officially to the highest place in the gift of any Republican majority, they have, in the main, shown themselves moderate and manly in their behavior. It was natural for them not to follow the leadership of the white classes referred to; while it was, on the other hand, natural for them to follow the leadership of that other class, the new-comer from the North, added to the Southern population by the war, contemptuously called " The Carpet-Bagger ;" for this class came as the representative of that sentiment and power which made them free and promised their enfranchisement and protection ; bringing them schools and books; to their more needy, food and clothing; and everywhere showing himself the friend of that power, so ill defined to the Negro intellect, which had brought the goodly things of freedom and equal rights to him who was formerly a slave.

Following the leadership of this class the Negro as naturally allied himself to the Republican party as the old master class did to the Democratic ; and here commenced that gulf of difference which has continued to widen, as reconstruction has been fixed by constitutional enactment and indorsed by the public sentiment of the country.

Of course the Republican immigrant, American by birth and education, reared in the midst of free institutions, and taught to value manhood, freedom and equal rights, obedient to law, and yet tenacious of every right, privilege, and immunity belonging to him, conceding nothing but what he demanded, and demanding nothing but what he conceded, —I say it was impossible for such class to locate in the South, surrounded by the newly-emancipated and enfranchised Negro, without becoming political leaders and representative characters in the work of reconstruction. Their influence, of course, while it tended to enlighten the Negro and establish him in his freedom, tended to draw him away from the control of the classes in the midst of whom he had lived, been enslaved, and served, to those who came as the representatives of freedom and conservators of the Republican party.

It did not improve the feeling of the defeated classes of

the South to contemplate, at first, the amendments of the Constitution of the United States, which not only established the freedom of the slave, but established his citizenship beyond question, and putting into his hands the ballot made him the politica equal of his former owner. Objecting not only to the law, but to that practice und

made it intolerable, the former master class became greatly exasperated, and resolving, if possible, to overcome this condition of things, organized bands of "White-liners," "Ku Klux," and "Bull-dozers," and entered upon that systematic. warfare upon Republicans, white and colored, which, resulting in violence, intimidation and murder, has necessitated the use of the army to maintain the peace, and protect the loyal people of the South against that domestic violence, which at times seemed to threaten utter destruction, interfering even with legislatures, and disturbing the operations of the Government.

This condition of things has continued from 1865, growing rapidly worse, up to and through the last presidential canvass, and seemingly, culminating in the massacres of South Carolina and Louisiana during the summer and fall of last year.

Were I to tarry here in my description of classes composing the population of the South, I should do great injustice to two other classes, of whom I make mention with special pleasure. I refer, first, to the very respectable class of white men found in the South, known as original Union men, latterly sneeringly called "Scallawags;" and, secondly, to a considerable class of white men who, going into the rebel army and being defeated in honorable warfare, have accepted the situation in good faith, and yield a cordial obedience to the law. These, too, have also been sneeringly designated by the same appellation.

If I might be permitted to particularize still further I would mention, for the purpose of bringing to your attention, with due emphasis, all the peculiar classes with which we have to deal in settling the Southern problem—a class of white men peculiarly and intimately related to the colored class by ties of blood and kinship. I refer to a class of white men who have not hesitated to establish the relations named, by recognizing, in many instances, the offspring of their slave women as their own children; not infrequently providing for their education, and otherwise manifesting a fatherly interest and affection for such children. How far such offspring, the children of white men by colored women, in many cases educated, as intimated, by their fathers, are to aid in bridging the social and political differences between the classes of the South, white and colored, Providence only knows and will determine. The prediction that this class will play, in the future, an important part in this work may not prove wholly untrue.

The classes now described are diverse in origin, unlike in instinct, and have by no means enjoyed equal educational advantages; in fact, the Negro and the poor white were wholly without educational opportunities during the days of slavery. One great class were formerly the slave-masters; another, their slaves; a third, the poor whites, during the existence of slavery, were almost as destitute of civil and political rights and privileges as the slaves themselves; and, in fact, their social and moral condition was even lower than that of the Negro. And these classes differ widely in polit. ical purpose and affiliation, as well as in political understanding and aspiration. Is it possible to bring these classes to such agreement with regard to their common welfare, the material and moral good of their section, and thus remove the differences, political and other, to which reference has been made, and also to establish peace, good order, and consequent prosperity and happiness, under the Constitution, as the results of pacific reconstruction?

The proposition of peaceful reconstruction is surrounded with serious difficulties, awaiting solution.

The first of these is found in the fact that the dominant classes of the South, united in purpose, and animated by common feelings, forming a compact social and political organization, easily and effectively wielded, as necessity required, has hitherto formed a firm alliance with the Democratic party, which promises, though its influence, direct and indirect, success to their sectional plans and measures. This party, always false in the presence of high moral and patriotic requirement, stands ready to promise all things in return for any support which brings it success and power. Its leaders act as if it had been organized, and were still maintained, rather to achieve mere party success and party ends, than the enduring good of all sections of the country, the lasting welfare of all the people. This party taught, first of all, the false doctrine of State sovereignty as opposed to the supremacy of the National Government; and it to-day must be held responsible for the blighting consequences which have followed therefrom. It is responsible, too, in no insignificant sense, for the late Rebellion, in connection with which there is no feature of its conduct, as a party, as far as the South is concerned, or the Government, which reflects upon it special credit, Having promised to aid the South in its attempts to make practical the lessons of political philosophy, which it had taught, in the hour of trial it proved itself cowardly, and ever after as unworthy of confidence. If, as a party, it affected to give the Government support, its acts proved insincere and pretentious.

Estimated in the light of its past record, weighing its purpose and integrity in the light of its recent behavior, one must conclude that the sagacious and earnest leaders of the South, always requiring, in those with whom they deal, decision, courage and truth, cannot longer confide in such party, nor trust the destiny of their section to its control. The character and behavior of the Democratic party, so inconsistent and unreliable, furnish no ground of hope for good to the South.   As the Southern leaders lose confidence in this party, its teachings and its policy, its disposition and ability to discharge its promises, the alliance mentioned will be weakened, sooner or later annulled, and other and more advantageous affiliations sought and formed.   The conduct of prominent leaders, members of the House of Representatives from the South in the last session of Congress, in connection with certain decisions of the Electoral Commission, bears with peculiar force upon this particular point.   It is admitted on all sides that it was the vote of Southern men —men who were expected to vote with fillibustering Democrats from the North—which thwarted the purpose of such Democratic members, and sustained the action of the Commission.   This must be regarded as a step in the direction of just and peaceful reconstruction.   With this beginning we may reasonably hope for an ending as beneficent as it is wise.

A second difficulty is found in the indisposition, heretofore existing on the part of the dominant class of the South, to brook opposition of opinion and judgment in matters of politics.   Taught from their cradles, by the influences of their peculiar institution, as it formerly existed, to believe themselves the owners and masters of men, and learning early, and witnessing constantly, the utter dependence of the non-slaveholding whites, living among them, upon their power and whim, it was altogether natural, inevitable, that they acquired the habit of command, exacting ready and unquestioning acquiescence. Politically, the course of treatment pursued by the Government toward the South on all subjects relating to that section, affecting its interests, directly or remotely, really or imaginarily, compromising too often, even at the expense of freedom and national honor, has tended greatly, and not unnaturally, to create and foster the feeling to which reference has been made.

The experience of the past sixteen years, the lessons of law and ethics, freedom and equal rights, free thought and free speech, the right of every individual, without denial and unchallenged, to form and express his own judgment, being amenable, according to law only, for the abuse of this privilege, have done much to correct this state of mind, and to beget and sustain largely a spirit of honest difference of sentiment, even on political subjects. The progress made in this direction, though far from being all we could wish, is of great value and promises well.

Free thought, free discussion, earnest and honest agitation are the indispensable conditions of reformation and progress in the South, as well as everywhere else, among all people. Is this condition possible by means of peaceful reconstruction?

A third difficulty following close upon the one just named, although distinct from it, is found in the inaccessibility of the masses, as well as leaders, now, as heretofore, dominant in the South. Will they hear? Can they be reached? The first question is partially answered in what has already been said. It may be added that: "The old wall of partition has been broken down," and the teacher and the agitator are now among them. If allowed to remain their influence must tell for good. The little leaven may leaven the whole lump. **N**

Following the revolution which has just been wrought in the South, breaking up institutions, changing the system of labor, necessitating the remodeling of law and legislation, the establishment of other and better educational organizations, the submission of the political and the religious opinions of the people to a new crucial test, the deposing of many old, and the advancement of other leaders, the condition of the public mind, now upon inquiry, the best, the most gifted and learned seeking knowledge, makes this the time pre-eminently to speak and be heard. The public address, the considerate editorial, the pamphlet or book, in which are discussed, with wisdom and moderation, the problems of reconcilement and pacification, the material and moral welfare of the South, its just local self-government, will be read, and their sentiments considered and diffused to the good of all the people. This is the hour for its performance, and this is the work which should be done for the South. The truth and the light should be given the people of this section.

A fourth difficulty connected with peaceful reconstruction is discoverable in the fear of many that efforts in that behalf tend to jeopardize the rights of the colored people, through the probable success of the Democratic party.

If what has already been said be true there can be no well-founded fear that peaceful reconstruction in the South would result in the success of the Democratic party, and in jeopardizing the liberty and rights of the emancipated class. Many good men, earnest and tried friends of the colored people, find it difficult to give their consent to the new policy of pacification, for the reasons here indicated. The Democratic party they justly fear; and they would keep it out of power at all hazards. The liberty and rights of the colored American they would sustain, even by the use of the army and navy. Such purpose I indorse and shall sustain, whenever needful, as far as possible, without violating the rights of others, and doing violence and damage to the interests of all concerned, the black as well as the white man.

In the first place, mere party success is not, in my judgment, indispensable to the greater good we should seek to accomplish, nor in any sense comparable with it. Party, I hold as a means. The end to be gained is the incomparable and enduring good of the people. The success of the Democratic party does not follow necessarily the adoption of the policy of pacific reconstruction. On the other hand, I fear the continuance of the use of the army in the South will hasten such result in the defeat of the Republican party. Let us not, in our anxiety as to Democratic success, fail to secure the continued success of the party of freedom.

But will pacific reconstruction prove injurious to the colored citizen? I believe not. I believe it will prove to him, as to all other residents of the South, an inestimable blessing. Of all others thus located, he is most ill prepared for a continuance of political strife, so costly of time, industry, the fruits of toil, personal safety, life, liberty, and the pursuit of happiness. Reconciliation—the peace, the rest, the opportunity and blessings which come of this, he needs. And if he is to gain positive footing as a citizen of character, means, and influence where he lives, this he must have. With harmony and good neighborhood existing between him and the white classes, his life, under the 13th, 14th and 15th amendments of the Constitution of the United States and the laws passed in pursuance thereof, with his liberty and rights duly protected, as emergency may require, by the State or Federal Government, will prove, it may be, at times rugged and hard, but on the whole, successful and profitable. Relieved from too pressing and absorbing political excitement, he will cultivate industry more thoroughly and advantageously, locate his family, educate his children, accumulate wealth, and improve himself in all those things which pertain to worthy life.

He will become, in this way, a valuable and influential member of society, respected and honored, it may be, by his neighbors and fellow-citizens. He will become, indeed, interested in all matters which concern the State in which he lives, and like his fellow-citizens, by voice and vote, advance and conserve the welfare of the community. He will become self-reliant and self-supporting; no longer a pariah, but a man and citizen in fact. Having passed thus his life in honest industry and noble endeavor, winning honors, official and other, no distinctions made against him on account of his color—distinctions offensive and harassing—he will spend his declining years in the midst of a happy family, his children respected, as they show themselves honest, honorable, and worthy. Is this condition possible? May we justly contemplate this as the promise of peaceful reconstruction to the former slave? God grant that it may be so!

I will not pass, I will not treat as a thing of small account, the hatred, intense and seemingly implacable, exhibited since the war by the dominant class of the South against the enfranchized colored citizen. The intensity and the implacability of this feeling cannot be denied, and this fact we must not fail to appreciate. In an amicable readjustment, however, and under the milder sway of truth and justice, law and liberty, it is to be hoped that the condition of things indicated will be established, and an intelligent and permanent friendship secured between these classes.

Several important circumstances, now existing facts, must contribute directly and largely to the accomplishment of this result. The improved condition of the colored people, their advancement in education, property, and social character, in their knowledge of their rights as well as their courage to assert earnestly their claim thereto; the presence and residence of many Northern white men in the South, with their broad and liberal education, their knowledge and appreciation of the beautiful and ennobling lessons of Christian civilization, their value of manhood and the best methods of developing and fostering its noblest qualities, their energy, their industry, their thrift, their progress, their love of liberty, equal rights, and free institutions; the influence of the native-Union white man of the South, his brave assertion of loyal sentiments, and his fearless maintenance of the doctrines of our amended Constitution and the equal rights of all, as therein enunciated, must all aid in producing and sustaining such state of society.

The last and crowning difficulty which I shall mention, is the wrong political education of the white classes of the South. The tendency of political thought in the South has always been towards aristocracy and feudal institutions—the right of the few to govern, that right being founded upon wealth, landed estates, and consequent social position and influence. It may be stated with truth that the central and controlling idea of the American Government, tersely and graphically described by Abraham Lincoln as "the Government of the people, by the people, and for the people," has never been incorporated in the political judgment or policy of the South. How else could it be, with the overshadowing institution of slavery existing there for quite two hundred and forty-five years, while under this institution 365,000 slave-holders constituted the body of property-holders, and the ruling class, to all intents and purposes? In addition to the political heresy, through the teachings of certain eminent and distinguished Southern statesmen, the doctrine of State-rights and secession prevailed, and was tenaciously held generally.

Besides, the South had not accepted as the basis of political action, prior to the war, those great and fundamental principles which distinguish the American Revolution. The principles of the Declaration, the doctrines of the Constitution, the sentiments of the wisest and best statesmen of the country were generally treated as " glittering generalities," void of practical significance. But now they profess to accept all these; and no one is found to advocate the re-enslavement of the Negro, or to oppose universal suffrage. Freedom and popular government are accepted and established facts. Everybody admits the utter absurdity and impracticability of secession, and yields a cordial and supreme allegiance to the General Government. Indeed, professedly, all the results of the war are accepted, including the amendments of the Constitution and the reconstruction acts, so-called. Taught, in a baptism of blood, the utter absurdity and futility of their former political training, its unreasonableness and want of foundation in truth, it is to be hoped that, like wise men, the Southern statesmen will build anew upon sounder principles of philosophy and law, as illustrated in the history of the best and most exalted civilization of mankind.

More than this. Revolutions always prove moral sources of education to the people. The revolution of the South will form no exception to this rule. And among the valuable fruits which it will bring to the people finally, as I believe, is a system of common schools, founded and supported by the State, aided, it may be, by the National Government, which will become nurseries no less of liberty and labor, learning and piety, than sentiments of humane consideration and kindly regard of the one class for the other.

The humanizing influences of letters, the liberalizing tendencies of knowledge, the purity of purpose and elevation of character produced by culture, the new feelings and consequent change of habits and conduct, products of enlightenment, must be treated as positive moral agencies, having to do with the problem which we are now considering.

In a carefully prepared address, delivered by the Hon. Roscoe Conkling, at Utica, New York, during the late presidential campaign, occurs the following truthful statement:

"Two hundred years ago two hostile systems of civilization started on this continent. They came from other lands. One was the idea of free thought and action, of equal rights for all; of dignity of labor—the idea that every man was his own master and peer of any other man before the law, however poor and humble his calling, however hard his lot. This idea, and the system it founded, were planted at the North. The other was the idea of aristocracy and caste, of lawful superiority of man over man, of the right of one class to dominate another and appropriate its labor, and to enjoy class immunity and privilege. This idea, with the system it founded, was planted in the South."

Our late war was, indeed, nothing other than the last bloody contest of these two ideas and systems in mighty and desperate appeal to arms for the mastery. The result of the contest has been chronicled; and the mastery—the eternal mastery of the Northern idea and system, matchless in the glory of its triumph, promising, in peace, prosperity, and happiness, such priceless blessings to the entire country—must, shall be maintained! If the professions of dominant classes at the South are sincere, if they have put away indeed the old things and really accept the new, the task of reconcilement and pacification is easy; and, accomplished, our nation moves forward, henceforth cultivating the one idea and the one system, thereby achieving the largest possible results under a common, harmonious, Christian civilization.

The Republican party, at its late national convention, expressed, with clearness and force, its judgment and purpose as to the permanent pacification of the South, and the complete protection of all its citizens in the free enjoyment of all their rights. Its expression on the subject is significant, and is alluded to here as wise and true. The third section of the platform reads :

"The permanent pacification of the Southern section of the Union, the complete protection of all its citizens in the free enjoyment of all their rights, are duties to which the Republican party is sacredly pledged. The power to provide for the enforcement of the principles embodied in the recent Constitutional amendments is vested by those amendments in the Congress of the United States, and we declare it to be the solemn obligation of the legislative and executive departments of the Government to put into immediate and vigorous exercise all their constitutional powers for removing any just cause of discontent on the part of any class, and securing to every American citizen complete liberty and exact equality in the exercise of all civil, political and public rights. To this end we imperatively demand a Congress and Chief Executive whose courage and fidelity to these duties shall not falter until these results are placed beyond dispute or recall."

Commenting upon this portion of the platform, President Hayes, in his letter of acceptance, says :

"The resolution of the convention on the subject of the permanent pacification of the country, and the complete protection of *all* its citizens in the free enjoyment of all their constitutional rights, is timely and of great importance. The condition of the Southern States attracts the attention and commands the sympathy of the people of the whole Union in their progressive recovery from the effects of the war. Their first necessity is an intelligent and honest administration of Government, which will protect all classes of citizens in all their political and private rights. What the South most needs is peace, and peace depends upon the supremacy of law.

"There can be no enduring peace if the constitutional rights of any portion of the people are habitually disregarded. A division of political parties, resting merely upon distinctions of race or upon sectional lines, is always unfortunate, and may be disastrous. The welfare of the South, alike with that of every other part of this country, depends upon the attractions it can offer to labor and immigration, and to capital. But laborers will not go, and capital will not be ventured, where the Constitution and laws are set at defiance, and distraction, apprehension and alarm take the place of peace-loving and law-abiding social life. All parts of the Constitution are sacred, and must be sacredly observed—the parts that are new, no less than the parts that are old. The moral and material prosperity of the Southern States can be most effectively advanced by a hearty and generous recognition of the rights of all by all, a recognition without reserve or exception. With such a recognition fully accorded, it will be practicable to promote, by the influence of all legitimate agencies of the General Government, the effort of the people of these States to obtain for themselves the blessings of honest and capable local government. If elected, I shall consider it not only my duty, but it will be my ardent desire to labor for the attainment of this end. Let me assure my countrymen of the Southern States that, if I shall be charged with the duty of organizing an administration, it will be one which will regard and cherish their truest interests, the interests of the white and colored people, both and equally, and which will put forth its best efforts in behalf of a civil policy which will wipe out forever the distinction between the North and the South in our common country."

True to this declaration, faithful to the promise it contains, President Hayes, in his inaugural address, elaborates and enforces the same sentiments in the following words:

"The permanent pacification of the country upon such principles and by such measures as will secure the complete protection of all its citizens in the free enjoyment of all their constitutional rights, is now the one subject in all our public affairs which all thoughtful and patriotic citizens regard as of supreme importance.

"Many of the calamitous effects of the tremendous revolution which has passed over the Southern States still remain. The immeasurable benefits which will surely follow, sooner or later, the hearty and generous acceptance of the legitimate results of that revolution have not yet been realized. Difficult and embarrassing questions meet us at the threshold of this subject. The people of those States are still impoverished, and the inestimable blessing of wise, honest, and peaceful local self-government is not fully enjoyed. Whatever difference of opinion may exist as to the cause of this condition of these things, the fact is clear that, in the progress of events, the time has come when such government is the imperative necessity required by all the varied interests, public and private, of those States. But it must not be forgotten that only a local government which recognizes and maintains inviolate the rights of all is a true self-government.

"With respect to the two distinct races whose peculiar relations to each other have brought upon us the deplorable complications and perplexities which exist in those States, it must be a government which guards the interests of both races carefully and equally. It must be a government which submits loyally and heartily to the Constitution and the laws —the laws of the nation and the laws of the States themselves—accepting and obeying faithfully the whole Constitution as it is.

"Resting upon this sure and substantial foundation, the superstructure of beneficent local governments can be built up and not otherwise. In furtherance of such obedience to the letter and the spirit of the Constitution, and in behalf of all that its attainment applies, all so-called party interests lose their apparent importance, and party lines may well be permitted to fade into insignificance. The question we have to consider for the immediate welfare of those States of the Union is the question of government or no government, of social order and all the peaceful industries and the happiness that belong to it, or a return to barbarism.

"It is a question in which every citizen of the nation is deeply interested, and with respect to which we ought not to be, in a partisan sense, either Republicans or Democrats, but fellow-citizens and fellow-men to whom the interests of a common country and a common humanity are dear."

These utterances—the one, that of the great national party, which is responsible for the conduct of our Federal and State affairs beyond question for the past sixteen years; the other the utterances of a sagacious and judicious statesman occupying conspicuous place among the leaders of the party— teach the threefold lesson: first, that pacific reconstruction, if possible, ought to be accomplished; second, that if accomplished it is to be done only in the adoption of "such principles and measures as will secure the complete protection of all citizens in the free enjoyment of all their constitutional rights;" and third, that such attempts at pacification are not only not inconsistent, but are in perfect accord with the principles and doctrines of genuine Republicanism. The lessons of history, not less than the precepts of our religion and the fundamental principles of wise statesmanship, justify and sustain such treatment of the Southern section of our country. But how shall this peaceful theory of reconstruction, so beautiful in ideal, whose results are so delightful to contemplate, be reduced to practice without injustice to any, and with the largest good to all?

I have designated the various classes composing the population of the South. I have indicated certain difficulties, and in that connection dwelt upon changes of institutions, and feelings of the people, which, as I suppose, have taken place; and I have presented in the language of the platform lately adopted, and in the language of his letter of acceptance and his inaugural address, the sentiments of the Republican party and the President of the United States, with regard to this subject. And now, with the field before us, the difficulties of its cultivation presented, the practical, all-important question of how shall we proceed confronts us.

The importance, the magnitude, and difficulty, as well as the necessity, of reconstruction by peaceful means will be conceded. And however we may regret it, it will be conceded that the method heretofore pursued proves by no means satisfactory in its results. Whether this failure is owing to the unhandsome and obnoxious conduct of political adventurers; the unnecessary and too constant political excitement and agitation of the people, the injudicious and oppressive acts of Republican legislatures and officials, the former composed, frequently, largely of ignorant, unqualified, and impecunious persons, white and black, and the latter frequently not only incompetent, but offensive and exasperating in their conduct; the too frequent interference by the National Government in State affairs with the army, seemingly for party purposes; the general bad temper and purpose of the native dominant white class—whatever the cause, as to the failure of the former method, there is but one opinion. The failure is a fact, and some new and, if possible, better method must be tried. This the welfare of those immediately concerned, as well as the general good of the country in all its material and moral interests, requires.

We must remember, however, in dealing with this subject, that there is to be no compromise, no surrender of principle, no betrayal of plighted faith. And there need not be; for with us it is not a question of new principles and measures; it is simply a matter of administration or policy, involving the mode of applying the principles and measures already accepted and fixed in the Constitution and the laws.

The present administration, in its efforts at pacification, in dealing with States, classes, races and individuals, proposes, as one must believe, to stand on the law, as now written and determined, insisting upon the cordial recognition of the equal rights of all citizens, the practical guarantee of their protection in such rights, the establishment and maintenance of such condition of good order and peace as to encourage immigration, the introduction of capital, and the advancement of labor, as well as the inauguration of such local self-governments as in all their departments and acts shall be harmonious with the altered status of the former slave, the new provisions of the Constitution and the enactments of the State and General Government passed in accordance therewith. Occupying such position, and insisting upon such conditions as precedent and indispensable, the good omens of its initials efforts promise a happy success. The acceptance of these condititions as precedent and indispensable constitutes the only correct and sure test of the willingness and the fitness of the dominant white classes of the South, for properly considering and appreciating efforts for the permanent pacification of that section. Did such condition of public feeling exist, discoverable in the acts and utterances of the leading and influential men of the South, in their treatment of the classes and persons differing with them in political sentiments and party relations, in the solution and determination of those questions, material, educational and political, which more especially affect the newly-enfranchised people, we might wisely give ourselves no further anxiety with regard to this subject, resting assured that the general management of it by the Government would improve and sustain it.

Our anxieties, our fears come of the fact, that too little such public feeling is now discernible; and that it is to be created and fostered largely by agencies and influences brought to bear mainly, from without and through the instrumentality of the Government, upon those who are to be reconciled and made obedient, law-abiding subjects of the State. The thing to be done, then, is to manifest in bold and decisive manner such impartial and patriotic disposition and purpose, with reference to the management of the Southern problem, as to convince all concerned of the sin-

cerity and wisdom of the pacific yet positive intentions of
the Government and country with regard to their case.   In
this way win their confidence, if possible, and secure an
earnest and hearty response to such beneficent purposes.
We do not calculate wisely regarding human impulses, nor
the power of kindness over the hearts of men, if the result
does not prove satisfactory.

The acts, expressive of such disposition and purpose—
whether by the appointment of a distinguished former rebel
to the Cabinet, and prominent Southern men of the same
class to conspicuous official positions, are matters of detail,
which may be very properly, under the law and the admoni-
tions of public opinion, entrusted to the President.   It must
be insisted, however, as both wise and just, that, in the dis-
tribution of official patronage, Republicans, especially native whites and blacks of the South, shall not be neglected,
and that the recognition accorded them shall be of equal
dignity and responsibility with that accorded the other class.
For in this way the aristocratic feeling already mentioned,
the hatred of the Negro, and the political repellancy existing between the classes, will be the more speedily corrected
and removed.   It must also be insisted, where no such domestic violence as that described in the Constitution exists
in a State, although there exist therein dispute as to the
fact and legality of one of two governments, that the Federal
army shall not be used to interfere therewith ; but decision
as to the dispute shall be made under the law in accordance
with the mode and methods provided thereby.   Thus an
exciting, irritating, and exasperating cause is removed, and
Government and people remitted to the established methods
of the law.   The experience, the habits of thought and
feeling of Americans, ill prepare them for tolerating the
use of the army in the settlement of political differences;

and in the presence of any such real or supposed condition of things, permanent peace is impossible in any section of our country.

The pleasing contemplation of the people of the South, engaging in the wise and profitable cultivation of all the industries, agricultural and other, peculiar to and remunerative in that section; human life and human rights, without regard to class or color, properly valued and protected; just local self-government established; the vexed and trying question of reconstruction settled; the union of our States and the Government no longer endangered by any exciting sectional dispute, but adjusted upon enduring principles of justice, law and liberty, excites in our minds the deepest feelings of hope, the profoundest purpose to do all that is practicable to secure such consummation, so devoutly to be wished.

This condition of reconcilement and peace secured, in the prosperity and happiness of our country, heretofore "rent by fratricidal strife," we shall realize the picture so strikingly drawn by the Bard of Avon when dwelling upon the restoration of peace at the close of civil war:

> "No more the thirsty Erinnys of this soil
> Shall daub her lips with her own children's blood;
> No more shall trenching war channel her fields,
> Nor bruise her flow'rets with the armed hoofs
> Of hostile paces; those opposed eyes,
> Which—like the meteors of a troubled heaven,
> All of one nature, of one substance bred—
> Did lately meet in the intestine shock
> And furious close of civil butchery,
> Shall now, in mutual, well-beseeming ranks
> March all one way, and be no more oppos'd,
> Against acquaintance, kindred, and allies;
> The edge of war, like an ill-sheathed knife,
> No more shall cut his master."

THE EXODUS.

THE CAUSES WHICH LED THE COLORED PEOPLE OF THE SOUTH TO LEAVE THEIR HOMES—THE LESSON OF THE EXODUS.

OFFICE OF THE EMIGRANT AID SOCIETY,
WASHINGTON, D. C., *September* 16, 1879.

HON. JOHN M. LANGSTON.

DEAR SIR: You are aware that during your absence from the United States there has been a movement initiated on the part of the colored people of the South which, owing to its magnitude and the peculiar combination of causes by which it was brought about, is necessarily fraught with much interest to the entire country. This movement, which as yet is apparently seen only in its incipiency, promises to result in transferring large numbers of the colored people from that section of our country in which they were recently held in bondage, and in linking their destiny for weal or woe with that of the young and thrifty States of the great Northwest. Involving, as it does, consequences which are destined to have an important bearing upon the future material and intellectual development of the race, this modern exodus has called forth serious thought and utterance from many distinguished statesmen and friends of the colored people. While by many regarded as really the most practical or available solution of one of the most vexed political problems which has thus far menaced the Republic, it is by all conceded to be at least a manly and dignified step in the already eventful career of the colored race of America.

In view of your identification with this race, and in recognition of your distinguished ability and sagacity as a leader, we are authorized by the Emigrant Aid Society of this city to solicit from you a public address upon the subject of Emigration, in Lincoln Hall, at such time as shall suit your convenience. Assuring you of a generally expressed desire on the part of the public to hear your views upon the subject named, we trust it may meet your convenience and pleasure to accept the society's invitation at an early day.

Very respectfully,
O. S. B. WALL, *President.*

J. M. ADAMS, *Secretary.*

WASHINGTON CITY, *September* 20, 1879.

GENTLEMEN: I have the honor to acknowledge the receipt of your kind favor of the 16th instant, in which you present, in the most flattering manner, in the name of the Emigrant Aid Society of the District of Columbia, an invita-

tion to me to deliver, at Lincoln Hall, a public address upon Emigration. In
accepting your invitation I beg to tender therefor my grateful thanks, and to
name Tuesday evening, October 7, as the time when it will suit my convenience to speak on the subject mentioned.

With sentiments of high consideration, I am,

JOHN MERCER LANGSTON.

Messrs. O. S. B. WALL, *President.*

J. M ADAMS, *Secretary.*

Seventeen years ago, on the 22d day of September, Abraham Lincoln published his preliminary Proclamation of
Emancipation, and one hundred days thereafter, on the 1st
day of January, 1863, he issued the proclamation in which
he designated the States and parts of States in which the
abolition of slavery, as a war measure, was declared. The
abolition of slavery in the border States soon followed; and
those persons who, prior to this action, had been held and
designated as things, chattels personal, sustaining in the eye
of the law only the status of four-footed beasts and creeping
things, were given emancipation, and, as supposed, all those
dignities which are implied in self-ownership and manhood.

The measure of emancipation, however, was not granted
as the consequence of a healthy, moral, public sentiment per-
vading the country; not upon political considerations advanced, elucidated, and enforced by our leading statesmen; not
in answer to appeals of abolition reformers and philanthro-
pists, but as a military necessity at the time felt by the Government and the loyal North engaged in a struggle with and
against the slave oligarchy of the South. Had emancipation
rested upon moral and political bases, as the result of agitation and debate, the condition of the emancipated class
might have been considerably changed. Some distinct governmental provision might have been taken for its due settlement, even upon lands appropriated specially for this purpose; and some system of education provided whereby it
might have, in an earlier and more thorough manner, mastered
lump.   O

and more fully appreciated the lessons taught and impressed in freedom and by civil responsibility. But emancipation as a war measure, was instant and speedy; and its consummation, characterized by no prior consideration and debate as to the subsequent situation of the freedman, left him in simple ownership of his person—otherwise destitute in the extreme.

Hence the Negro, yesterday a slave, finds himself to-day, as emancipated, in the enjoyment of the simplest and merest self-ownership. Without property on the one side, and destitute of educational and moral appliances for his elevation on the other, he can look only to the philanthropic, the Christian, the benevolent public even for food; clothing, and those simpler elementary matters of instruction which tend to confirm him in the consciousness of the self-ownership which had just been conferred. All honor to the philanthropic, the Christian and benevolent public of this and other lands for the liberal and generous manner in which responses were made to the wants of the emancipated colored American. Many noble families of the North gave their best son and their best daughter to educate and to elevate, as far as practicable, the newly-made freedman; others their money by thousands to advance his material and educational interests. It was a sight worthy of the civilized, Christian country in which we live to witness how the noble sons and daughters of such heroic, devoted families attempted this work; with what earnestness, vigor, and matchless moral heroism. And the little good we find to-day already accomplished among the freed people of the South is more largely due to the efforts and offerings here referred to than to any Government assistance, State or national, which has been given.

With regard to the emancipation of the American slave, there have existed from the foundation of our Government

two opinions, the one favoring and the other opposing it; and
as slavery itself grew hoary-headed, the institution becoming
more and more deep-seated, hedged about and defended by
State action and national recognition, public sentiment against
its abolition became more general and fixed. So much was
this the case that we have not to travel far back in the history
of our country to find when the two great political parties,
the Whig and Democratic, pledged themselves to its maintenance and support as a positive, moral, legal, and political
finality. Every one of us recollects with the most vivid dis-
tinctness the action had by these parties with regard to the
compromise measures of 1850; and the American Church, in
several of its important branches, as if it would not be outdone
by the great political organizations of the day, was not slow
in making solemn and positive utterances founded, as was
claimed, upon the philosophy and logic, the theology and
teachings of the Old and New Testaments, favoring this institution, which made and sustained property in the bodies
and souls of men created in the image of our Heavenly
Father. It is also within our memory, that memory running
back not beyond a quarter of a century of our past, that the
leading doctors of divinity, the conspicuous pulpit orators of
our country argued, with an ardor befitting a better cause,
with an eloquence frequently to the common mind irresistible
and overwhelming, that slavery was a divine institution,
sanctioned and sanctified by the teachings of Moses and Paul.

It was out of this state of things, a state of things implied
in the declarations which I have just made in regard to the
national parties and the church, that the great Republican
party, organized in 1854, avowing its purpose to stay the
extension of slavery, had its origin, and entered upon that glorious national career which is so distinguished by its triumphs
in favor of freedom, equal rights, the support of free institu-

tions, the maintenance of the Government, and the perpetuation of the Union of the States. It was upon the vote of this party finally that Abraham Lincoln was made President of the United States; it was the triumph of this party that gave occasion to the slave oligarchy to move in the establishment of a Southern Confederacy, and the severance from the union of those States in which this new government was to take control. And as the old Democratic party passed out of power, James Buchanan retiring to the eternal shades of night, forever disgraced by the action which he had taken, or failed to take, (for his sin is at once one of commission and omission,) the great slave-power received that death-blow, under which, staggering, it fell, dying in the midst of the thunders of the great guns, whose echoes, lasting through the ages, are a warning to those who would break our Union and sunder our Government; while they are glad music, the perpetual song of joy to those who, accepting the sentiments of our Declaration and the doctrines of our Constitution, hold life, property and sacred honor in pledge to the maintenance of all those institutions which protect, defend and eternize American freedom with its sacred blessings.

But in the discussions had with regard to the non-extension of slavery, the distinctive principles of the Republican party and its purposes should it come into power, nothing had been said really, with reference to the immediate abolition of slavery in the several States where it existed, and no well-defined position had been taken, no measures suggested for ameliorating the condition of the slave in such States, should he be emancipated. Indeed, the one great purpose, the sole object which the most advanced leader of the Republican party advocated and expected to realize, was the prevention of the spread of slavery into territory then free. But it was discovered in the midst of our war against the rebellion, that the abolition of slavery, as just indicated, was a fitting and necessary war measure; and the brave and true Lincoln, with one mighty stroke of his pen, decreed the emancipation of the Negro, who went out from his prison-house of enslavement, but in the poverty bequeathed by centuries of hard and cruel oppression. He was landless; he was homeless. Destitute mainly of those things which distinguish the humblest life, he has been battling for the past seventeen years of his freedom, in a material sense, for the merest, simplest necessaries of a lowly condition. In fact, the merest emancipation of person and body has been practically the only thing, up to this hour, which has been guaranteed him. In this connection it is our duty to discriminate between simple emancipation, accompanied by a destitution characteristic of slave existence, and practical freedom, in which such destitution does not ordinarily exist; for if provision is not made for the newly emancipated by State or national regulation, opportunity, with fair wages, ought to be given for regular and remunerative labor, with intelligent investment of its proceeds in those things which are indispensable to well-ordered and prosperous life.

This brings me directly to the consideration of the condition of the American ex-slave as we find him to-day, struggling for life, with its common, usual rewards, in the South. This condition ought to be considered in its several relations of protection, industry, and politics. In dwelling on this branch of the subject we are not to forget that our national Constitution has been amended so as to guarantee freedom, civil rights, and the ballot to the freedman; that Congress has legislated in support of any rights, immunities, and privileges claimed by this class of our citizens; and that it is true that generally in the States of the South laws have been enacted the purpose and object of which seem to be the protection and conservation of the rights, civil and other, which belong to the same class. In a word, as far as mere legislation is concerned, the condition of the freedman seems to be altogether tolerable—indeed good. In a material and industrial point of view, however, as well as political, the difficulty in his case seems to be even more deep-rooted and hard of management. His real condition is described and duly appreciated only when we recollect that although emancipated and legislation has been had in this case, as stated, still he has not been given *practical independence* of the old slave-holding class, constituting the land-proprietors and employers in the section where he lives and labors for daily support. And besides this, he is left to seek existence in the midst of those classes who of all others are most interested in demonstrating that emancipation is a failure; that the freedman is incapable of cultivating those things that pertain to dignified, honorable life; and that slavery is his natural and normal condition. Not only holding the lands, the old slave-holding class control the wealth and intelligence, as well as the social and governmental appliances of that section. They are masters in the church, masters in the courts, masters in the schools, masters in politics, masters at the polls, and masters of the legislatures, as well as the plantations, directing and controlling according to their caprices, their interests, their prejudices, and their predilections. The non-landholding white of the South must do their bidding; and the non-landholding Negro, also, occupies a subservient position to them. Depending, then, for labor, food, clothing and shelter upon his former master—the property holder—who is his abusive, tyrannical employer, making even harder exactions than he was wont to make of him when a slave, the condition of the freedman is certainly sad.

If what is here stated with regard to the condition of the

freedman be true, reasoning *a priori*, to say the least, one might naturally conclude that the measure of protection accorded him would be limited and inadequate; that his industrial situation and prospects would be anything other than prosperous and promising ; and that his exercise of political powers would be circumscribed and obstructed—as far as possible entirely hindered.

Mere philosophying, however, finds no place in this connection. The facts that bear upon this point are clear, positive, and undeniable. The freedman is without protection. His condition as a laborer, whether he work for wages, as a share-farmer, or renter, is not favorable; indeed, it is lamentable; while as a voter, it is well known that he cannot safely cast a free ballot according to the dictates of a wise and patriotic judgment. The "bull-dozing" record of the South is well understood, and the knowledge of the bloody deeds of its instigators and supporters is widespread and fully appreciated by the people of our country. Nor do his appeals to the courts of justice for redress of wrong meet with any success. If he make an appeal on law and fact to a jury of his fellow-citizens, who should, even from their own interest, if from no other and higher consideration, do him justice, what is the result ? Even if the facts be plain and the law clear in support of his claim, the jury disagree ordinarily, and the judicial remedy which would naturally work him justice is defeated in its operation. This is true in civil as well as criminal proceedings, especially where the interests of the landed class as against the freedman are involved. In this regard the black man seems to have no rights which the white man is bound to respect.

After seventeen years of emancipation, in a condition of life even worse than that of serfage, in struggles against want and hardship, taxing his utmost endurance, the freedman has at last discovered his real situation and necessities, and has resolved, if possible, to relieve himself by escaping thence. What more natural than his effort in this regard, what more manly, what more worthy of him? What effort is better calculated to relieve him of his servile dependence? This movement is a declaration of the purpose of the freed-man to assert and maintain that independence in his own behalf, without which no individual and no people can rise to the level of dignified and honorable manhood. His exodus, if justified on no other ground, is justified thoroughly and entirely by the fact that it is, on his part, an effort to relieve himself of his present condition of utter dependence upon the old slave-holding class which he has served so faithfully in the past, and thus secure to himself the fact as well as the consciousness of real freedom.

The history of the emancipated classes of the world, whether they have been serfs or slaves, abundantly sustains the assertion that in most cases in which emancipation has occurred, and the emancipated class has been left under the control of the former master class, in the midst of the old associations of its slavery, upon the plantations or estates where it was wont to labor, such class thus situated and thus controlled does not and cannot rise until it has by some means freed itself from the dependence connected with such condition. It remains, in fact, in a servile position, without self-control, self-reliance, or independent character; without the purpose to make earnest, courageous effort to accomplish those things which are worthy of manhood.

It is not astonishing that centuries of enslavement imbed in the very soul of the enslaved the spirit of servility and dependence; nor is it astonishing that this feeling once mastering the soul of man, holds it enchained to those things which work degradation and ruin to freedom. The soul of man is only relieved of this feeling as it becomes conscious of its own power in the assertion and maintenance of its own purposes in the struggles and achievements of life. And until the soul is emancipated from this feeling, man does not enjoy real, substantial freedom. While one man leans against another, or in his soul fears him, he is subservient; and in his subserviency loses his freedom as he does the real dignity of his manhood. And this is especially true of a class once enslaved.

To really comprehend the condition of the freed class, it is necessary to understand and appreciate that on the part of the ex-master class there still exists the feeling of superiority; the feeling of the right to rule, direct, and, in fact, to own, if not the body and soul, certainly the services of its former slaves; while on the part of the dependent and serving class, there exists, from long habit connected with its slave condition, the sense of inferiority, of subserviency —a disposition to go and come as commanded. Either the relations of the two classes must be changed entirely, and the change thoroughly recognized and admitted by both, or the former masters will attempt the continuance of their old conduct and ways of mastership; while the other class, not conscious of its freedom, will continue to serve as formerly from fear and force of habit, their freedom being only recognized as something ideal, without the practical benefits which it should bring.

If there be any doubts in the mind of any intelligent person in regard to this matter, he has only to read carefully the history of the emancipation of the serf of Russia and consider his present condition ; the history of the West India bondman and consider his situation, to be entirely convinced that the statement is true. Wallace, in dwelling upon the emancipation of the serfs in Russia and in considering the question as to how their condition may be improved, states, in addition to other considerations offered, that "it would be well to organize an extensive system of emigration by which a portion of the peasantry would be transferred from the barren soil of the North and West to the rich fertile lands of the Eastern provinces."

It may be claimed that in this case the only reason why emigration is recommended is that the emancipation law did not confer upon the peasants of Russia as much land as they required, and consequently the peasant, who has merely his legal portion, has neither enough work nor enough revenue. But to one who considers the case of the Russian serf dispassionately and with care, it will be apparent that the real difficulty in his case is that although provision has been made for him, as far as land is concerned, he has been left practically in a state of dependence, if not upon the land proprietors, upon the Commune; and up to this time has not been able—discovering his real condition—to assert his independence of surroundings which tend to hold him in servile position. It will be remembered that the three fundamental principles of the law of emancipation in Russia were, as stated by Wallace, first, that the serf should at once receive the civil rights of the free rural class and that the authority of the proprietor should be replaced by Communal self-government; second, that the rural Communes should, as far as possible, retain the land they actually held, and should in return pay to the proprietor certain yearly dues in money and labor; third, that the government should, by means of credit, assist the Communes to redeem these dues, or, in other words, to purchase the lands ceded to them in usufruct. These conditions constitute the substantial features of the emancipation law of Russia. Upon close examination of these provisions, it will be discovered that although the emancipated serf is given, through the Commune, an interest in the soil, he is not relieved of a dependence which, in fact, keeps him in a servile condition; and until he has that freedom, which is indispensable to the cultivation of the highest possibilities of honorable manhood, he will be restless and his condition unsatisfactory, as it is unfortunate and unhappy. Let him but change his condition, emigrating from the old places so familiar to him, where his oppression and his real condition can never be forgotten, and settling in our own new and free country, where the blessings of liberty are guaranteed to every son and daughter of any and all nationalities, without money and without price, without stint, and without limit other than legal, and he enters upon new life, with new prosperity and new joy. It is emigration with its new conditions that gives to him and his posterity, the blessings of real freedom, which are more precious than rubies, more to be desired than any other human possession.

But that we may understand this subject from the slaveholding standpoint rather than that of serfage, and as connected with our own rather than the Eastern continent, it may be well to consider for a moment the condition of the emancipated bondman of the West India Islands. Here reference need only be made to the Islands of Barbados and Trinidad. In an excellent little work, entitled "The Ordeal of Free Labor in the West Indies," written by William G. Sewell, it is stated, in speaking of the condition of the laborers in the former island, that : "Under the new practice, still in force, a laborer has a house and land-allotment on an estate for which he pays a stipulated rent; but he is under an engagement besides, as a condition of renting, to give to the estate a certain number of days' labor at certain stipu-wages, varying from one-sixth to one-third less than the market price. The rate of wages in Barbados is about twenty-four cents per day; but the laborer, fettered by the system of tenancy-at-will, is compelled to work for his landlord at twenty cents per day. He is, therefore, virtually a slave; for if he resists the condition of his bond he is ejected by summary process, and loses the profit he hoped to reap upon his little stock. This remnant of coercion must be abolished wherever it exists—and it prevails, with some exceptions, in all the West India colonies—before it can be said that emancipation has been thoroughly tested." After making this statement the author gives account of the organization of an association in Barbados for the improvement of the social and moral condition of the laboring population, stating that in the preamble to the resolutions adopted at the first meeting thereof, it was declared that "one of the main barriers to social progress" in the island "arose from a want of confidence between the employer and the employèd." He regrets the fact that the proprietor-body set their faces at once against this movement, and he says: "The planters, tenacious of their privileges and like aristocracies all the world over, anxious to retain their power over the masses, met to counteract the new movement, denounced the society for attempting to arouse unjust suspicions in the minds of the ignorant touching their rights, viewing with alarm and as a political movément the demand for a more liberal tenure, and as an effort to jeopardize the successful system of plantation management" as adopted. They maintained that the best of feeling existed between them and their tenants; and, finally, they declared their inherent right to adopt such measures as they might think fit for the good government, safety, and well-doing of their properties. Here is the master class asserting its right to be masters, and in effect believing it to be the duty of the laborer, even when emancipated, to consent to remain in a servile and slavish attitude.

If we turn from Barbados to Trinidad, it will be found that the people in the latter island, having left the estates upon which they were slaves, and thus exchanged a condition of servitude for one of independence, " as, a natural consequence are more enlightened, better educated, and more wealthy than their brethren in Barbados." Herein, claims Mr. Sewell, we discover the distinction that should be made between the Negroes in Trinidad and in the other islands where they have been able to leave the estates and work for themselves, and those in Barbados, where, by force of circumstances, they have been compelled to remain on the estates and work for others.

While it is true that in Barbados the ex-slave has shown himself a valuable and persistent laborer, to such a degree and extent that that island is said to be in its culture a beautiful garden, unnatural, unjust distinctions, on account of color, exist to this day, against the black and mulatto classes, and it may be said that the real condition of such classes is that of the free Negro where his social and civil rights are not recognized and respected.

Under the title of " Social Distinctions in Barbados," the author to whom I refer states that " the distinctions of caste are more strikingly observed in Barbados than in any other British West India colony. No person, male or female, with the slightest taint of African blood is admitted to white society. No matter what the standing of a father, his influence cannot secure for his colored offspring the social status that he himself occupies; and the rule is more rigidly carried out among women than it is among the men."

Dwelling still on this subject, Mr. Sewell says: "But when he (the Barbadian planter) and all the other white inhabitants of the island make a difference of color their only line of distinction, and parade their reasons in an offensive and obnoxious way—when white planters refuse to associate with colored planters, white merchants with colored merchants, and white mechanics with colored mechanics—simply because they *are* colored, the question ceases to be a purely social one and assumes a dangerous political complexion. As long as the colored people were slaves, their heart-burnings and jealousies might be disregarded with impunity or contemptuously ignored. But freedom has opened to them the way to progress and power, and if their present progress and present power have proved, as they *have* proved, that color is no insuperable barrier to social, intellectual development and refinement, it is but wise to make it no longer an insuperable barrier to social advancement."

But such social discriminations are apt to continue, fostered always and everywhere by the master class against the laborer, especially if the latter has been a slave, and, on his being emancipated, is left thereafter in the conditions and under the control which were connected with his enslavement. Such distinctions will last until, by some manly utterance or courageous deed, he demonstrates his independence of the old servile condition, and his capacity to dare and achieve upon his self-reliance, as a fearless, independent man. It is in recognition of the principle here elaborated that Cassagnac, in his "History of the Working and Burgher Classes," in speaking of the mode of emancipation in France and the allotments of land allowed upon leases made with regard thereto, especially the contracts made for long terms, removing thereby the emancipated far from the influence and control of the former master class, says: "This kind of contract had this advantage, that when they were for a long term, as, for example, for three generations, a century passed, during which the action of the master upon the slave was restrained and weakened; while the slave, almost free in fact, acquired the manners and customs of the father of a family, became industrious, economical, settled, prudent, accumulated small profits and left them to his children. At the end of a century, when three generations had passed away, the master was much less a master, the slave was much less a slave. Both had forgotten whence they came by only seeing where they stood."

The inference to be drawn from the facts adduced is this : In proportion as the emancipated class is relieved of the presence and control of the class formerly owners and masters, from the conditions of its former enslavement, the spirit of servility is removed and that of self-assertion, self-reliance, and independence is cultivated, while steady, solid progress is made in the accumulation of the valuable fruits of industry.

The feeling too generally entertained by the old master toward his former slave, and by the latter toward the former, after emancipation, is strikingly illustrated in the story told by Herodotus with respect to the Scythian, who advised his comrades as to the manner in which they should meet and resist the army of their slaves, who, having taken possession of their households, their wives, and the management of public affairs, resisted them on their return from a protacted military expedition. He counselled his comrades to throw away their weapons, their arrows and their darts, and meet their opponents without any means of defence save the whips which they used upon their horses. Said he : "Whilst they see us with arms, they think themselves our equals in birth and importance ; but as soon as they shall see us with whips in our hands, they will be impressed with a sense of their servile condition, and resist no longer." The historian reports that the plan suggested was adopted, and proved to be entirely successful.

How shall the American ex-slave, who has served for two hundred and forty-five years under the influence of which I speak, be relieved of the presence and control of a class h006etofore his masters ?   The history of the world offers but one solution of this question, and that solution is found in his exodus.   Let him go forth; and where sympathy and the recognition of liberty and equal rights are accorded him ; where labor is to be performed; where struggle is to be made; where the stern realities of life are to be met, there let him demonstrate his courage, his self-reliance, his manly independence.   Under such new conditions his capacities, his powers and his efforts will win the crown which befits the brow of noble manhood.

The exodus of the colored American is intimately connected with and inseparable from the continued existence of the old order of things in the South.   Up to this time there seems to have been in this regard practically little, if any, change.   It is very true that a few plantations, comparatively speaking, have changed hands; a few even of the former slave class have here and there possessed themselves of small homes, have bought small pieces of land, and erected thereon small houses; but "the great house" has not disappeared, nor has the Negro quarter; and in some of the Southern States the old whipping-post, with its proverbial thirty-nine lashes, is still recognized as a judicial institution. Nor have the modes of industry, or the crops grown in that section, been materially changed.   Cotton and sugar are the chief products of the South to-day, as they were a half century ago.   Nor has there been any change, certainly no general and fundamental change, in the feelings and purposes of the old slave-holding class as to their right to work, drive, and scourge the Negro laborer. Having been his master once, their conduct would indicate that they believe, even in spite of the action of the General Government and the results of our great war, that their mastership is to continue forever. Nor has the feeling of the non-slaveholding class of the South undergone any material' change with respect to the freedman. Indeed, it seems to be true that this class hates the colored man more now than when he was a slave; and stands ready at the command of the aristocratic class to do its bidding, even to the shedding of his blood. As showing that this condition of affairs is true and that little advancement has been made, one has only to pronounce in your hearing certain terrible words coined in connection with the barbarous, cruel treatment that has been meted out to the emancipated class of Mississippi, Louisiana, and other States formerly slaveholding. What is the meaning of the frightful words, "Klu-Klux," "Bull-dozers;" and the terrible expression, "the shot-gun or Mississippi policy?" The meaning is clear. It is that neither the old slaveholding spirit, nor the old slaveholding purpose or control is dead in the South; that plantocracy, with its fearful power and influences, has not passed away; that the colored American under it is in a condition of practical enslavement, trodden down and outraged by those who exercise control over him. Such things will continue so long as the spirit of slavery exists in the South; so long as the old master class is in power; so long as the freedman consents to remain in a condition more terrible than any serfage of which history gives account. How can this condition of things be broken up? How can the planter-rule be changed? How can the master class be made to realize that it is no longer slaveholding, and that the slave has been set free? And how can the freedman be made to feel and realize that having been emancipated, practical lib-

P

erty is within his reach, and that it is his duty to accept and enjoy it in its richest fruits; fearing neither the responsibilities of enfranchised manhood, nor trembling as a coward in the presence of trials and dangers?

To the intelligent and sagacious inquirer, who, without feeling, without passion, but philosophically and in a statesman-like manner considers this matter, there can be, as it seems to me, but a single answer. It is this: Let the freedman of the South, as far as practicable, take from the old plantocracy, by his exodus, the strong arms, broad shoulders, stalwart bodies, which, by compulsion, have been made to prop and sustain such system too long already in this day of freedom. Let him stand from beneath and the fabric will fall, and a new and necessary reconstruction will follow.

But is it possible to transfer all the freedmen from the Southern part of the country? Perhaps not. It is, however, possible and practicable to so reduce the colored laborers of the South by emigration to the various States of the North and West, as to compel the land-holders—the planters—to make and to observe reasonable contracts with those who remain; to compel all white classes there to act in good faith; and address themselves to the necessary labor upon the plantation, as well as elsewhere; obeying the law and respecting the rights of their neighbors.

Thus the old order of things would be speedily changed, and the industrial interests of that section greatly advanced; while the civil and political rights of all would be, through necessity, respected and sustained. Even the exodus movement just commenced, small as it is, insignificant as it appears to be, has produced in this regard a state of feeling in the South which justifies entirely the opinion here expressed.

It is well to recollect that in the South we find a barren, *effete* civilization—a civilization the natural product of slavery and slave-holding institutions. The school, the college, the institution of learning, publicly or privately established by the State or in connection with the church, has not taken deep root there, bearing fruit in natural abundance. The masses of the freed people are illiterate. How could it be otherwise? But a large portion of the whites are also illiterate. The existence of slavery accounts for the condition of both these classes in this respect. All those things which appertain to an advancing civilization—healthful, vigorous and manly—seem to be wanting in the Southern section of our country.

Let the freedman come to the North, let him go to the West, and his contact with new men, new things, a new order of life, new moral and educational influences will advance him in the scale of being in an incomparably short time, even beyond. the expectations of the most sanguine. In his new home he will cultivate personal independence and free thought, acquiring in the meantime experience, knowledge and wisdom, which will enlarge his mind, ennoble his soul, and fit him for those higher walks of life, as merchant, mechanic, lawyer, doctor, minister, scientist or scholar. In other words still, the same benefits, the same blessings enjoyed by the newcomer from Ireland, England, and other foreign countries, tending so largely to elevate the thought, the purposes of such person, will be given to the ex-slave, and operate with equal power in the improvement of his mind and condition.

But as things are at present constituted in the South, the old methods of slavery and slave labor still prevailing, there is a large excess of laborers in that section. It is to be remembered that in slavery seven men, at least, were required to do the work of a single man in freedom. The exodus works at once the salvation of such surplus laborers by furnishing them a field for their muscle and labor in the unimproved acres of the West and North, thus not only benefiting them, but aiding in the development of the sections where they may locate. This consideration the people of the West and North appreciate, and their invitation to the poor freedman comes from them cordially and heartily. Cassagnac, in his work heretofore referred to—"The History of the Working and Burgher Classes"—in dwelling upon the Proletariat, says that it embraces: First, working men ;. second, mendicants; third, thieves; and fourth, women of the town. In explaining what he means by these several designations, he states that a working man is a proletary who works and gains wages for a living ; a mendicant is a proletary who will not or cannot work, and who begs for a living; a thief is a proletary who will neither work nor beg, and who steals for a living ; a woman of the town is a proletary who will neither work nor beg nor steal, and who prostitutes herself for a living. As the friend of the freedman, as one who would see him other and better than either of the classes here named composing the Proletariat of Cassagnac; who would see him more than the ordinary working man in the sense explained ; who would see him a landholder and owner ; who would see him master, as he is father, of his own household, rearing his family and his children in the fear and the admonition of his Heavenly Father ; growing sons, indeed, to the State, with shoulders broad and Atlantean, fit to bear the responsibilities of earnest, dignified, manly life, I do not fear but approve and advocate his emigration.

Where shall he go? It has already been indicated that the North and the West furnish the localities open for the freedman, and to which he should go. It certainly would not be wise for him in large numbers to settle in any one State of the Union; but even in thousands he would be received and welcomed to kind, hospitable homes in the various States of the sections named, where labor, educational advantages, and the opportunity to rise as a man, a citizen and a voter would be furnished him.

But to his emigration there are objections :

First. It is claimed that the Negro should remain in the South, and demand of the Government protection from the wrongs which are perpetrated against him, it being asserted that for him to emigrate at this time therefrom is to surrender the fundamental principle of protection which is guaranteed him, as well as every other citizen of the Republic, by the Constitution of the United States. Here it must be remembered that in emigrating from the South to the North the freedman is simply moving from one section of our common country to another, simply exercising his individual right to go when and where it suits his convenience and his advantage. In the next place, it is the exercise of such constitutional right that he leaves a section of the country where slavery has created a barbarous and oppressive public sentiment, the source of all the abuses which he suffers, and which it is impossible, certainly impracticable, to reach and eradicate by any legislative enactment had by the General Government, or by any legal fiat ; and which, in fact, can only be changed and improved by educational and moral appliances brought to bear upon the masses of the people of the South for an indefinite period. This objection is urged, too, in disregard both of the considerations just now suggested, in reply thereto, and in disregard of the fact that the freedman emigrating to the North or West puts himself in far better condition than he is in the South, in every sense ; while he makes himself useful upon a larger and better scale to the country generally.

But it may be claimed, and doubtless is, that if the freedman leaves the South under the oppressions which are heaped upon him, he yields to an unconstitutional proceeding on the part of the dominant classes, and thus weakens, if he does not surrender, the right to demand protection generally. In answer to this opinion it may be justly replied, that the freedman has a right to protection, and it ought to be granted to him at once, if possible; but it can hardly be required of the freedman who desires to leave the South to remain in his present condition and sacrifice himself, make himself a martyr in such manner.

Secondly. It is claimed that the freedman cannot endure a northern and western climate. It is said that the winters of these sections are too severe for him ; that in their chilling winds, their biting frosts, their deep, freezing snows, he will find himself sickening and speedily dying. Upon what facts and data this opinion is presented and sustained it is difficult to imagine. It is true, as justified by observation, and as facts and figures would show, could they be secured, that the colored man as he goes north into colder regions adapts himself with ease to the climate. While it is true that in no part of our country does the colored man show more robust health, finer physical development and endurance, and consequent longevity, than in the northern and western portions of our country. In fact so much is this the case that latterly it has become a thing of general observation and remark. It is where the zymotic and malarial disorders prevail that the Negro sickens and dies; and this is abundantly shown in the fearful death rate that is given by sanitarians as connected with the warm and tropical regions of our own and other countries.*

---

*The following statements will show the difference in death rate in several of the Southern cities as compared with a like number of Northern cities for the year 1878:

The death rate per 1,000 of population during that year ran as follows: New York city, 24 93; New Orleans, (exclusive of deaths from yellow fever,)

In the third place it is objected that if there is any considerable emigration from the South the freedmen who are left behind will be forgotten—their case ignored. But if the views already presented be correct, if emigration will work the results which are claimed, then this objection is fully and completely met. The old plantocracy is abolished; the slave system is entirely overthrown and the industrial systems of the South reconstructed; all oppressions and abuses are removed; protection and fair wages with the prospect of general agricultural improvement and the enjoyment of all civil and political rights are guaranteed; and thus the vexatious Southern problem is solved.

Again it is urged that the freedman is too poor to emigrate. Those who urge this objection ought to remember that it is the poor and oppressed in all ages and in all countries who have emigrated. One never emigrates only as he seeks to improve his condition, to relieve himself and family of want, to escape oppression and abuse, to gain such position as that, while he enjoys his freedom and rights, it is possible for him to cultivate as to himself and his children those circumstances of property, wealth, and intellectual, and moral, and religious culture, which distinguish desirable, wise, human existence.

Is it wise for the poor, starving, oppressed Irishman to quit the country of his nativity to seek a new home in our goodly land, where opportunities of culture, the accumula-

---

30.02; Philadelphia, 17 96 ; Savannah, 30 25; Cincinnati, 17.23; Mobile, 23 02 ; Chicago, 16.60; Nashville, 23.11 ; Cleveland, 16.72 ; Jacksonville, 21 10 ; Milwaukee, 14.35; Augusta, 18 33 ; Boston, 21.53; Charleston, S. C., 28 98.
In the city of Charleston, South Carolina, the death rate of the white population was 20.95, while that of the colored was 35 14. In the District of Columbia, the death rates of whites was 16.37; while the colored was 32 24. In all the Southern cities where the death rate is given comparatively, that of the colored race far exceeds the whites, and the very large number of deaths among the colored people resulting from what is known as the zymotic or preventable diseases is especially noticed.

tion of wealth, advancement and success await his endeavors? From whom comes the negative response? Then let no man either despise or oppose the exodus of the freedman, who now, realizing his real condition, emigrates from the old plantation and Negro quarter, from the scenes of his former enslavement, from the hateful and oppressive control of a stupid and tyrannical landed aristocracy, from poverty, from ignorance, from degradation to a home among those who value freedom, free institutions, educational and material, moral and Christian worth, individual effort and achievement—to a home among those who, loyal to God and man, never fail to give sympathy, succor and hospitable welcome to the needy son of Ireland, or the yet more needy son of Mississippi, who comes seeking not only liberty, but the opportunity to labor, to live, and achieve in their midst.

Our own national experience furnishes a valuable lesson upon the subject under consideration; and pondering such lesson wisely, the freedman and his family will do well to act in its light. This lesson is presented in the two-fold character of individual and family emigration, and the success and prosperity gained in connection therewith.

The family of a New England farmer is numerous. His sons are not needed at home; and there is no remunerative labor, manual or other, to be had in the community where this family lives. What is done? What has always been done in such families under such circumstances? Let the well-ordered and worthy household, the beautiful, fertile and productive farm, the substantial and enduring success, the political, the official, or the professional distinction which have been gained, and which now belong to the eldest son of such family, who, leaving home, settled fifty years ago in one of our nearer or more remote Western States, give the answer. But the community is overcrowded. Whole families are without work and pinching want seems to be near the door. What has been, and what is done in such cases? We know full well; for the populous, rich, prosperous, growing, vigorous,_matchless West, with its thousands of free, Christian homes, noble sons, intelligent, heroic daughters, makes the answer in full, clear, positive, eloquent manner.

Then, too, in Ohio, Michigan, Indiana, not to mention other States in connection with which the same thing is true, the colored American has moved heretofore from the South, and establishing settlements in the States named, has proved by his complete success the benefit and advantages of emigration. His rich and prosperous settlements in Pike county, Ohio, and in Cass county, Michigan, deserve in this connection special mention. But why dwell on these facts ? For the colored man is seen now in all parts of the North; and wherever he is, earnest, sober, and industrious, he makes reasonable advancement, commendable progress, in the honest ways of life.

In view, then of the considerations presented; to secure the highest good of all the parties concerned by the overthrow of the plantocracy of the South and the reconstruction of the industrial system of that section, on the basis of free labor, justice, and fair dealing; to relieve the ex-slave from his dependent and practical slavery, and while giving him the fact and consciousness of his freedom and independence, furnish him the opportunity to cultivate, not only ordinary labor, but to build up his present interests, industrial, material, educational, and moral, with reference to that future of which his past conduct, his capabilities and powers, his loyal and Christian devotion, give such reasonable promise,

I do most reverently and heartily accept the lesson contained in the words—

".I have surely seen the affliction of my people which are in Egypt, and have heard their cry by reason of their task-masters; for I know their sorrows; and I am come down to deliver them out of the hand of the Egyptians and to bring them up out of that land into a good land, and large, a land flowing with milk and honey."

FUTURE OF THE COLORED AMERICAN.

HIS CIVIL RIGHTS AND EQUAL PRIVILEGES—MENTAL AND PHYSICAL QUALITIES—ADAPTATION TO SKILLED LABOR.

BALTIMORE, *October* 31, 1875.

PROFESSOR JOHN M. LANGSTON:

DEAR SIR: At the regular monthly meeting of the Progressive Union and Co-operative Association, held in September, the following resolution was adopted:

Resolved, That Professor John M. Langston be specially invited to lecture in Baltimore, in behalf of this Association, on Thanksgiving evening, November 25, 1875, upon the following subject: "The Duties of the Hour as they Pertain to the Colored American Citizen;" and that he be furnished with a copy of the declaration of objects of the Association.

Whereas, it is an undeniable fact that a strong and powerfully organized opposition exists in this country to the colored man's full and complete enjoyment of all the rights and privileges of American citizenship; and

Whereas, we believe that the full enjoyment of said rights is to be obtained and preserved only by combination, organization and perseverance by colored men; therefore

Resolved, That we organize for the following objects under the name of the "Colored Men's Progressive and Co operative Union:"

1. To secure equal advantages in schools of all grades, from the primary school to the university.

2. To secure a full and complete recognition of our civil rights, and to defend by all proper means any abridgment of the same.

3. To use all justifiable means to obtain for our children admission into the workshops of our country, that they may obtain a practical knowledge of all mechanical branches of business.

4. To labor for the moral and social elevation of our people.

I hope you will discuss at length the right of the colored boys' admission into the workshops and the unjustifiableness of their exclusion. This is the second letter written to you on this matter. I did not know it until yesterday. I saw Mr. Isaac Myers and he told me that you had not received my first letter. If you have suggestions to make with reference to the lecture I will be happy to receive them. Respectfully, GEORGE MYERS.

MR. PRESIDENT: I am not insensible of the distinguished honor shown me in the invitation which brings me before you on this occasion. I experience and express to you and the

" Progressive Union and Co-operative Association " the liveliest feelings of gratitude. As I value the honor you do me,
through your invitation, I trust I in some proper sense appreciate the dignity and importance of the task it imposes,
as well as the difficult and perplexing character of its wise
and conscientious performance.

I despair of my ability to perform the duty, self-imposed
by the acceptance of your invitation, in such manner as to
interest and edify you and promote the welfare of that large
class of our population described in the phrase, " colored
American citizen." With no large confidence in my ability,
and with no purpose to cultivate oratorical art or display in
its discussion, I bring to the consideration of the subject
which you have named as the theme of my address the deepest and most abiding loyalty to those on whose behalf you
have organized your association. And, like you, I would
discover not only the excellent qualities of character, the
commendable facts of conduct, and the more important and
valuable achievements which render memorable the history
of the colored American, but, exploring the hiding places of
his weakness, the secret haunts of his insidious foes, the
destroyers of his physical, industrial, educational, moral,
social and civil greatness, I would induce him to erect and
sustain the strongest defenses against these enemies.

I may, I ought, to congratulate you and our fellow-citizens,
especially our colored fellow-citizens, upon the organization
of an association whose purposes, generous and philanthropic,
are so clearly and tersely set forth in its declaration of objects,
in the following words :

Whereas it is an undeniable fact that a strong and powerfully organized opposition exists in this country to the colored man's full and complete enjoyment of all the rights and
privileges of American citizenship; and whereas we believe
that the full enjoyment of said rights and privileges is to be

obtained and preserved only by combination, organization and perseverance by colored men; therefore

Resolved, That we organize for the following objects under the name of the "Colored Men's Progressive and Co-operative Union:"

1. To secure equal advantages in schools of all grades, from the primary school to the university.

2. To secure a full and complete recognition of our civil rights and privileges, and to defend them by all proper means against any abridgment.

3. To use all justifiable means to obtain for our children admission into the workshops of our country, that they may gain a practical knowledge of all mechanical branches of business.

4. To labor for the moral and social elevation of our people.

Upon the organization of such association and its public inauguration on this Thanksgiving evening, under auspices so favorable to its extended usefulness, I do indeed congratulate you. Its success is assured in the disinterested and earnest devotion of its projectors and members; the humane and Christian purposes which it seeks to accomplish.

According to a resolution unanimously adopted by the association I have been invited to speak on this subject: "The duties of the hour as they pertain to the colored American citizen."

I infer from the statement of my subject and your declaration of objects that I do not travel beyond legitimate and proper limits if, in dwelling upon this theme, I speak of certain duties which we are bound to perform in our own behalf as well as those which our white fellow-citizens ought to acknowledge and respect as binding upon them. At this hour in our history I consider the former of not less importance and their performance not less imperative than the latter; and as I progress, if we do not agree now, I feel assured that we will ere I conclude.

Since our emancipation a great deal has been said with regard to our "dying out." Within a few days a gentleman put into my hands a Democratic weekly journal containing what he called a well-considered and philosophical article, in which I found these words:

"The decree of emancipation was a sentence of death to the Negro race upon this continent; none the less inexorable because it is self-executing. If to that sentence there is any alternative, it is barbarism—the loss of all that three centuries have gained—and a lapse into the old and normal character and condition. This, in the face of multiplied efforts to overcome and to avert it, is what experience show to be inevitable. In the tropical and semi-tropical countries of the Western hemisphere it is possible that the Negro, left to his own guidance, will survive; but his survival will be upon the terms of his own native instincts and propensities —the permanent elements of his character. In the temperate regions he will go out, slowly or rapidly, in proportion as the climatic influences are more or less adverse to his constitution."

Continuing, the writer says:

"Admitting that the climate is, other things being equal, such as to allow of the continuance of the Negro upon this continent, the fact of his survival depends upon another condition—that he shall become industrial. No race of people, not spontaneously industrial, can maintain a permanent existence in a temperate climate. Slavery made the Negro involuntarily industrial; perhaps, in the process of time, it would have made him voluntarily so. In order to elevate the Negro, and fit him for his material environment, and insure his survival in it, it is proposed to school him; give him what is called an education. The effect of schooling upon the white is to make him, as an individual, non-industrial. The *rationale* of the matter is something like this: A race of men in order to survive must be industrial. The blacks, as a race, are not industrial; the whites are. Schooling makes the individual white non-industrial. Therefore, in order to make the individual black industrial, he must be schooled. And this is no more feeble than the rest of the educatio-philanthropic systems of ideas."

Again, he says:

" Death or—so far as the relations of the race are concerned —its equivalent was the doom pronounced upon the African by the decree of emancipation. The Negro in the United States is dying out. Whether or not he is elevated is, there-fore, either to himself or the white, matter of small, and, at the most, temporary concernment. In the race between education and extinction it matters little which comes out ahead when the latter is inevitable. But, admitting the pos-sibility, under favorable circumstances, of educating the Afri-can into the equivalent of a European, there is one condition of race advancement which is absolute, and with which the Negro cannot comply. A race of people which, through the cir-cumstances of their environment, or through defects in their own constitution or disposition, or through both of these com-bined, do not keep good their own numbers, cannot progress ; can only deteriorate. The stamina or the character or the constancy essential to the one is an inflexible condition to the other. Multiplication and advancement, and dimunition and retrogradation are things co-ordinate and inseparable. The history of the world does not furnish an example of a people who were fallen off numerically and advancing spiritually at one and the same time. Such are the relations between the physical and the psychical in humanity that the thing is im-possible. Stamina and robustitude in the one is stamina and robustitude in the other, and there is no instance in which a diminution or reproductive capacity and consequent diminu-tion in numbers has not been found associated with reduced intellectual audacity and moral constancy. This law is so absolute that each ratio of increase and diminution has its corresponding mode and degree of intellectual and moral manifestations."

If we carefully and critically examine the words I quote we shall find that the writer makes these three assertions:

1. That the decree of emancipation is a sentence of death. to the Negro race.

2. That in the temperate regions the Negro will go out slowly or rapidly in proportion as the climatic influences are more or less adverse to his constitution.

3. That no race of people not spontaneously industrious can maintain a permanent existence in a temperate climate. The Negro is not spontaneously industrious. Education will not make him such. Therefore the Negro in the United States is dying out.

He does not quite believe his first assertion himself; for after speaking of the sentence of death as "none the less inexorable because it is self-executing," he declares that if "there is any alternative"—insinuating that there may be such—it is "barbarism." Neither logic nor the presentation of facts in support of his conclusions are offered; and that, too, when the history of the world, as regards all oppressed and outcast races, in all regions and all periods, all complexions and nationalities, shows that emancipation, freedom, with its blessings, its infusion of manly aspiration and ennobling purposes, has always proved the best, the most valuable and dearly prized of human benefits; never a curse, always a blessing; never death, always life, precious indeed.·

There is nothing in his second assertion to assist him. For his statement finds an irresistible and perpetual answer in our daily observation of the colored man living in our climate to a like age, in many cases to a greater, with his white fellow-countrymen. And this after an enforced service of centuries in slavery; fed and clothed in a manner and in the use of articles the effect of which upon the body could not have been specially life-giving.

Nor is his third assertion particularly fortunate. I know of no "spontaneously industrial race." I do know that, according to my observation, there is about as much spontaniety in the industry of the Negro as in that of the white

man. It seems to me that both races work as they must, they
following the law written in our nature by our Creator, from
which no race may plead freedom, but in obedience to which
every race reaches its highest industrial eminence. It is the
sense of want that leads to industrial endeavor. It is this
sense, the love of gain, the laudable ambition to promote the
special good of those who are nearly related to us, or the general good of our race, countrymen, or mankind, or that selfish
ambition which seeks to perpetuate one's own name and deeds,
that prompt, sustain, and make valuable industrial enterprise. Want makes us all work. As we rise above want,
lose our interest in the welfare of mankind, and cease to
value endeavor in that behalf, or the selfish purpose sur-
renders its control of our minds, any of us, all of us, show
ourselves anything other than "spontaneously industrial."
Taste we may cultivate; we may even find ourselves endowed
by nature with feelings and inclinations leading us in peculiar ways of industry; then habits of industry, like other
habits, may so fasten themselves upon us that we seem to long
for work as the drunkard does for drink or the libertine for
lustful gratification. All that can be said of any other of
the human races in this regard can be said with equal truth
and force of the Negro. And so I can but believe the writer,
whose statements I combat, must really admit, since he uses
this rather remarkable language: "Slavery made the Negro
involuntarily industrious, perhaps in process of time it would
have made him voluntarily so." It cannot be that slavery
could have added to the powers or elements of our souls.
This cannot be claimed.

All, surely, that can be meant is that enforced service
might have produced the result indicated. This result would
certainly be more easily attained under the influence of free
and intelligent labor, even in the case of the Negro. I use

Q

the word intelligent.   I mean thus to deny the absurd sentiment that "schooling makes the individual white non-industrial."   A false education may lead a white man, as it
may a colored one, to shun and despise labor.   But a sound
education, one which imparts that knowledge of life and the
dignity of labor, as a means of happiness and civilization,
essential to all real wisdom, begets a different, a nobler feeling and determination, and, therefore, where education has
been cultivated labor has been dignified and industrial
enterprises of private and public character have been
inaugurated and perfected.   Otherwise education and labor
would be inimical, and we should find the grandest industrial achievements among the most illiterate and intellectually degraded.   No one other than a person who has the
vulgar and mistaken conception of labor and laborers, the
equally false and pernicious opinion of the master class,
engendered and fostered by slavery, would advance and
pretend to support by positive asseveration such unjust and
unfounded declarations.

Underlying the statements of the writer upon whose words
I dwell are these two glaring absurdities.   First, that in proportion as we educate a people they become non-industrial,
and being non-industrial, die.   If this be true, then deaths
among the white people of our country should be largely in
excess even of a like number of Negroes, since the whites
are much more generally educated, and the number of idle
and worthless persons among the whites should greatly
exceed the number of the same class among the blacks.
Can this writer make such admissions ?

In the second place, it may be true that education takes
many persons from the merely manual occupations of life
to literary, artistic, scientific and professional; but that the
interests of human society may be conserved these latter

callings must be cultivated. And fortunately for the poor white, even the poor black boy, in our country and under our law, no aristocratic class may fix limits to the callings to which malice or cultivated taste, interest or consideration of humanity, patriotism or religion lead us.

I do not feel any alarm, in view of these and such statements, as to our dying out. There are, however, certain facts connected with our physical condition which we as wise men will do well to consider. As showing what I mean, and as showing a condition of things which must be improved, I beg to submit the following facts and figures as respects our death rate in the cities of Philadelphia, Baltimore, Richmond, and the District of Columbia.

The entire population of Philadelphia is 800,000—the white 775,000, the colored 25,000. The total number of deaths for twelve months ending September 30, 1875, is 17,702—16,714 white, and 988 colored persons. Percentage of deaths, 2.15 of white and 2.45 of colored persons. Deaths per 1,000 inhabitants, 21.57 white and 24.50 colored persons. Here is a showing greatly against us.

The entire population of Baltimore is 350,000—the white being 305,000 and the colored 45,000. The total number of deaths for the twelve months ending September 30, 1875, is 7,585—6,036 white and 1,549 colored persons. Percentage of deaths, 1.98 white and 3.44 colored persons. Deaths per 1,000 inhabitants, 19.80 white and 35.40 colored persons. Here, again, is a showing against us.

The entire population of Richmond is 72,5000—the white 41,400 and the colored 31,100. The total number of deaths for twelve months ending September 30, 1875, is 1,632—701 white and 931 colored persons. Percentage of deaths, 1.69 white and 2.99 colored persons. Deaths per 1,000 inhabitants, 16.93 white and 29.94 colored persons. And here is a showing adverse to us.

The population of the District of Columbia, white and colored, is 160,000—115,000 white and 45,000 colored persons. The total number of deaths for twelve months ending September 30, 1875, is 4,352—2,210 white and 2,142 colored persons. Percentage of deaths, 1 92 white and 4.76 colored persons. Deaths per 1,000 inhabitants, 19.20 white and 47.60 colored persons. Still the showing is against us.

If we extend our examination we shall find that the number of births reported for the time named, white and colored, in the District of Columbia, is, of the first class, 2,518, and of the second, 1,397; total, 3,915. The percentage of births is, of the white 2.19, of the colored 3.10. Births per 1,000 inhabitants are, white 21.89, and colored 31.04. There is an increase of white births over deaths per 1,000 inhabitants of 2.69; but a decrease of colored births over deaths per 1,000 inhabitants of 16.56. As we extend our examination facts and figures seem to stand against us.

As confirmatory of the statements made in reference to the District of Columbia, and as indicating the cause of our very great death rate, and the remedy therefor, in the fewest possible words, I offer the following letter from Dr. D. W. Bliss, one of the most skillful physicians, and, at the same time, one of the most earnest and laborious sanitarians of our country, a friend of our race of many years' standing, and of devotion and tried character. He is at present a member of the board of health of the District of Columbia, and registrar of vital statistics of the same board. His letter, addressed to me, reads as follows:

WASHINGTON, *November* 16, 1875.
PROF. JOHN M. LANGSTON, *Washington, D. C.:*

SIR: In reply to your letter of the 13th instant, requesting certain information from the records of this office, I have the honor to submit the following, viz:

The colored population of the District of Columbia is estimated at 45,000.

The number of colored births reported during the twelve months ending September 30, 1875, was 1,397, of which number 733 were males and 664 were females.

The number of deaths of the same class during the same period was 2,142—2,141 native and 1 foreign. Of the whole number 1,029 were males and 1,113 were females.

The mortality of the same class was at the rate of 47.60 per 1,000 per annum, while the mortality of the white population was at the rate of 19.21 per 1,000 per annum, showing that the death rate of the colored population lacks but twenty-three one-thousandths of one per cent. of being one and one half times greater than the mortality of the white; in other words, the deaths were at the rate of 247 colored to 100 white.

In reply to your interrogatory, as to the "diseases with which this class seems specially afflicted," I respectfully refer you to the accompanying table, which contains thirty-one of the most prominent of a total of 212 causes of death, affecting this class for the same period.

The number of marriages reported of this class for the same time was 321.

The number of illegitimate colored births reported during the same period was 250, or 18.61 per cent. of the entire colored births reported.

The number of colored still-births reported for the same period was 223, of which number 123 were males and 100 females.

In reply to the question asking my opinion as to the cause of the large death rate of the colored population in this District, I would respectfully refer you to my opinion on this subject, expressed in my annual reports to the board of health for 1873 and 1874. It is not surprising that the mortality of the colored population is so very great, if we consider the great influx of this class into the District during and since the late war, bringing with them the filthy and careless habits of the plantation, occupying, from necessity, unsuitable habitations, located in the alleys, in the lowest and most unhealthy portions of the city, subjected to all the unwholesome influences of overcrowding and poverty, combined with absolute ignorance of the laws of health.

These, the most patent causes affecting the sanitary condition of this class of inhabitants of the District, operate in a very great degree to produce the result shown in our statistical tables.

The data for the present year will afford me additional evidence as to the cause of the great mortality of this class, which I shall present to the board of health in my next annual report, now in course of preparation.

Very respectfully,   D. W. BLISS, M. D.,
Registrar Vital Statistics.

Table showing thirty-one of the most prominent, of a total of two hundred and twelve causes of deaths, of the colored population of the District of Columbia during the year ending September 30, 1875.

Diseases.	Number of deaths. *	Colored.	White.	Total.
Atelectasis pulmonum	33	13	6	19
Anasarca	41	16	10	26
Bronchial catarrh	18	7	1	8
Bronchitis	133	52	24	76
Cholera infantum	296	116	154	270
Congenital debility	61	24	20	44
Congestion of lungs	71	28	40	68
Convulsions	303	119	78	197
Dentition	33	13	9	22
Diarrhœa	199	78	52	130
Enteritis	33	13	19	32
Entero-colitis	61	24	14	38
Erysipelas	20	8	15	23
Fever, typhoid	100	39	61	100
Fever, typho malaria	20	8	61	100
Gastritis	28	11	18	29
Gastro-enteritis	33	15	11	26
Hydrocephalus and tubercular meningitis	77	30	36	66
Inanition	110	43	48	91
Meningitis	89	35	47	82
Nephria, (Bright's disease)	28	11	14	25
Paralysis	49	19	19	38
Pericarditis	33	15	16	31
Phthisis pulmonalis	95	272	307	579
Pneumonia	621	243	187	440
Premature birth	84	33	44	77
Rheumatism	13	5	5	10
Tabes mesenterica and morasmus	294	155	56	171
Trismus nascentium	153	60	17	77
Valvular disease of the heart	56	22	45	67
Whooping cough	204	79	45	124
Thirty-one diseases		1,566	1,434	3,000

* The white population is 2.5-9 more than the colored. If the colored population was the same in numbers as the white the figures in this column would indicate the number of deaths from each cause.

On examining the table referred to by Dr. Bliss, and which is presented with his letter, it will be found that the diseases with which the colored residents of the District of Columbia have chiefly died are zymotic and preventable, or such as, though constitutional, are no more peculiar to persons of the African race than to others in similar circumstances and of similar habits.

Dr. Bliss does not so state in his letter, but it is a fact that the records of his office will show that a large proportion of the deaths of colored persons is of children dying under five years of age. This fact, showing that too large a number of our babes and infants are unable to survive the trying circumstances into which they are so often born, is significant. Nor does the Doctor state that the number of births given is simply those that are *reported*, while we very well know that many children are born in the District among persons of all classes, which are not reported, as required by law. It is, perhaps, true that thirty per cent. of the births in the District are not reported; the percentage of births not reported of the colored people being probably even larger than those of the whites.

I have not been able to get any reliable information with regard to births of either white or colored people in the cities named. However, I am of the opinion that were we able to secure the facts, the result would not materially vary the condition of things, as shown in the city of Washington and the District of Columbia.

The facts and figures adduced admonish us that we should at once enter upon the work of improving our physical condition.

The Negro, naturally tenacious of life, even under the oppressive and life-exhausting conditions of slavery, over-worked, ill-fed and poorly sheltered, lived, multiplied his numbers and largely by natural increase became numerically a great people in this land.

Like other classes of the human family, however, he can not live and multiply his numbers in conditions where pure air and the essentials of sound bodily health are denied him. In ill-constructed, cold, leaky, damp, filthy and foul shanties and structures, overcrowded and poorly and insufficiently ventilated, located in alleys, narrow and unimproved streets, and back places where noisome odors and noxious gases, generated in filth of every conceivable name and kind, death-breeding, poison and destroy, he must die. The number of our people finding their homes in such places, in such miserable substitutes for dwellings is altogether too large, and our mortality must grow yet more alarming if we continue in them. Where pure air, the life indeed of the body, is denied admission; where there exists a condition of things which constitutes a perpetual injunction against its presence, the Negro cannot live—no human being can live. All sicken and die, for we violate the law of our being which God himself has made, whose penalty is death.

As bearing upon the general subject already so fully considered, and as indicating our future situation as to health and life, should we improve our physical condition, I introduce an extract from a letter written by Dr. Verdi, a member of the board of health of the District of Columbia, a gentleman occupying eminent place in the medical profession and as a sanitarian, in answer to a question propounded by me with regard to the mortality of our race. The question was: "Is the cause of the great mortality of the colored people of our country, as indicated by statistics within your knowledge, in your opinion a permanent one?" To this he says:

"I answer, temporary; probably mainly confined to the

present and the next generation. In his contest with the white—for his position is a contest—he must learn that the strongest wins, and then learn how to make himself strong. Legislation cannot do it. He must learn to improve his own condition, by keeping his dwelling free from the filth that poisons its atmosphere; he must know that dry and well-ventilated houses are conducive to health; he must learn that healthy food preserves his life and makes his children strong; he must learn that constant labor only will give him the means to provide healthy food; he must learn economy, and save when he is well and at work, so as not to be in want when sick or without employment; he must learn that pork, although cheap as an article of diet, will only perpetuate his liability to disease, which he will transmit to his child. All this he will learn in his contest with other races; hence, the mortality of the present generation will lessen in the next, and so on until he can stand abreast of the white contending for supremacy in industry, art and labor. Many will die in this period of probation, but those that are left will be stalwart men, and statistics will not threaten him with the extinction of his race."

I have considered the matter of our physical condition, adducing and commenting upon the facts and figures presented, not for the sake of combatting what I conceive to be false theories with regard to our mortality, not for the purpose of exciting undue alarm or unnecessary feeling of any kind as to this subject, but for the purpose of inducing, if possible, as far as may be practicable, such improvement as may insure sound health and long life to the colored people of our country. The improvement which I urge is one which each family must make for itself; and the obligation to make it is imperative and absolute. It is a dictate of paternal as well as patriotic duty; and to urge its religious observance is justified by considerations of the highest good of all concerned. Our first duty, towering above all others in importance, whose performance is indispensable to our permanent welfare, is the one of which I speak. It may be well to care for our dead, to commit their remains "decently and in order," to the earth; it is far more important that we care for our living, making the largest sacrifice, foregoing all indulgence of appetite and mere pleasurable gratifications, husbanding every resource, that we may be able to improve our residence, making our homes, in all the essentials conducive to sound bodily condition, in structure and cleanliness, models.

As to our industrial condition. It is no part of my purpose to say that we do not work, and work hard and perseveringly. It is altogether true that we, as a class, are industrious and laborious. The well-worked fields of the South, luxuriant and beautiful with that rich plant once called king, attest our devotion in slavery or freedom to work. Driven as beasts of burden in our former condition of servitude, we never rebelled against labor. Emancipated and sent empty-handed to seek our living or die, we have demonstrated our acceptance of the ancient law, that in the sweat of man's brow shall he gain his bread. However otherwise we are vulnerable to charges derogatory and degrading, no one can, with any degree of justice, pronounce us as a class idle. Individuals of our number are idle; individuals of all classes are; but, as a class, we compare favorably with the very best as to habits of industry.

As the laboring class, however, of a large and important section of our country, our position is subordinate and menial. Not one word is to be said against any necessary and honorable labor. In no sentiment of opposition thereto could I expect you to agree with me or any other. But I have no such word of opposition to utter. Nor do I advise you to abandon those humbler walks of industry, along which you have, for so many years, by diligence and perseverance, honesty and obedience, gathered the means of an honorable and happy, though humble, living.

What I advise is that we grow our children, especially our sons, to those occupations—mechanical, artistic and other— whose cultivation not only brings wealth and independence, but desirable and influential social position. It is the duty of the father, as far as practicable, to lift his son from the lowly condition which he occupies. It is the duty of the son to improve upon that condition as far as possible. With the father acting under a due sense of his obligation, and the son appreciating his duty and the purpose of his parents, much can be done to accomplish the result proposed, even where workshops are closed against us and our children denied a knowledge of those trades and callings without which industrial enterprises of every character must fail.

Considerations of justice and patriotism, one would feel, must induce the mechanics of the country, upon reflection, to open their shops to our sons. If, however, they do not relent, but continue to deny to them the knowledge and skill desired, let us combine to sustain those white workmen, and establish and support such colored ones, as will give our children the instruction and labor which they need.

If we cannot, as individuals, accomplish this object, let us organize ourselves into associations and aggregate our small sums of surplus funds to sustain those workmen who will deal justly with our sons.

If we cannot find situations for them in the cities, towns or country places where we live, let us send them to distant places, where men are found who will instruct them. Then, when their apprenticeship has been served, have them return to establish and conduct business among those who deny them opportunity to learn and labor.

Were you to read the history of the outcast races of Spain

and France you would, in the course of your reading, find a peculiar and despised class, called the Cagots. Why they were despised no man knows, any more than he does whence they came or how or where they get their name. As a class possessing a lobeless ear and afflicted with goitre, aggravated by burden-bearing, they were hated and maltreated without the least humanity or mercy shown them—as if they had been cursed by God and branded as the objects of His hot displeasure.

This statement you will believe when you are told that if they entered a church they did so by a special door, being compelled to occupy a special part of the church by themselves. The priest refused them confession, and they were compelled to take holy water from a separate and special vessel. The consolations and benefits of religion were practically denied them. They were refused civil rights and political privileges. When witnesses were needed the testimony of several of their own class was required to contradict that of a single witness of ordinary character. They were compelled to wear shoes lest the touch of their naked feet soil the pathways. That they might the more readily be recognized they were compelled to wear, attached to their clothing, a piece of red cloth, cut after the pattern of the goose or duck's foot. All social intercourse was denied them, and they were compelled to live in the outskirts of the towns and cities of Spain and France, an outcast race. When it is added that they were for many centuries slaves, ignorant and degraded, forbidden intermarriage with any other than their own class, and having born to them children condemned like themselves to slavery and misery, you will exclaim, "How strikingly their condition resembles our own!" And yet the Cagot was a mechanic. He was permitted, in spite of the inveterate prejudice which existed against him, to become a sawyer and a carpenter. His tools were esteemed by him his most valuable property, and they were the only weapons which he was allowed to possess.

When we were slaves the selfish interest of our owners in many cases led them to put us to trades of various kinds. Many free colored persons, even in slave States, also followed different kinds of mechanical occupations. We are not, ·therefore, wholly without good workmen, though the number be small—too small in all parts of our country where colored men reside. These workmen, denied opportunity to labor in the shops generally, and with white mechanics upon the larger and finer edifices and structures, public and private, have steadily pursued the humbler and less profitable walks of their calling, displaying frequently taste, skill and workmanship of the best order. Such persons deserve special commendation. Whenever it is practicable they should be given our patronage, for their course is at once honorable to them and creditable to us.

In many places, and among many of our first-class white mechanics, the prejudice which has heretofore existed against us is giving place to a better and more humane feeling. Colored mechanics in such localities, and as engaged by this class of white employers, are steadily advancing to the most desirable and renumerative positions in their callings. This fact is prophetic of large and permanent good to us.

Among our sons many are found who desire to leave menial occupations, to learn and pursue mechanical and commercial callings. Let us foster, encourage and sustain this feeling till it becomes a settled purpose, as discovered in efforts to master the occupation to which their inclinations lead them. In pursuing such course we will resist and overcome, as we ought, the tendency connected with our former and our present condition, toward a permanent state of slavish dependence, which is menial and degrading. Against labor, even the humblest, I repeat, I do not say a single word. For in my thoughts, when man shall have reached his best earthly estate, labor and learning stand perpetually conjoined, conspiring to elevate his thoughts, purify and ennoble his feelings, sustain his aspirations, direct and support his purposes, softening his humanity, conserving his highest interest, promoting his most lasting good.

We often feel, very erroneously, however, that through what are termed the learned professions, the legal, the medical and theological, alone do we, or can we, rise to distinction. In obscure and humble industrial pursuits not unfrequently do the youthful, aspiring subjects of future greatness catch that spirit which sustains and bears them forward in those more conspicuous and influential paths of reform, legislation and politics.

To-day we mourn the loss of a Senator and statesman, whose name, associated in our memories with those of Giddings, Lincoln, Hale, Stevens, Lovejoy, Birney, Chase, Henry Winter Davis, Gerrit Smith, and Charles Sumner, lives in immortal freshness and beauty, lovely and precious, through all the ages to come. We pause to drop a tear of the profoundest sorrow over the death of Henry Wilson. In all his relations in life, domestic, social, and official, he did not—his friends could—forget that he rose from humble, dignified labor to high public station. Let no man despise the early, lowly condition of real greatness!

Dr. Edward Young, in his excellent special report on "Labor in Europe and America," just published, in dwelling upon the condition of the feudal period in England, says:

"In the former period two-thirds of the people are said to have been either slaves, or in a state of bondage approaching slavery, to the remaining one-third. They might be put in bonds and whipped; they might be branded, and on one occasion are spoken of as if actually yoked. Cattle and slaves, in fact, formed a common measure of value under the denomination of live money, and were a medium of exchange in which the prices of commodities were computed.

" The operatives and handicraftsmen of this period, as well as the agricultural laborers, were mostly slaves. The clergy and nobility employed as domestic servants persons of this class who were qualified to supply them with such things as were then considered the necessaries of life.

" Hence in monasteries we find smiths, carpenters, millers, illuminators, architects, agriculturists and fishermen. Smiths and carpenters were the most numerous and important as ministering to the chief secular pursuits of the time, both in war and husbandry. Bancroft

" Great as were the politic il effects of the Norman invasion it did not materially alter the condition of the masses of the people. Their services were as necessary to the new masters as to the old, and the terms on which these were rendered could hardly have been made more onerous than they had been. In order to maintain more firmly the ascendancy of the invaders the feudal relations were enforced with somewhat greater strictness than before, but no changes were made in the chain of subordination which had already been established.

" Hence for a long time after the conquest the Saxon subdivisions of society were maintained, and the inhabitants of the country continued to be divided into the two great classes of freemen and serfs or slaves. Except the baronial proprietors of land and their vassals, the free tenants and socmen, the country people were depressed in servitude, which was uniform in this respect, that no one who had either been born in or had fallen into bondage could acquire any absolute right to property. Aside from this, however, there were distinctions in the degrees of servitude. One class of villeins, or villagers, though bound to the most servile offices of rural industry, were permitted to occupy small portions of land to sustain themselves and families.

" Other ranks of men, equally servile, are noticed in the

ancient records, particularly the bordars and cottars. The former, in consideration of being allowed a small cottage, were required to provide poultry, eggs and other articles of diet for the lord's table ; and the latter were employed in the trades of smiths, carpenter and other handicraft arts, in which they had been instructed at the charge of their masters. Inferior to these were the thralls or *servi*, principally employed in menial services about the mansion.

"Their lives were professedly protected by law, and with the consent of their owners they were allowed in some cases to purchase their freedom ; but, in other respects, they were in the lowest degradation, so much as to be considered mere chattels and regular articles of commerce."

From this condition, so strikingly descriptive of our own, in many respects, as slaves, and even now as freedmen, as the centuries have passed, these classes and their descendants have advanced in intelligence, industry and civilization, till their achievements in all those things which distinguish national greatness command the admiration of the world. Industrial effort inspired and sustained intellectual and moral endeavor, and those reacting upon each other not only led the people to value, assert and maintain their freedom and independence, but to make the progress and accomplish the results which their history records.

Our industrial future—the future of industrial triumph, is still before us. Properly appreciating the future, while we labor to open avenues of honorable and dignified industry to our children, we may justly feel that in this way largely we shall gain wealth and its blessings, elevate ourselves and our posterity from our present low moral and social condition, while we demonstrate the possession of that industrial capacity and power which signalize individual and national vigor and purpose.

Let us remember that the ancient and mediæval nations and races are no more distinguished for moral and intellectual than industrial accomplishments.

The immortal pyramids of Egypt, frowning upon the ages attest the industrial triumphs of the once proud people of the Pharaohs. And the monuments of Greek and Roman greatness are seen and admired not less in their industrial than in their intellectual achievements. This is true of all the nations and all the races of the past which have won renown and gained eminence and influence in the world's history.

As having relation to our general educational condition, I would present the following letter of Hon. John Eaton, Commissioner of Education of the United States:

DEPARTMENT OF THE INTERIOR,
BUREAU OF EDUCATION,
WASHINGTON, D. C., *November* 16, 1875.

DEAR SIR: Your request that I should furnish you with " the number of schools organized among the colored people since their emancipation, giving the number of pupils and the progress that has been made by them," is received. In reply, I would respectfully say that on these points full statistics cannot be given, because they are not received by us.

In the State reports on education from the old non-slaveholding States there is rarely ever any separation of schools for colored children, with their pupils, from the others; and in many of those from the States in which slavery existed there is no such such separation—none, for example, in the reports from Alabama, Florida, Kentucky, Louisiana, Mississippi or Texas. And even in the States which do make returns on this point there is considerable difference as to the character of the returns. Such as we have, we give:

For instance, from Delaware we have, from the secretary of a society which has thus far attended to this work, a report of 1,125 colored pupils in 28 schools, under 28 teachers; from Virginia a report of 37,267 colored pupils enrolled in 669 schools, number of teachers not given; from South Carolina a report of 56,294 such pupils under 814 colored teachers, number of schools not given; from North Carolina, in 1873, a report of 40,824 pupils in 746 schools, number of teachers not given; from Virginia a report of 994

R

schools, with an enrollment of 52,086 (out of a colored population of 177,317,) under 490 colored teachers; from Tennessee a report of 103,856 colored school population, with 923 schools, 921 colored teachers, and in 1873 a colored attendance of 23,446; from Missouri a report of 282 schools, for a colored population of 38,243, attendance not given; and from West Virginia a report of 2,461 colored children (out of 5,540) in 63 schools.

Of the other slave States, Alabama appropriated $163,-469 for schools among a colored school population of 172,506; Arkansas had no public schools to report in 1874. Louisiana, by law, gives all her children access to the schools without distinction of race or color, and perhaps one-half out of her school population of 280,387 may be colored, with perhaps a like proportion out of 74,309 enrolled in schools. Maryland seems to have given to her colored schools $68,-506, these schools numbering 245, with 269 teachers, and an enrollment of 8,756 pupils. In Kentucky a system of schools for colored children was commenced in 1874, and there is yet no report from it. Out of the 152,785 enrolled in schools in Mississippi, and the 98,308 in Texas, you may form your own estimate of the number of colored pupils. We suppose that it may be about one-third.

Of the former free States California reports 694 colored children in public and private schools; Indiana, a colored school population of 9,470; Ohio, 5,950 in colored schools; Illinois, an attendance of colored children with the whites in a large majority of the counties, while in ten counties they attended separate schools; number of colored pupils not given.

The above refers throughout to elementary schools. Beyond these we find 15 graded schools, sustained by the American Missionary Association in five Southern States, and several of kindred character sustained by the Protestant Episcopal Church. The former had, at the time of the last report, 66 teachers and 4,654 pupils. The statistics of the latter are not in our hands.

Then the State of Alabama sustains, or helps to sustain, as a part of her public school system, two normal schools, at

Huntsville and Marion, for the training of colored teachers, with about 200 pupils in them. Maryland has one, at Baltimore, with about 250 pupils, and New York city one, with 18 to 20 pupils. One is sustained by the colored people themselves at Jefferson City, Mo., and others for them at Lincoln University, Oxford, Pa.; Wilberforce University, Xenia, Ohio; Fish University and Nashville Normal and Theological Institute, Nashville, Tenn., with one at Maryville, in the same State; at Tongaloo University, Miss.; at Straight University and New Orleans University, New Orleans, La.; at Talladega College, Talladega, Ala.; at Atlanta University, Atlanta, Ga.; at Shaw University, Raleigh, N. C.; at St. Augustine's school in the same place. In Petersburg, Va., the Rev. G. Cook, a colored minister of the Protestant Episcopal Church, sustains one, with about 70 pupils, while at Hampton, Va., is a large and important one, and at Howard University one, as you know. The number of colored pupils in most of these cannot be determined by us, as they are not separated in the statistics from the whites who may also be attendant.

In all the above universities and colleges, too, the colored people have admission to the advantages of both superior and professional instructions ; as also at Berea College, Berea, Ky.; at Central Tennessee College, Nashville, Tenn.; at Alcorn University, Rodney, Miss.; at Leland University, New Orleans, La., and at the University of South Carolina, Columbia. Oberlin College, Ohio, is open to them. Yale and Trinity, Conn.; Harvard, in Mass ; Dartmouth, in N. H., have admitted colored students, and few, if any, would exclude them now. At most of the theological schools in the Northern States, too, colored pupils are believed to find a welcome. How far this is the case at law and medical schools, your own researches have probably determined.

As to the progress made by colored pupils in the various kinds of institutions thus organized for them or opened to them, no absolute general statement can be made. In the effort to secure equal advantages to pupils of every color, there has been less and less showing of the different races in statistics. It is, however, certain that, in many instances which come clearly beneath our observation, the colored children in the schools and colored youths in colleges have advanced as fast and as far as white ones with the same advantages.

Trusting that this information may serve your purpose, I am, very respectfully, your obedient servant,

JOHN EATON,
Commissioner of Education.

PROF. JOHN M. LANGSTON, *Washington, D. C.*

In colored schools managed by boards of trustees or commissioners having charge of the white schools as well, in which uniform regulations as to text books, the employment and control of teachers, the examination and conduct of pupils are enforced, though the schools be separate, in many instances, the progress of the scholars has been marked and commendable. In schools where the children attend without reference to complexional peculiarities their progress has been greater, and the intellectual and moral condition of the scholar more thoroughly improved. In such schools no inconvenience or injury is experienced by either class, white or colored, while their contact improves both in feeling and friendly regard for each other. The schools only will bring perfect reconciliation to the races. Such colleges as Oberlin and the schools of New England furnish proof of the correctness of this opinion. And the trustees and officers of such colleges and schools deserve the grateful commendation of all classes. They but pursue that path of national reform essential to the highest good of the colored, and conducive to the permanent welfare of the white American. And success in this regard will win for the philanthropic Christian educator the golden crown of the nation's noblest reformer.

As to this subject, I need not weary your patience with protracted remarks. Upon the dignity, importance and necessity of education, our minds are fully settled. We have only to give ourselves anxiety and care as to the thoroughness and skill with which the children and wards are educated. We are justly solicitous as to the wholesome character of food eaten by our families. Nothing poisonous and deleterious is knowingly suffered to be brought into our houses. And were we convinced that our cook, or any other, had given such article of food to our child, our indignation and wrath would be kindled and burn at highest heat. Were the object of our anger by his act brought within the meshes of the law, no delay would be made in bringing him to justice. Mankind would applaud our conduct in this case. Let us be solicitous! It is well. But, if we care thus for the body, should we not be even more careful of the soul, with regard to the food upon which our minds are fed? Articles of one sort strengthen and invigorate; those of another debilitate and destroy. Mental robustness, strength and vigor of soul we need no less than bodily health and endurance.

Here I bring to your consideration two facts: First, in many schools and colleges, established and conducted in the interest of the colored youth of our country, scholars and students are taught, as they are generally treated, as if they were of, and destined to live and labor only among, a peculiar caste or class. They are frequently told that they *are colored*, and that when they complete their course of study they are to find occupation among colored people. In the second place they are impressed, by teaching and conduct, too, generally, that an imperfect mastery of the various branches of study, even the commonest, will answer all purposes for them. Their study, therefore, often is of that loose and unreliable sort which in no sense strengthens, but confuses and weakens the understanding. The same mastery of learning and science, the same careful discipline and culture of the mental powers, the same consciousness of power developed and sustained by such mastery, discipline and culture, are needed in the case of the colored American youth as in that of any and all others. In our country, famous for its composite nationality, the equality of all its citizens before the law, with the avenues of the State, the Church, the school, open to all alike, with the largest rewards awaiting his endeavors who brings into requisition, in labors of literature, science, art or reform, the largest powers of heart and brain, no child, the children of no class of our people, should be taught, or in any wise impressed, that anything less than the most perfect educational accomplishment will suffice.

If we would grow sons strong in intellect, rising in feeling and purpose to the moral plane of the truly educated, accomplishing those results in life which distinguish earnest and true men, let them forget that they are of, and must live and labor for and among, a particular class. Let them see to it that they are prepared for service in behalf of any employer, and in any direction promising the largest harvest of blessing to mankind.

With regard to our moral, social and civil condition I had intended to speak at this time. Upon each of these topics much remains to be said, and much remains to be done, to improve our condition. I may not, however, detain you longer.

Your association, this night entering upon its mission of benevolence and reform, will find much along the path over which I have conducted your minds by my remarks for reflection and effort. In the name of those whose advancement you seek, I bespeak for it the most cordial and generous support.

THE END.